The Dream
of Water

ALSO BY KYOKO MORI

Shizuko's Daughter

One Bird

The Dream of Water

A MEMOIR

Kyoko Mori

ONE WORLD

Fawcett Columbine • New York

A One World/Fawcett Columbine Book
Published by Ballantine Books

Copyright © 1995 by Kyoko Mori

All rights reserved under International and Pan-American Copyright Conventions. Published in the United States by Ballantine Books, a division of Random House, Inc., New York, and distributed in Canada by Random House of Canada Limited, Toronto.

This edition published by arrangement with Henry Holt and Company.

Library of Congress Catalog Card Number: 95-90673

ISBN: 0-449-91043-1

Cover design by Min Choi

Manufactured in the United States of America
First Ballantine Books Edition: January 1996
10 9 8 7 6 5 4 3 2 1

*for Vince Broderick and
Sylvia Navarro, whose generosity
made this book possible*

The Dream
of Water

Distant
Water

On March 16, 1969, the night his marriage ended, my father, Hiroshi, went to sleep as usual in his small room off the kitchen. The undertaker had dressed my mother, Takako, in her best kimono and left her on a futon in that room. For the first time in nearly ten years, Hiroshi lay down next to her and closed his eyes. The drapes in the room still smelled of the gas she had breathed in that afternoon by taping the windows shut, unhooking the gas line, and holding the tube to her mouth. She had even covered her head with a plastic bag, to make sure. There was no doubt that she really meant to die.

After sleeping fitfully all night, Hiroshi jumped off his futon at dawn, wide awake. Someone was snoring. Takako was alive after all. But when he sat down and touched her forehead, her skin was cold. Hiroshi tiptoed out to the living room and found his father-in-law, Takeo, stretched out on the couch in his undershirt, his mouth wide open. My grandmother, Fuku, was curled up into a tight ball on the armchair. They had arrived from the countryside in the middle of the night and decided not to wake us up.

Later that morning, Grandmother made rice and miso soup for breakfast, completely forgetting that my younger brother, Jumpei, and I did not eat Japanese food in the morning. Jumpei poured honey over his rice the way we did over oatmeal. I stirred my rice with the chopsticks but didn't eat it. We were all listening to Hiroshi in silence. Grandfather's eyes were dry but red.

"For a minute, I thought it was Takako snoring," Hiroshi said. "Funny, isn't it? I don't think she ever snored. At least not like you were, Father." Hiroshi wasn't smiling or crying. He was just stating the facts: our mother was dead, and he mistook one set of breathing for another.

Grandmother suddenly got up from the table and ran out to the yard, where she began pacing back and forth with small quick steps. I could hear the dog straining at his leash, excited to see her. While my father continued to talk, I went to the refrigerator and poured myself a glass of milk. Almost every morning, my mother and I had bickered because I hated drinking milk, which she insisted was good for my bones. I had complained endlessly about how the sticky aftertaste made me sick on the way to school. Some mornings, I knocked over the glass, pretending to be careless. Sitting back at the table now, I lifted my glass and sipped slowly. I held my breath and kept swallowing each small mouthful till the glass was empty.

Jumpei and I stayed home all that afternoon while the undertaker's men rearranged our living room for the wake. Around four o'clock, a man from a photography studio brought back a portrait of my mother in her red sweater, smiling and squinting at the same time, her hair blown slightly to the left. When the picture had been taken the previous fall, I was standing next to her on a hiking path and we were both smiling at Jumpei, who was learning to use the camera. This was the only good picture he took that day. The others were blurred or cropped wrong. The man from the studio said she looked kind and happy in this picture. He sat at the dining room table in the morning and cut out a square around her face and shoulders so that he could enlarge just that small piece. As he brushed the rest of the picture—thin glossy strips—off the table into the wastebasket, I sensed how my mother might see the world now: small and insignificant, lighter than an eggshell. She had been cut loose from life as easily as the photographer's scissors separated her face from mine, her shoulders from the mountains in the background.

By early evening, our living room was covered with white drapes and incense, with an altar in the front next to the coffin. People started gathering for the wake in their formal black kimonos and suits. The priest from our family's Buddhist temple read the sutras for an hour, his monotonous chanting broken up now and then by the brass bell he struck with what looked like a small black chopstick. Though the priest left immediately afterward, people stayed on— they were mostly my mother's relations: her parents, brothers and sister, cousins, second cousins. Because most of them were staying overnight, they were still talking when I went upstairs. All day long, my grandmother and aunts had been watching me with worried looks on their faces. I closed the door behind me, glad to be alone finally. I laid out my futon and fell asleep immediately.

It was still dark when I woke up and saw my father sitting on the floor next to me.

"Wake up," he said. "I need to tell you something important."

I started going through the same thing I was to experience every morning for the next few weeks: reminding myself that my mother had really died and I was now alone.

"Remember when you went to your mother's cousin Takeshi Ogata's funeral?" he asked.

I nodded but didn't sit up. I couldn't decide whether the sky was gray because it was cloudy or because it was so early. Takeshi's funeral had been two years back. My mother had been sick with the flu so I had gone in her stead with Hiroshi and my mother's brothers Shiro and Kenichi.

"You remember what Takeshi died of?" Hiroshi asked me. He was sitting cross-legged. His gray pajamas smelled of stale cigarettes.

"Heart attack," I said. Though Takeshi and my mother had been friends in childhood, they hadn't seen each other much as adults. I hardly knew him and often confused him with his two brothers, who were also doctors.

"That was a lie they told us," Hiroshi said. "Takeshi killed himself just like your mother. He had manic depression, a mental disease. Your mother must have had it, too."

I said nothing. Sparrows were gathering in the ginkgo tree outside. They were chirping and fluttering.

"I always thought there was something suspicious about his death," he went on. "Heart surgeons don't die suddenly from a heart attack. They kept his suicide a secret till last night. Finally, his brother Akira told me. There's something wrong with your mother's family. Both Takeshi and your mother had some problem with their minds. It must run on your grandmother's side. It's bad blood. Mental disease is hereditary. I want to make sure you and your brother turn out differently. Do you understand? You can't be like them."

He edged closer. I rolled away just a little.

"Your mother spoiled you and Jumpei. But I'm in charge of you now. I won't let you be like her. I'm going to help you by being strict." He abruptly got up and started walking away. "You can get up," he said.

I covered my head with the blanket and tried to remember something about the funeral or Takeshi's family. He had a daughter a day younger than I, but I had only met her that time at the funeral and wouldn't recognize her if I saw her again. All I could remember was the train ride to northern Kyoto, where his family lived. After the train had gone over two big bridges in Osaka, my uncle Shiro said we had crossed the same river twice. He breathed on the windowpane and drew the curve of the river and the tracks crossing it twice. Once the picture had faded, I could make it appear again and again by breathing on the glass.

I lay on my futon thinking, but I wasn't particularly surprised by the way my father had talked about my mother's cousin's suicide or about the bad blood he thought her family had passed on to me. He had never shown me any consideration because I was only twelve or even because I was his daughter. I didn't expect him to be kind. The day before, when we had come home from shopping and found my mother on the floor with a black bag over her head, my father called a doctor he knew and walked down the hill to meet him, leaving my brother and me alone. I made Jumpei go to his room upstairs while I opened the windows to let out the gas. I covered my mother with a blanket and waited. The doctor came but could not revive her. As soon as the doctor shook his head and pronounced her dead, my father told me to go and call my mother's relations and his own sister, Akiko. After that, he had me call my sixth-grade teacher, Jumpei's second-grade teacher, and our school friends. When I was done with all the phone calls, he sent me to the police station with the doctor to give our statements while he made calls to keep the incident out of the newspapers.

At the police station, the doctor told me to wait in the car. "You shouldn't have to do this," he said. "You're too young. I didn't want your father to send you. I told him so, but he wouldn't listen. He thought you should go as a witness. But I'll just go in by myself and ask them not to question you." When he had been inside for a few minutes, a young policeman came out to the car. He showed me into a small room at the station and gave me a cup of tea. He didn't question me. We scarcely talked except he kept asking me if I was warm enough. It was raining outside and chilly. *Even this policeman must have a mother,* I thought. The world was already rearranging itself. It was like a big gym with everyone who had a mother standing against one wall and the few of us who didn't standing against the other wall. The doctor came to get me, and we drove home in the rain.

I continued to lie on my futon though my father had told me to get up. While our guests were still sleeping, he was in the kitchen broiling some dried fish for his breakfast. The oily, salty smell reminded me of the rare mornings he had stayed home, when my mother had prepared him that same meal. I could picture the blue flames of the broiler leaving black marks on the leathery skin of the fish. No one else was getting up. The house stayed quiet except for his footsteps. Reaching under my futon, I pulled out the red notebook in which my mother had been keeping her journal for the past two years. I had known about the journal during her life, though I would never have touched it then. But when I came back from the police station, I took the notebook to my room and read it that night while my father was sleeping next to her body. I wanted to be the first, perhaps the only person to read her words. If necessary, I was prepared to burn the notebook to protect any secrets she might have wanted to keep.

But she had already destroyed the last few pages. The white thread that held the paper to the spine had popped in places when she tore them out. The last entry left intact was dated December 16, 1968, three months earlier. Most of the entries before that were from the preceding fall, though there were a few from the summer and from the previous winter, when we had first moved into our new house.

Sitting on my futon, I began to reread the notebook backward, starting with the most recent entry. Nothing my mother had written surprised me. Most days, sitting alone in the house made her sad; she wondered if her life had any real purpose.

"I am going insane," she wrote in October 1968. "I will become a madwoman. If my husband doesn't return home again tonight, I want to kill my children and commit suicide. I wish I were already dead. I cannot leave my children with him. They would only be a burden to him as he no doubt will remarry and start his life over. They and I are better off dead."

That was the only reference to killing my brother and me, unless there had been more in the pages she destroyed. The entries from the previous winter were no different, full of sadness, crows cawing, dead leaves stuck on the window, the times she wished she could simply evaporate and become nothing. Her thoughts had gotten stuck in that terrible sadness till death seemed the only way out. None of that—even the one mention of killing us—surprised me. I had slept next to her every night. I could easily imagine what she might have written in January, February, and early March and torn out.

Just about every night during that time, I woke up to the sound of her crying. Sometimes she would talk; other times we held hands and were silent. One night in the last week of her life, she turned on the light and woke me up. It must have been three or four in the morning. She wasn't crying this time. She looked pale and serious, her cheeks and jaws set hard.

"Are you okay?" I asked, sitting up. "You look sick."

She didn't answer. As we sat side by side on our futons, she took my hand and held it. Her hand was cold. She must have been sitting up for a long time.

"If I asked you to do something important," she asked after a while, "would you do it?"

"Of course," I said.

She squeezed my hand. "What would you do if I died? Could you go on living by yourself? Or would you wish you were dead, too?" She let go of my hand to wipe her tears.

I pulled my knees up and rested my forehead on my kneecaps, trying to think. My mother didn't say anything more. She was waiting for my answer. Finally, I said, "I don't want to die."

"Even if I were gone?"

"No. I don't want to die even if you were gone. But you are not going to die. I don't know why you keep talking about it. I wish you would stop." My voice sounded harsh, but I kept saying, "I want to go back to sleep. I'm so tired." I turned away from her and started crying.

"I'm sorry," she said. "Maybe I'm going crazy. All I can think of is how I would be better off dead."

Alone now in the room where she had said these things, I knew that my mother would never have forced my brother or me to die with her. That night when she woke me up, she might have been on the verge of asking me. She must have been relieved, then, to hear me say that I didn't want to die. I had told her what she wanted to believe: that I would continue to live with or without her. My words became the go-ahead she had been waiting for in the last few months. I reread her last journal entry from December: "Many times, I wish I could die in my sleep. I look around my house. I feel no attachment to my furniture, my clothes, everything I've worked hard for all these years. Even my children, I believe, would be happier with someone else. Someone stronger and more competent would be a better mother to them even if she were not related to them by blood." I closed the notebook. What I had said must have sounded like the final confirmation to her. *Now,* she must have thought, *I can go ahead and do it.* I wished I had said something entirely different. Why hadn't I told her that I didn't want to die but I didn't want to live without her, either? I should have shown her that I wanted both of us to be alive for a long time.

Downstairs, my father was sitting down to his solitary breakfast of salty fish and rice while, in the various rooms in the house, my mother's family who had stayed the night were beginning to get up. I could hear them walking about and getting dressed. I put the notebook under the pillow and closed my eyes. Soon I heard footsteps coming up the stairs. The door slid open with barely a sound. I opened my eyes just enough to see it was my aunt Keiko, my mother's younger sister. She sat by my futon for a long time while I pretended to be asleep. She did not want to wake me up, I knew, because in my sleep I might have forgotten about my mother's death, and she didn't want to remind me. Finally, she reached out her hand and touched my shoulder.

"I'm awake," I said. "Don't worry. I'm awake."

I sat up. She leaned forward and put her arms around me. We sat holding each other a long time before I got dressed for the funeral.

May 20, 1990, Green Bay, Wisconsin. At four in the morning, the air outside is already warm and humid. The screen door creaks shut behind me. As I begin to run without my glasses, everything looks blurred in the gray light from the sky. Daisies and clover spread a fuzzy green on the roadside, like moss. Above the sidewalk, the branches of oaks and maples are black shadows without clear edges. In the residential areas, porch lights are still on, cars and vans parked in driveways. Behind them, houses look larger than life and slightly tilted, as though they were sinking into water or floating out of it. Two miles into the run, I think of all the time and distance ahead of me.

I am taking a trip to Japan for the first time in thirteen years. "A trip" is how I think of it, not "going back" or "returning," which would imply that my destination is a home, a familiar place. As my running shoes pound the predawn sidewalk of this small midwestern town, Japan seems like a place that exists only in dreams or on television. Even my itinerary, which I have almost memorized, seems unreal.

My plane leaves Green Bay at seven this morning for Minneapolis. From there, I will fly to Seattle, Narita, then Osaka. Because of the time change and long layovers, I won't arrive in Osaka till the late afternoon of the day after tomorrow. I'm not sure how many actual hours I will be flying. Up in the sky, time is arbitrary. Hours will flow backward first as I travel west toward Seattle; then somewhere over the Pacific, time will reverse directions and rush forward at double speed, erasing one whole day in the blue light outside the window.

"Do you go back often?" people ask me when they find out that I was born in Japan, even though I have spent the last thirteen years—most of my adult life—in the American Midwest. I invariably wince at the words *go back* and say, "No. I'd like to visit some time, but there are other places I'd rather travel to if I had the money." Still, last fall when I was putting together my sabbatical application at the college where I teach creative writing, I included a trip to Japan. I'd heard the committee favored proposals that featured research. *Why not go to Japan?* I thought. After all, it is the only foreign country where I can speak the language. Besides, most of my short stories are set in Japan, and my poems tend to juxtapose my memories of Japan with my life in the Midwest. There is no better place for me to gather material. So I proposed that I go to Japan for seven weeks and write some new poems and stories. My proposal was accepted, my seven weeks are just beginning, and I have made very few plans.

For one thing, nobody in my family knows that I am coming. I have prepared letters to mail to my father and to my maternal grandmother from the airport this morning. All I say in the letters is that I am arriving in Japan soon as part of my sabbatical project, that I will travel around the country first on my four-week rail pass, and that I will contact them before the end of June. I know the letters are abrupt, even rude; anyone else who grew up in Japan would have contacted his or her family months ago. But I could never get on the plane this morning if I had to see my family first thing upon arrival. I need an interval, a transition period. I want to see the Japan I have never seen before—the Japan that is truly a foreign country—before I can deal with my hometown, my family, the Japan that has become foreign to me.

As I turn the corner by the river and head back, the shadows overhead are changing back into maples and oaks. It will be midsummer here when I return from Japan. Back in April, when the maples were shedding their red flowers on the sidewalks, I began to think that I might not see many more springs and summers here in Green Bay—that I would like to move on, start over someplace else, with my husband or even alone. There isn't anything wrong, in particular, with my life in Green Bay. I have been here for seven years now. I have finally gotten used to my job so I can teach and write at the same time and not agonize over the lack of time and energy. I no longer feel the sort of urgent but unspecific anxiety I felt in graduate school or even in the early years of my job. Still, some mornings, I sit on my couch at home or in my office at school and feel that the walls and furniture could simply dissolve around me. It seems strange, unlikely even, that I am living this stable life—tenured and married though childless—in a small Wisconsin town where the old women in diners don't look anything like my grandmother and the children playing in front of the ranch houses at the edge of town do not resemble any children I could possibly have. The life I am leading cannot really be my life, I think from time to time, especially while I am running or driving through the city.

I sprint the last block and stop in front of our house, its door painted a dark red. Going up the steps into the house, I am sorry that my run is over. I need to hurry now. There is just enough time to shower, pack the last-minute things. The flight ahead seems like a long time to sit still, to be stuck in one place against my will. I tell myself that I can sleep through most of it, I won't even notice the hours passing.

By the time the plane lands in Narita, it's late afternoon. I have already lost the day in the middle. Though I fell asleep shortly after Seattle and only got up in the last hour to put in my contact lenses, I am tired and groggy. I collect my overnight bag and follow the other passengers toward the door. We step outside into the humid heat and then get on a shuttle bus that takes us from the plane to the terminal building, where we disperse to our various gates.

My plane to Osaka won't leave for another hour. The windows of the waiting area where I sit overlook an endless stretch of green rice paddies. Flat and rural, the view is nothing like the Japan I know. If anything, it's more like the American Midwest I have just left. Still, looking away from the window and surveying the waiting area, I know that I am in Japan. Most of the people waiting for the Osaka flight are businessmen in black or blue suits: *sarariman,* Japanese people would call them—men who work to earn their salary. Every trashcan and bench around me is painted with advertisements. "Pokkari Sweat," the nearest one says, with a picture of what looks like a bottle of soda. This is the kind of English used only in Japan, by advertisers who think that foreign names make their products sound more sophisticated, even though often the names make no sense. A few seats away from me, a woman dressed in a mustard-colored two-piece suit is carrying her belongings in a paper shopping bag from the Seibu Department Store instead of in a suitcase. The shopping bag is immaculately white and uncreased; the name, Seibu, is printed in English, in a fancy italic script. I look away, overwhelmed.

The man in the next seat looks at me and smiles. One of the few non-Japanese waiting for the Osaka flight, he is wearing a red T-shirt and blue jeans. Like many of my friends, he is slightly overweight but not fat. I smile back at him. Everyone else in the waiting area is staring straight ahead, trying to avoid eye contact. In Japan, one does not smile at or talk to total strangers.

"Are you visiting someone in Osaka?" I ask the man.

"No," he says. "I'm going on to Singapore."

For a moment, I wish I were going to some exotic-sounding location as well. "That's great," I say. "Have you ever been there?"

"No. This is my first time."

I am envious of him because he is going to a place where he has never been. "Is this your vacation?" I ask him, "or is it work?"

"Both," he replies. "How about you? Where are you going?"

"I'm going to Kobe, twenty minutes from Osaka. I used to live there, a long time ago." I want to explain that I am not really going back, that I will be leaving on a four-week trip right away rather than staying to see family, but suddenly I feel too tired for the more complicated conversation it would take to explain that, so I turn away from him toward the window. Maybe the view doesn't look exactly like the Midwest after all. The paddies are a deeper green than the wheat- and cornfields of Wisconsin and Iowa. Water shines in jagged slivers beneath the deep green. In the distance, the air has that luminous quality it gets from being near water. I stare at the horizon to see if what is beyond is just the sky or perhaps a distant sea, but my eyes tear from the hazy light, and I can't tell.

Suddenly, there is a lot of commotion at the next gate. Three men in navy blue uniforms enter the gate, their big white name tags identifying them as immigration officers. Two East Indian women walk by, squeezed between these officers. The women look about thirty; they are dressed in saris, one in pink, the other in blue. Neither of them speaks; their faces are serious but blank. A fourth officer, a woman, stands slightly apart from them, talking into a walkie-talkie. I can't hear what she is saying. When the gate opens and the flight to Montreal is announced, the three men take the women by the arms and go on board. Nobody comes back. The woman officer stands by watching until the plane has taken off.

"You think those women were being deported?" I ask the man who is going to Singapore.

"Sure looks like it," he says.

I get a sudden tight knot in my stomach as I lean toward the window. The green of the rice paddies looks too lush. I wish I had not come so far from home, that I could take the next plane and head back. But as soon as I think that, I'm not sure what I mean by *home*. My blue American passport is tucked in the outside pocket of my overnight bag. I am no longer a citizen of the country in which I was born; I have been thinking of moving to another city, another state. After seven weeks here in this foreign country that was once my home, perhaps I will not feel that returning to Green Bay is going home, either. I might feel more as if I am going from one foreign place to another.

A few hours later, the last plane I am to ride begins its descent toward the Osaka airport. As we break through the cloud cover, the plane tilts sideways toward the dense foliage below. This is Rokko, the mountain ridge that borders the Kobe-Osaka metropolis. The green of the trees here is completely different from the green of rice paddies or the green of midwestern corn. It's dark and lush at once, textured. The plane rights itself and continues to lose altitude. Whatever city is directly below us now—either Osaka or its suburb Itami—glitters like a rock split open next to the moss-colored mountain ridge. The city is a jagged sprawl of concrete, metal, and glass, with sharp teeth like those of quartz. The plane tilts again, this time to the other side. Across the aisle, out the window, the Seto Inland Sea stretches dark blue. The water is wrinkled where the waves are rough, like the globe I made in a grade-school geography class and did not paste very well. The Bay of Osaka curves in the bow shape I learned back then. My ears are ringing from the air pressure. I take a deep breath and swallow hard as we descend toward the landscape of my childhood.

Minnows

A few minutes away from the airport, the taxi begins climbing a steep ramp onto a raised highway. Tilted back in my seat in the air-conditioned cab, I can see nothing for a few seconds except the sky, violet with the glow of neon. Next to me, my friend Vince is silently watching the other cars. The cab picks up speed as we merge into heavy traffic and rush toward a tangle of intersecting ramps and concrete high-rises. I don't know what happened to the familiar shapes of land and water I saw from the airplane. Now that I am on the ground, the scenery reminds me not of my childhood, but of the science fiction movies I have seen in the past few years. I could be the Harrison Ford character in the opening sequence of *Blade Runner,* cruising a strange future city, on the hunt for killer androids. The cab zooms into the farthest right lane to pass. Every move of the traffic is the reverse of what I am used to, driving in the States. The digital clock on the dashboard says it's 9:00 P.M. I have no idea what time it is back in Green Bay.

"Are you tired?" Vince asks me, craning his neck to look into my face. In the thirteen years I have not seen him, his dark brown hair has gone gray in the front and along his temples, but his eyes look the same. They are narrow, sharp eyes—dark green with a brown glint.

"I'm all right," I assure him. "I slept on the plane."

"I'm sorry my house is such a mess you can't stay there," he apologizes. "But Sylvia has a lot of room, and you'll like her. She'll enjoy having company. Her husband is away for the summer."

"Thanks for finding me a place to stay." I put my hand on his wrist, just above his watchband. His skin feels cold from the air-conditioning in the cab.

Vince is one of the few people I still know from my time in Japan. He came to teach in Kobe in the early 1970s, after finishing graduate school, and has not gone back to the States except for brief visits. Our lives mirror each other's. He has spent all of his adult life in Japan; I have spent all of mine in the American Midwest. In 1976, when I was nineteen and he was thirty-one, he was my writing teacher at the Japanese college I attended for two years. Now I am two years older than he was back then; I teach writing in Wisconsin. The way our lives intersected seems suddenly terribly weird, but I am too exhausted to think about it. I press my forehead against the window, watching the buildings and neon signs whip by.

In a few minutes we get off the freeway and head north through streets that get narrower as we drive uphill. Past a station of the commuter trains, there is a park with a pond, then a high-rise condominium. What I see out the window is no longer like a movie. I know exactly where we are. Around the next bend in the road there will be a hospital. "Konan Hospital," the sign in front will read. This is Mikage, an eastern Kobe neighborhood where I used to visit my friends in high school. My best friend, Machiko Imazu, lived in one of the new subdivisions near the top of this hill, in a house with a big paper lantern hanging over the stairway. Last I heard, Machiko had married and moved to Tokyo. She has two sons. In the dreams I still have about her, we are both teenagers, even though we might be walking in my garden in Green Bay or sitting down to dinner at a restaurant in Chicago. I twist back in my seat. Through the back window, down the hill, I see the lights of the train station and of the small stores where Machiko and I used to buy bread or flowers or sweets. The cab clears the bend and is passing the hospital with its sign. I face forward. I can't quite believe that I am really here: riding up the hill with Vince, suspended between memory and dreams.

The cab lets us off in the subdivision north of Machiko's old house, as close as you can get to the mountain ridge. I follow Vince up the steps to the front door. A woman with long reddish hair lets us in. After we take off our shoes, we go into the kitchen where a young girl is sitting at the table. Red, blue, and purple balloons are taped to the kitchen door; colored tissue paper and paper rings hang from the ceiling.

"Was it someone's birthday?" I ask the girl.

"Mine," she says, brushing back her long brown hair with her hand. "Yesterday."

"This is my daughter, Cadine," the woman with the red hair says to me. "I'm Sylvia. Please sit down."

"So how old are you now?" I ask Cadine, making small talk in the way I always do at people's houses.

"Twelve," she says.

"Are you guys hungry?" Sylvia asks Vince and me. "I can offer you some soup." She's already getting up.

"Don't go to any trouble for us," Vince says.

"It's no trouble. The soup's already made. We just had supper."

"Actually," I say, "I should tell you now. I don't eat meat." It's my policy to be up-front about my vegetarianism, though I have been worried about how to handle that in Japan. When people offer you food here, you decline it twice out of politeness, and then, when it is offered the third time, you accept it and give great compliments while the host says it was nothing. The ritual leaves no room for the possibility that you might *really* want to decline the food.

Sylvia smiles. "We are vegetarians, too," she says. "One of our cats eats fish cake. That's about the only meat we ever buy." She goes to the stove and brings bowls of cream of cabbage soup.

We talk about my flight, my plans to travel around the country. Vince and Sylvia both suggest places I should visit. When I'm done with the soup, I bring the bowl back to the sink and rinse it out—almost as if I had eaten here many times already. Soon I am so tired I can hardly keep my eyes open. I follow Sylvia upstairs with my suitcases.

"Here," she says, opening the paper *fusuma* doors to a Japanese-style room with *tatami* mats and cypress-wood pillars. The paper shade is drawn over the large windows to one side. Sylvia goes to the closet and brings out the bedding—an odd mixture of Japanese-style futon and stiff linen sheets, a big feather pillow, and a Hudson Bay blanket. I start laughing.

"This must be your culturally diverse bedding," I say.

"Quite a mishmash, isn't it?" Sylvia laughs, too.

"It's great."

"Do you think you'll be warm enough? It could get cool here in the mornings yet. We're up on the hill."

"I'll be all right."

We say good night, and Sylvia goes downstairs, closing the fusuma doors behind her. I am relieved that she is casual about putting me up—giving me whatever bedding she has, not standing on ceremony or apologizing about things. I can feel at home and sleep well in any house so long as my host is not endlessly apologizing and giving me the "I'm sorry the house isn't as clean as it should be" line. I change, turn off the light, lie down under the Hudson Bay blanket, and close my eyes. I even drift off for a while. But ten minutes later, I am wide awake and staring at the ceiling.

Getting out of bed, I walk to the windows and pull up the paper shades. Outside the windows, which face south, a wooden porch juts out over the front of the house. I go out there through the small door to my right. Below, my hometown is outlined in the white and orange lights of the streetlamps and houses, the bright blue and purple neons clustered near downtown. "The million-dollar night view," the tourism bureau called it. For all I know, people here still say that. It's the view I saw almost every night of my life in Japan. Right now I am standing only two or three miles west of my mother's last house. The condominium where my father lives must be about four miles east of here. I go back inside, close the shades, and lie down again. Still, I stay awake for a long time, feeling stranded, somehow, on a mountaintop.

A week after my mother's funeral, in March 1969, the school year was over, leaving Jumpei and me on vacation till early April. My mother's youngest brother, Kenichi, was a high school chemistry teacher. Since he was off when we were, he came to stay at our house. He was thirty and single; we called him Ken Nichan—*Nichan* means "Big Brother"—rather than *Ojichan,* "Uncle." Every morning and evening, Ken Nichan burned incense at the Buddhist altar for my mother's soul. The three of us sat in front of the altar thinking about her and asking the spirits of our ancestors to watch over her. My father, Hiroshi, had gone back to work the day after the funeral. He left the house before we got up and came home past midnight, just as he had done during my mother's life. Sometimes he was gone for days on business trips.

A few nights before school started again in April, Hiroshi came into my room at midnight and woke me up. Kenichi and Jumpei were already asleep in the next room. Hiroshi sat down by my futon and said that Jumpei and I would be moving to the house of his widowed father, Tatsuo, in Ashiya, the closest suburb of Kobe to the east. Tatsuo lived with my aunt Akiko and her daughter, Kazumi, who was my age. Akiko's husband worked for a shipping company and was seldom home. My brother and I must move there, my father stated, so that Akiko could take care of us. I sat up while he was talking.

"It's not very far away," Hiroshi said at the end. "It's walking distance."

That was true. Our houses were only about two miles apart.

"What about our things?" I asked him.

"A truck is coming in the morning to move them," he answered. He meant the next morning.

"How about Ken Nichan?"

"He won't be staying here for long now."

"Why not? He doesn't have a family. Maybe he can stay on with us, and then Jumpei and I won't have to move."

"Nobody asked your opinion." Hiroshi frowned. "You should leave important decisions to adults. It's none of your business. Your uncle Kenichi and I aren't related. He's not going to live in my house."

"Will Jumpei and I ever come back to live here?"

Hiroshi shrugged. "I don't know. You are not old enough to keep house for me. You and your brother can't live here until you are old enough or I can get married again. You can't stay here without someone taking care of you."

The next morning, after Hiroshi had gone to work, Akiko and Kazumi came to help us move. They packed my brother's clothes and books while I told the movers what to load onto the truck and what to leave behind. We were ready in a couple of hours. I went to get my dog, Riki, from his kennel outside, but he growled at the movers and would not get into the cab my aunt had called. While we were standing around trying to coax him, my brother started crying. "Shut up. Don't be such a crybaby," I scolded Jumpei. The dog began to whimper. I yanked at the leash, trying to drag him toward the cab, but Riki wouldn't move. My brother was crying harder now. I almost felt like crying, too, but I just kept pulling at the leash.

Ken Nichan put his hand on my back and suggested, "Maybe you and I can walk to their house and bring the dog that way. It'll be a good walk."

I hesitated.

"Come on. You like taking walks." Ken Nichan reached out for the leash. Everyone else got into the cab.

"You did a very good job with the movers," Kenichi said to me while we were walking.

"I shouldn't have told Jumpei to shut up," I said. "I only made him cry harder."

Kenichi just shrugged. That reminded me of my mother—how she never used to criticize me if I admitted that I had done something wrong.

Later that night, when my grandfather came home from the paint company he owned and managed, he scolded Akiko in front of my brother and me for having allowed me to bring the dog.

"You know I don't like animals," he muttered in a low, angry voice. "All they do is dirty up my patio and make noise to keep me awake."

"But I couldn't leave the dog," I said. "Father wouldn't have taken care of him."

"I'm not talking to you," Tatsuo snapped at me and then turned back to Akiko. "You should have taken the animal to the pound."

"Try to be a little more tolerant," Akiko replied. "Your grandchildren just lost their mother. How could you expect them to give up their dog at a time like this?"

Tatsuo got up and walked into his room without a word.

Kenichi stayed on at our house for two more weeks, until the first forty-nine days after my mother's death had passed. During that period, her soul was supposed to be traveling to Buddhist heaven. The white smoke of the incense, going straight up, was said to point the way and guide the soul's journey, so Kenichi wanted to make sure someone would be at our house to tend to the altar and burn incense.

Even after he went back to another part of Kobe, where he lived with his sister, Keiko, and her family, Kenichi visited us almost every day after school. He had always been good friends with my aunt Akiko. Now he sat talking with her in the afternoon and then stayed for supper. I had started my first year at Kobe Jogakuin, a private girls' school that had junior and senior high schools and a four-year college on a big campus up on a hill. Because we took the same commuter train line to our schools, Kenichi and I usually waited for each other at the station and walked back to the house together. It was as though he had continued to live with us after all.

Hiroshi visited us for a few hours every other Sunday. Almost all of his visits ended with him yelling at me and hitting me. "Don't look at me with that impertinent face," he would say as his hand flew toward my cheek. It didn't matter whether I was frowning, smiling, or trying to keep my face absolutely blank. My face was always an impertinent face. If we disagreed about something and I explained my view, he got angry at my talking back. If I said nothing, he got just as angry because, then, I was being sullen and stubborn. After a while, I expected him to hit me regardless of what I did or didn't do. Nothing made any difference. The only important thing was to keep absolutely still while he hit me so that he would not miss and get angrier.

I had heard somewhere that in bad traffic accidents, people who were asleep in the backseat were the least likely to suffer severe injury. They didn't have time to panic, tense up, and do the wrong thing in trying to avoid being hurt. Hiroshi's rage seemed as inevitable as a head-on accident. Often, I tried to picture myself sleeping in the backseat just as he was getting ready to hit me. As he lifted his hand,

I would imagine the car swerving on a wet road. Then I would think of myself slumped against the seat, breathing deeply and easily with my eyes closed.

Hiroshi relented only once, when I made fun of the sideburns he was growing. They had reached halfway down his cheeks in the two weeks I hadn't seen him.

"You're too old to try and look like a movie star," I taunted. "You look like a thug."

He was standing by the window next to Akiko's sewing machine. He stuck his hand into her sewing box, pulled out a pair of scissors, and turned to me. I flinched, stepping back toward the door, and then stopped. But he brought the scissors up to his face and snipped off both sideburns without looking, tossed the hair into the wastebasket, and jammed the scissors back into the box. He had no hair left above his ears. His skin was the color of clay.

"Is this what you want?" he yelled.

"No," I said. "You cut them too short."

He shook his head and walked out of the room. He was the only person I knew who could look stern and ridiculous at the same time.

During my mother's life, my father had spent little time at home. On the rare occasions when I saw him, he was either eating, or watching television, or sleeping. We scarcely talked to each other. Though I didn't like him, I wasn't afraid of him. It was different with my brother, who had spent every Sunday with Hiroshi the previous year at junior league rugby practices. My brother hated rugby. He cried on Saturday evenings just thinking about how rough the practice was going to be the next day. Even so, he never told Hiroshi that he wanted to quit. He was able to stop toward the end of December only because Hiroshi became too busy with his own rugby league. I now understood why Jumpei had been so afraid of him. Everyone avoided Hiroshi.

Kazumi took my dog to the park on those Sundays and didn't come home until Hiroshi was long gone and I was sitting alone in the room we shared. I could hear her tying the dog to the chain outside, coming in the house, and washing her hands. After that, she came upstairs and turned on the light because, by then, it was dusk. She always brought me a piece of cake or an apple, which I would eat in silence. She never asked me how the visit went. Instead, she just sat there with a worried look on her face, watching me eat; then she would ask me, "Do you want anything else?" or "Do you want to watch television?" "No, nothing else," I would reply, or, "Okay. Let's go watch television." I smiled, to let her know that I was all right, no matter what had happened. Kazumi didn't force me to say more. She nodded and smiled back or patted my shoulder in silence.

My mother used to praise Kazumi for her kindness. "Kazumi is a very considerate person," she had said. She was right. On the day I moved in, Kazumi slid her clothes to the right half of the closet to make room for mine. When both of our jewelry boxes didn't fit on top of the bureau, she emptied all her bangle bracelets and beaded necklaces into my box and put hers away. I wondered how things might have been if our situations had been reversed, if she had come to my house to share my mother and my room. I didn't think I could have been as kind and understanding toward her as she was to me.

One Sunday in early May, Hiroshi canceled his biweekly visit to referee a rugby game. On the telephone, he told me to meet him the next afternoon at his house. "Come by yourself right after school," he ordered. "Don't be late."

But I was late. I missed two trains because they looked too crowded and I was afraid to get on. When I arrived at the house, Hiroshi was sitting in the kitchen with his jacket on. The ashtray on the table was full of squashed stubs.

"Keep your coat on," he said. "We'll talk on the way. It's late."

"Where are we going?" I asked.

"I'm walking you back to Ashiya. There's no time for anything else."

Outside, it was getting dark. We walked down the hill without talking, Hiroshi a few steps ahead of me. I had a hard time keeping up because I was carrying my schoolbooks and gym shoes.

At the bottom of the hill, as we turned east toward Ashiya, he said, "You and Jumpei can come home next week. Someone's coming to take care of you."

"Who's that?" I asked, thinking of my aunt Keiko and some of my mother's friends. I didn't see how any of them could come and live with us since they had their own children.

"Things would have been different if you had been older or if your mother had trained you better to do housework," he replied. "But you have school and friends. I can't ask you to stay home to do housework and take care of Jumpei." He stopped to light a cigarette. The white smoke came out of his mouth and gradually disappeared ahead of him. "I know there are girls your age who can keep house and take their mothers' places, so maybe you *are* old enough to do it. But your mother didn't teach you much in that way. She only encouraged you to study and play the piano and do artwork. Besides, I don't want you to make a big sacrifice. It wouldn't be fair."

He kept on walking ahead of me so I couldn't see his face. It was hard to concentrate on what he was saying. His voice went forward while I walked behind. My science book kept slipping out of my arms.

"The woman who's coming is a very good housekeeper," he added. "I'll bring her to meet you and Jumpei before you move back to the house. You'll like her. She's very tall and stylish."

I straightened out the books so I could hold on to them better. "I don't understand," I said. "You said I should stay with Aunt Akiko till I was old enough, unless you could get married again. Are you saying that you'll get married again?"

"Not until next April," he said. "You know we have to observe the one-year mourning period for your mother. We can't have a wedding ceremony before that's over with."

"But you are going to marry this woman."

"Yes."

"And she'll live with us even before that."

"She's coming the day after tomorrow."

We walked on. It was getting dark fast. Soon the streetlamps would be lit. I didn't know what to say. My gym shoes, tied together at the laces, kept bobbing sideways.

Finally, I asked him, "Do you love her, or are you going to marry her because you need a housekeeper?"

He stopped and turned around. I held my breath and stood still as his head whirled around toward me. The street was deserted. But he didn't hit me. He just said, "You must never ask adults about love. You know nothing about it. It's none of your business."

He didn't speak again all the way to my grandfather's house. I didn't want to ask him anything more. I was sure he was going to marry this woman because neither he nor I could manage the house and take care of Jumpei. He must have lied to her and said he loved her. Nobody would marry him just to take care of my brother and me. I tried to picture the woman. Even though he had described her as tall and stylish, I could only imagine a short and fat woman in a plain brown shirt and dark pants, a white apron over them. Perhaps we would call her *Obasan,* which was what we called the live-in maid our grandfather Tatsuo had hired one year when our aunt Akiko was sick. *I don't want to live with a strange woman. I want to stay with Aunt Akiko,* I wanted to say, but I knew it wouldn't do any good. What I wanted made no difference to him. The way he had talked, he had made me feel as though the whole thing was my fault for not being old enough.

At the door of my grandfather's house, Hiroshi turned and headed back to the train station. He was returning to the office to do the work he couldn't finish because he'd had to wait for me. I went alone into the kitchen, where Jumpei was crying. I knew that Aunt Akiko had told him the news. Kenichi had been sitting in the corner, helping Kazumi with something she was writing or drawing. He came over and took my hand. "Are you all right?" he asked me. I nodded quickly, swallowing down the hot lump that kept pressing against the back of my throat, but I couldn't say anything.

Jumpei and I moved back to our father's house on Friday the following week. We got there at dusk and found the woman alone, making supper in her bright green shirt and brown pants. Our father was going to work late, she said. We had only met her twice before, but we were supposed to call her *Okasan*, "Mother." I had told my father that I would prefer to call her *Michiko Obasan*, "Aunt Michiko." Hiroshi grabbed me by the arm and shook me. "Call her Okasan," he said. "Understand?" I nodded, thinking that at least in my mind, I would think of her as Michiko Obasan. My brother and I had called our mother Mama, anyway, so we were not going to have to address this woman in exactly the same way. Still, no one talked much during supper, and we avoided addressing her in any form. The chicken dish she served was brown with a thick sauce. The spices burned my tongue.

After dinner, Michiko took a bath and put on a sheer white nightgown that had pink ribbons at the neck. While Jumpei was taking his bath, she laid out a crimson futon in Hiroshi's room. I had never seen such a large futon. It covered most of the floor in the small room. The overstuffed quilted cover rippled like rough water. She put out her clothing for the next day—a white blouse, a mustard yellow skirt, balled-up brown hose, pink underwear folded up small as a handkerchief. She laid out each item separately, side by side. From the kitchen, where I was watching, they looked like small puddles, or stepping stones leading up to the crimson pond, which might, after all, be an island. The whole thing reminded me of those maps on which I could not tell what part was the sea and what part was the land.

I took my turn at the bath. When I came out, Michiko was showing Jumpei the beauty lotion she used to get rid of dead skin so she
would have nothing but smooth new skin. She squirted a small
amount on her palm and rubbed it into her left elbow. Her skin came
off in minuscule wormy shapes like pencil marks erased from paper.
Jumpei and I took off our robes, sat on bath towels, and proceeded to
rub the dead skin off our elbows and knees. When that was done, we
tried the small joints of our fingers, the flat bones behind our ears, the
disconnected vees at our throats. I hadn't known there was so much
dead skin everywhere. It took hours to get rid of it.

Against the wall, there was a new, shiny brown dresser with many
small drawers. From one drawer, Michiko pulled out a pink gown
that looked like the white one she was wearing.

"Here, you can have this one." She handed it to me.

"Thank you. It's very pretty." I slipped it over my head, trying
to be polite. The material reminded me of balloons blown up too
thin. My mother and I never wore anything but cotton, linen, or
wool.

Back in my old room, I laid out my futon and turned off the light.
I couldn't sleep. I lay with my face pressed tight against the pillow so
I wouldn't have to see the things hung up on the wall: my mother's
portrait over the black altar; by the window, a framed sampler of oyster shells and pearls she and I had bought in a seaside village the previous summer. There we had stood in the drizzle to watch a diver in
a white robe plunge from a small boat into the sea. I had been afraid
that the robe would get tangled around the diver's legs the way my
nightgown did at night and cause her to drown. Later that year, while
my mother wept at night in her unhappiness, I imagined seawater
flowing out of the frame into the darkness of the room. Now, sleeping in the same room, I was plunging endlessly into her tears: I was
that diver with the long robe tangled around my feet. I sat up to keep
from drowning. Getting out of bed, I closed all the curtains as tightly
as possible so no light from the street shone on the portrait or the oys-

ters; then I took my cardigan sweater from the suitcase and threw it over the altar so I would not see its black surface. But when I lay back down, I still could not sleep.

Before long the front door rattled. My father was home. I waited a little and then got up. I should be sure to greet him, I thought, since this was my first night back in his house. Right before I left her house, my aunt Akiko had taken me aside and said, "You must try very hard to show respect to your father and your new mother. You are the older of the two. Your mother would want you to set a good example for your brother." After she had said this, my aunt looked pale, her lips drawn tight as if she were going to cry; she had told me to do something she wished I didn't have to do, but all the same, I had to do it.

Downstairs, my father and Michiko were sitting in the small room with the door half-open. I was surprised to see him already in his pajamas. I stood in the doorway for a while not knowing what to say. I thought he would be changing and sleeping in my brother's room from now on.

Hiroshi and Michiko looked back at me. They were sitting on her futon and drinking from a glass they passed back and forth. I had never seen two adults drink from the same glass; only mothers did that with very small children. *Maybe he's wearing his pajamas,* I thought all the same, *because it's hot.*

"Why are you wearing that?" Hiroshi demanded, pointing in my general direction.

I looked at my gown and realized how ugly it was with that sticky candy pink.

"It's hers," I pointed at Michiko. "She gave it to me to wear."

Michiko said nothing to verify that. Hiroshi, too, remained silent. She passed him the glass they were sharing, and he took a sip.

"Jumpei's already sleeping," I said. "Sometimes he cries if you wake him up in the middle of the night. You can sleep in my room tonight if you want to. I don't grind my teeth anymore."

"Go back upstairs," my father ordered me. "Don't bother about other people's business. Don't come down here again."

I went back to my room, saw the cardigan covering up the altar, and was glad that my father hadn't taken me up on my offer. He would have been angry at me for hanging my clothes in the wrong place. I was only being polite when I had said he could sleep in my room. As I closed the door behind me, I could hear Michiko bursting out in a high-pitched laugh.

A month later, in the locker room after our volleyball practice, a ninth-grade girl, Junko, told me why Hiroshi and Michiko were sleeping in the same room. We had just taken our showers and were drying off. We sat in front of the lockers with towels wrapped around us. When Junko went into the particular physical details, I didn't even know what part of the body she was talking about.

"It's where you have your periods, you know," she said.

"But I don't have anything like that," I protested.

"You've heard about them, haven't you?"

As Junko began to dry her hair, I recalled the afternoon back in fifth grade when all the girls had been excused from gym class to hear a lecture in the auditorium. Two of the women teachers had told us something about bleeding, and my friends were very squeamish about it afterward. But my brother was having frequent nosebleeds at that time so blood didn't seem like such a dramatic thing to me. He could start the bleeding at will, sometimes, by scrunching his eyes and breathing through the nose. I had tried this myself with no success: I had wanted my nose to start bleeding while my mother was nagging me about practicing my piano or doing my math homework, so she would have to stop talking and tend to me instead. But she had thought I was making funny faces at her and had complained that I never took anything seriously. At any rate, I concluded that this menstruation business was like a once-a-month nosebleed I might get in some distant future. The lecture didn't alarm me like the other health presentations, about leprosy, for instance, or Japanese encephalitis, which you could get from being bitten by a certain kind of mosquito.

But now Junko was talking about people sleeping together and having babies. I leaned forward and covered my face with my hands because I was crying all of a sudden and could not stop.

"Maybe my father does that with her," I insisted after a while, my voice sounding high and weak. "But he never did anything like that with my mother."

"Don't be silly. You wouldn't be here if they hadn't," Junko laughed.

"But my parents never slept in the same room."

In the end, Junko said, "Okay. Maybe your parents only did that twice. To have you and your brother."

We finished dressing and walked to the train station. She ran into the bakery in front of the station, came out with two buns filled with sweet bean paste, and handed one to me.

"Look," she said, "I didn't mean to make you cry. I thought you knew more than you did."

Sitting on the bench on the platform next to her, I ate the bun even though I hated bean paste because it was overly sweet. The bread was too soft and fluffy while the paste was too sticky—purple, full of small lumps. I kept chewing carefully so I wouldn't choke or start crying again. When the train pulled in, I got up too quickly from the bench. Suddenly I was dizzy and out of breath. Everything looked purple.

Our two-month summer vacation was going to begin in late June. Until that year, Jumpei and I had spent every July and August with our mother and her family in her parents' village. Though most of our uncles and aunts lived away from the village, everyone came back—"came home," as they said—for the summer. One evening in

June, our uncle Shiro called and said that he and his family would meet my brother and me at the station so we could make the trip together.

"I don't know exactly when Father was planning for Jumpei and me to go," I said. "I can't ask him because he's still at work."

"That's all right," Shiro assured me. "I'll call him at his office tomorrow and make sure it's okay with him. Tell your brother that Kenichi and I are going to teach him how to fish."

"You should tell Ken Nichan to call me," I told Shiro. Kenichi hadn't visited us since we had moved back to live with my father and Michiko, though we went to see him and our aunt Keiko a few times. "I'm going out for the volleyball team. I want him to show me the roundhouse serve."

"So you're looking for a killer serve?" Shiro chuckled. "When will you start acting more like a girl?" Shiro had always been the uncle who teased me the most. He had a way of screwing up his face so you couldn't tell if he was smiling or frowning. I could see him, even over the phone, making that face.

"Never," I said.

After we hung up, I woke up my brother to tell him that we were going to our grandparents' house with Shiro's family. We talked about how Shiro and Kenichi would teach him to fish. Our other uncle, Yasuo, would be fishing alone, we imagined—he was such a good fisherman he liked to go by himself and not be bothered by people who were less serious about the sport. I could already see all of us eating watermelon in the backyard in the afternoons, everyone laughing and spitting out the black seeds. Though our father said nothing in the next few days about our visit, we assumed that everything was settled. The prospect made us even more eager for the end of the school term.

About a week later, Hiroshi told Jumpei and me to meet him at his father Tatsuo's house after school because he had something important to say. When he came in, around five o'clock, he ordered us into the drawing room, where Tatsuo, already seated in one of the armchairs, pointed at the couch for my brother and me to sit down. Hiroshi took the other armchair. Then, without any pause or preamble, he said, "It's about your grandparents. You're not to see them again." "That's right," Tatsuo continued. "Your mother is gone, and you have a new mother. It's time for some changes." Jumpei started crying right away. He kept wiping his face with his shirtsleeve and sobbing out loud.

"Be quiet," Tatsuo scolded.

"You mean we won't ever see them?" I asked.

"I'll make exceptions if somebody dies and you have to go to the funeral," Hiroshi replied. "Or if your uncle Kenichi ever gets married, you may attend the wedding."

"Other than that, I won't see any of them at all?"

"When the priest comes to read the sutras for your mother, I'll invite your aunt Keiko. She can come hear them."

"I'm supposed to go and see her soon. She wants to buy my summer clothes. She and Ken Nichan called the other day," I pointed out. "They want me to come over soon."

"You have a new mother to go shopping with. You don't need your aunt."

"I'll be at school when the priest comes to read the sutras. He always comes in the morning. May I stay home then so I can see Keiko?"

"Absolutely not."

"My mother let me stay home from school when I asked. She said I should just ask her. It was better than pretending to be sick. Just be honest, she said."

Hiroshi hit the table with his fist. "Your mother indulged you too much. She spoiled you and left you to me. You are not to talk about her."

I turned my face aside and squeezed my eyes shut. When I opened them, I noticed Tatsuo's purple vase, which was always empty. Tatsuo never put flowers in it because he never entertained guests. He sat in the drawing room alone or else scolded us there and locked us up afterward to reflect on our faults in the dark.

"May I write to my grandparents?" I asked. I had written them every Sunday since I had learned to write in the first grade. Before that, I had sent them pictures.

Tatsuo and Hiroshi looked at each other. Tatsuo said, "You may write so long as you show the letters to your father first."

Hiroshi nodded. Jumpei was wailing and hiccuping. Neither Hiroshi nor Tatsuo tried to comfort us; neither said they were sorry to cause us pain. I started thinking how much I hated them, how I would outwit them. I could not visit my relatives without Hiroshi finding out—my absence would be noticed. But I could write my letters without showing them to him first.

Every afternoon on my way home from school, I walked past a post office. I could write to my grandparents during my lunch hour and mail the letter from there. I could buy stamps with my monthly allowance and lunch money. To ward off suspicion, I would write letters now and then to show Hiroshi, but I would never mail the ones I showed him. No one had ever inspected my private letters before in my life. No one had forbidden me to see my own relatives.

Soon Hiroshi and Tatsuo told us we were dismissed. "Go see your aunt in the kitchen," Tatsuo said. "She'll give you supper before you go home."

Akiko and Kazumi came through the kitchen door into the hallway when they heard my brother and me. "Your father's too harsh," Akiko whispered with tears in her eyes. "I'm sorry I can't help more." She put her arms around my shoulders and hugged me so that her hair touched my neck. The moment I hugged her back, leaning into her shoulder, tears started coming out of my eyes. No matter how I tried to stop, my whole body kept shaking with the small jagged breaths I was taking. Out of the corner of my eye, I could see Kazumi holding Jumpei's hand and patting him on the back, trying to comfort him, but soon she was beginning to sniffle, too. Nobody said, "Don't worry. It's going to be all right." I imagined my grandparents standing in the road in front of their house and waving at us, the way they did at the end of every summer when we were leaving on the bus. Now maybe they, too, would be crying. And Aunt Keiko would have to come to our house alone to hear the sutras and never see us. My brother was beyond whimpering or sobbing; he was making a loud wailing noise. Hiroshi and Tatsuo did not come out of the drawing room to see what was going on, if we were all right. Letting go of my aunt and wiping my face on my sleeve, I thought how wrong my mother had been to think that we would be better off without her.

Someone is playing an organ or a horn in the street. It's the same tune over and over, played loud and harsh. I sit up in bed, automatically repeating the words in my mind.

> *medaka no gakko wa*
> *kawa no naka*
> *sotto nozoite metegoran*
> *minna de oyugi shiteiruyo*

> the minnow children
> go to school in the river
> look
> they're playing together

The tune begins to fade away in the distance just as I run downstairs.

"What was that?" I ask Sylvia, who is drinking coffee at the kitchen table in her pink jogging suit, her long red hair in a ponytail.

She looks at me as if she doesn't know what I'm talking about.

"Who was playing that song? It's crazy."

"Oh, that," Sylvia laughs. "That's the tofu truck."

"The tofu truck?"

"A guy selling tofu from his truck. He always plays that same song so we can tell when he's driving by—in case we need tofu."

"They should write him a tofu song," I tell her. "Not the minnow children. It's a song we all learn in kindergarten. It has nothing to do with tofu."

"Poor guy," Sylvia says, sipping her coffee. "Can you imagine hearing that over and over all day?"

"No."

"I know all the street vendors by their songs. There's a guy who goes around sharpening knives. And a guy who sells fish cake. They each have their own song."

I imagine my school friends now grown up and married, listening to our silly childhood songs blaring out of trucks to get them to run out and buy tofu. When we were young and talked about our future, we debated whether we would ever get married or pursue some artistic career, whether we would fall in love or find the right partner by allowing our parents to go through matchmakers. We were so serious about being happy.

"I was woken up by the tofu truck," I tell Vince on the phone while Sylvia gets ready for work. "He was playing the song about the minnow children."

"That's what they've done with electronic music here," he says. "In some cities, when the traffic light turns green, a tune comes on so you know which way to walk. I was crossing a street in Nagasaki once, when I realized I was listening to 'Coming Through the Rye.'"

We talk some more and agree to meet downtown for lunch. After we hang up, I continue to sit at the table, drinking the coffee Sylvia poured for me and thinking of last night's cab ride. With the raised highways intersecting at sharp angles in front of me, I felt as though I had been dropped into the middle of a high-speed chase from a science-fiction film. The bright glow of neon made the city look more like a Hollywood set than any real place. Now when I think of singing lights and musical vendors, this whole country reminds me of an amusement park, a big Disneyland with computerized lights and electronic wonders. The place I came back to seems absurd, comical, even silly.

But how can I possibly feel that way after last night, when, lying in the dark a few miles from the house where my mother had chosen to die, I realized it was fear that had kept me away for so long—fear of this city, this country, of being plunged back into my mother's unhappiness? I slept poorly all night because I kept remembering the past. Then, woken up by a silly tofu song, I find myself staying with people I have never met before in my life. I feel perfectly at home, safe, in their house. Accepting hospitality is my gift: I can make myself comfortable anywhere; I am good at being a guest. As I get up and pour more coffee, open the fridge to find some bread because I don't want to walk down the hill and ride the train on an empty stomach, everything, even my own concerns, seems so calm and banal, completely harmless. How can I feel this way after not being able to sleep last night? My memories are painful enough to keep me awake a long time, and yet some part of my mind is thinking about what to wear to lunch.

I put the coffee cup in the sink and walk up the winding stairway toward my room. To the left of the stairway, the wall is solid with wood panels that are stained a dark brown. To my right, from between the lighter-colored cypress pillars, I can look down at the front entrance. The door is open to let in the air. A light breeze is moving the glossy leaves of the orange trees planted near the gate. Ascending the stairway, I am suspended in midair between these two views, between two separate pictures I cannot bring together.

I walk down the steep hill from Sylvia's house to the commuter train station, a few miles to the south. Gradually, as I walk on, the view of the city and the sea gets blocked out; finally, I can't see them at all beyond the station building. When I look back to the north, the dark mountain ridge stands against the sky. The northern subdivisions crowd up against the green.

A train is gliding into the station just as I punch in my ticket and walk up the stairs. It's the same color as it used to be—a shade between dark brown and purple. The electric doors slide open. Inside, the seats are the same green, and posters hang from the ceiling advertising movies and gossip magazines. I sit down facing the mountains. Several young women get on at the next stop and stand together by the windows. Once in a while, all of them burst out laughing at the same time; their hands fly up to cover their mouths, which are carefully outlined in lipstick. They are wearing blue and gray tailored suits and carrying briefcases. They must be office workers on their lunch break. I close my eyes and feel the train rocking slightly as the wheels hit the crack between the rails. Everything about the ride is exactly as I remember from when I was a teenager taking this same commuter line to school.

When the train pulls into the downtown station, I immediately recognize the big department stores, the newspaper building, the hotels to the west. There must be some new buildings that I have never seen, but the old ones stand out. If the city has changed, I don't notice it.

"Maybe it was a mistake to come back here," I tell Vince at a health food restaurant, only a block away from the bookstore where I worked one spring break, typing order forms in English and German. "It's too much the same, but it also seems so weird." At the bookstore, old women were hired expressly to bring cups of tea to the male workers at their desks. All employees had to put on dark blue smocks over their street clothes. Sometimes I didn't button mine all the way up to my throat and had to be reminded. "It looks sloppy," said the man who was my supervisor. Maybe there still are old women pouring tea all afternoon in that building.

The waitress brings our plates of vegetable sandwiches and goes away. The restaurant is attached to a health food supermarket, both of them quite new. Most of the people shopping or eating here are Americans.

"Are you still going to travel around for a while?" Vince asks me as we begin to eat.

"I don't know," I reply. "I almost feel too tired to think of what to do next. But I suppose I should travel."

"I brought you something that might help." He pulls a thick red book out of his bag and pushes it across the table, his big hands maneuvering it around our plates. "This is a directory I use when I travel. It has all the business hotels and youth hostels listed in major cities. Here, you can borrow it."

"Thanks."

"Maybe it would be good to travel," he suggests. "You said you wanted to see parts of Japan you didn't see when you lived here. It'll inspire you to write. You'll feel better afterward."

We eat in silence. I know Vince is right. I have managed to come here only because of the sabbatical, which allowed me to say to myself, "I am here as a writer. What I am doing is part of my job. Seeing my family is just an extra thing." I can't keep saying that unless I leave Kobe and travel, as planned.

"You're right," I admit. "I didn't see that much of Japan when I lived here."

Vince smiles as he says, "This is a foreign country you are getting to know."

After Vince leaves to teach his night class, I walk to the tourism office of the Japan Railway Company, which is inside the downtown station. At the counter, I present my passport and my rail pass voucher to an old man who is wearing a uniform all rail workers wear: a starched white shirt, creased black pants, and a wide-brimmed black hat. He looks through my papers for a long time and finally asks me if I speak Japanese. Though I nod, he doesn't start up a conversation. All he says is, "Please wait," before he disappears into another part of the office.

He returns with the rail pass, which is a piece of embossed paper folded in two.

"When do you want this to be effective?" he asks me.

"When can I have it be effective?"

He shrugs. "Anytime," he says. "Today, if you'd like."

It's already four o'clock. I need a day to decide where to go and to make hotel reservations. I want to get in touch with Miya Ueda, the friend I wrote to in early May.

"The day after tomorrow," I say.

The man picks up the big silver stamp and readjusts the dates, rolling forward the days. I watch him as he stamps my pass: 5/25/90. The ink is dark and perfectly printed without a smear. He pushes the stamped pass toward me without speaking or even smiling. As I nod and turn to go, I realize how different this transaction has been from what I am used to: The man said nothing to me except what strictly pertained to the business at hand; he didn't ask me where I was going, where I was from, what I was doing in Japan. He made no small talk. He didn't even thank me for doing business with his company. For once, I miss what I am mildly irritated by in the American Midwest: people wishing me to have a nice day, perfect strangers engaging in small talk. Here a person could be isolated in polite silence for days.

Walking out of the station, I pass the golden statue of a dancer that has been here as far back as I can remember. Up ahead, across a busy street, I can see the Sony Building, the Mr. Donut store, the San-ai boutique, and other places I used to visit. On this side of the street, a crowd of people is waiting for the light to change: businessmen in dark suits, women office workers in their tailored dresses and medium-high heels, and young women shopping in what would be party outfits in Wisconsin—pink or white dresses with gathered skirts, silk flowers pinned to lapels. Here women wear clothes like these every day just to go to the store. I stop behind them. In my denim shorts and T-shirt, I'm out of place, but no more so than when I was thirteen or fourteen and wearing jeans and sweatshirts. I used to spend whole Saturdays walking up and down the same streets, window-shopping alone, because I did not want to go home to see my stepmother cleaning the house yet again. Every movement of her rag or broom announced that even the accumulation of dust was somehow my fault.

The light changes. Stepping into the intersection, I remember what Vince said about the singing traffic lights in other cities. Around me, everyone is taking firm, brisk steps, looking straight ahead. We could all be marching to silent music coming from our various childhoods. On the other side of the street, I break away from the crowd. Leaning against the window of a hat shop, I open the directory Vince gave me and start thinking of where I can spend the next four weeks.

Shapes of
Land

"Kobe. Kobe-San-nomiya," the conductor announces the downtown station in the singsong my brother and I used to mimic. "Thank you for using Japan Railways. Please be careful not to forget your umbrellas as you leave the train." Reaching out for my suitcase, I am irritated by the announcement, by the impersonal courtesy I cannot get used to— store clerks bowing and welcoming us into their stores without making eye contact, conductors reminding us, over the loud-speaker, not to forget our belongings. Every greeting sounds exactly the same, as if recorded, addressed to a large generic audience. Face-to-face, nobody says anything.

As I step onto the platform and walk toward the commuter line, I can already feel the humidity. In the four weeks I have been gone, the rainy season must have arrived in Kobe. The sky is heavy with clouds, and people are carrying umbrellas. The umbrellas remind me of Kyushu, the southern island where I spent two of my four weeks: there, old women walked down the street with umbrellas under the midday sun while, across the narrow channel, a volcano erupted on a small island. The volcanic ashes rained down on the streets of Kagoshima for a week. Though the ashes were invisible as they came down, every morning the pavement was covered with a half inch of white silt. I could not run without coughing. Except for the old women, no one showed any anxiety about the ashes. The young people sat in rooftop cafés to watch the smoke spewing from the island across the water.

The old women with their umbrellas reminded me of my grandmother Fuku. Like her, they had borne and raised children before and during the Second World War, before the Western diet of high calcium and protein. Their backs were bent, their necks foreshortened. Watching them, I remembered my mother's insistence that my brother and I drink milk every morning. "You have to have protein to grow tall and strong," she had said. She had discouraged us from sitting Japanese-style on the floor with our legs folded under in the posture called *seiza*, "correct-sitting," because she had feared that our young bones might get crooked or stunted. Every generation has its fears. My mother's generation worried about not being tall and strong, while my grandmother's distrusted anything that rained down, like bombs, from the sky.

It's drizzling when I get off the commuter train. I stand in line for a cab, and when my turn comes, I shove my suitcase in and sit down. The driver cocks his head when I give him Sylvia's address.

"That house belongs to a *gaijin* family, doesn't it?" he asks, using the word that literally means an outside-person and, therefore, a foreigner.

"Yes. My friend is an American."

"Are you a *nikkei*?" A nikkei is a foreigner of Japanese descent.

"I'm an American citizen," I reply, "but I was born here."

The driver puts his car in gear and pulls away from the curb in silence. I don't ask why he thought I was a foreigner. All over Japan for the last four weeks, people have thought I was a foreigner. Even other foreigners thought I was one of them.

Lost in the old castle town of Kanazawa during my first week, I met an American man sitting outside a temple and turning his map around to get his bearings. "When you get that map figured out," I said, "I'd like to see it. I'm lost, too." We decided to set out together to look for the train station. When we got to an intersection where two workers were fixing a streetlamp, I asked them in Japanese, "Which way do we turn here to get to the train station?" They told me; we walked a block and stopped for the light to change. The man I was with said, "Hey, I didn't know you could speak Japanese." "Why?" I asked; "I was born in Kobe." "But you're not dressed like a Japanese woman," he pointed out. "You don't even have a purse."

A few feet away from us, five young women, all in lacy pastel dresses, were waiting for the light to change. Each of them had a white leather purse with shoulder straps, medium-heeled shoes that matched her dress and pantyhose. Their hair was softly permed to frame their faces. In my T-shirt, denim shorts, and Reeboks, my long straight hair in a ponytail, I looked nothing like them. Instead of a purse, I carried a backpack especially designed for runners and walkers. "I guess I know what you mean," I admitted, and the two of us started laughing. Though I had just met this man and would most likely never see him again, he seemed like someone I had known a long time. He opened his mouth and tipped his head back when he laughed. He looked me in the face and smiled as he made half-ironic comments about the way people looked. He was like my friends. He was American.

In Kanazawa and in the other cities, I stayed at *minshuku*, private houses where you can get a room and two meals a day. The minshuku

I went to were run by older women, who stayed in small sitting rooms by the main entrance all day, making sure their guests had everything they needed. Except for me, the guests were businessmen on their sales trips. Perhaps they made regular visits to the same cities and always stayed at the same minshuku; they were very friendly toward the hostesses. As these men stood in the foyer putting on their shoes to go out, they would announce where they were going, when they would be back. "I am leaving for my meeting downtown now," they would call toward the room where the hostess was sitting. "I expect to be back at seven." They would wait for the hostess to come out to wish them a good day. Later, coming back into the house, the men would call loudly again, "Hi, I'm home. I got out of my meeting early," or "Hi, I'm home. My meeting was long, and I'm really tired." The hostess would come running out with slippers for the men to change into. Then, together, they would go into her room to talk over tea. It was almost as though these men were staying at their mother's or aunt's house.

In Japan, either you are an insider or an outsider, never anything in between. When an insider stays at a minshuku, it isn't at all like business; it's a family visit. With an outsider, on the other hand, the hostess does not even make small talk, much less fetch slippers and offer tea in her own sitting room. I was an outsider. When I wanted to leave for the day, I put on my shoes and left. When I came back, I got my own slippers and went to my room. Though the hostesses knew that I could speak Japanese, they kept their conversations with me to bare essentials: what time I wanted to have dinner served, what time I wanted to check in or out. They used the most formal and polite level of language, addressing me not by name but as *Okyaku-san,* "Our Honorable Guest." Most evenings, I could hear them talking to the other guests in the hallway, using the informal language people use with old friends or relatives. From the conversations I overheard, I knew that most of the hostesses were widows and had daughters who lived nearby raising children. Perhaps that was their idea of what a woman my age should be doing. They couldn't figure out why I was traveling around the country alone, visiting museums and craft centers. Because I was nothing like their daughters, I might as well have been a gaijin. For my part, I was glad to be left alone. I did not expect to feel "at home" at what was essentially a bed-and-breakfast. My staying there was just business, nothing like staying at the houses of friends. Silence was a relief and a protection.

As the cab climbs uphill now, I am protected inside the same silence. Though cabdrivers are probably the only people in Japan who chat with their customers, this driver isn't going to talk to me. He is staring straight ahead. In spite of what I said, he thinks that I am a gaijin, that my Japanese might be limited. He doesn't want to start a conversation we might not be able to finish.

I *am* glad, in a way, for his silence: I don't want to have to explain who I am, why I'm here. Still, it's odd to be driving up this familiar hill, passing the park, the hospital, the condominiums, the houses I used to see as a teenager, while being treated as a foreigner. Visiting the other cities was different. In most of them, people spoke slightly different dialects from the one I had grown up with. Often, over the phone, I had to ask them to repeat themselves. I got lost in every city, especially when I went running, which made me feel all the more that I was in a foreign place. But I had expected to feel that way from the start.

Using my four-week rail pass, I had first gone to Kanazawa, which is north of Kobe, and then all the way down to Kagoshima, the southernmost city on the southern island of Kyushu. I spent the last two weeks retracing my way back north toward Kobe: through the middle and northern parts of Kyushu and then the southwestern part of the main island, Honshu. In each city, I visited museums and craft centers to look at tapestries, ceramics, woodblock prints, gold-leaf painted screens. Nothing I saw made me feel "at home."

Just as I was lost in the unfamiliar cities, I was lost in the landscapes, the floral paintings, the color juxtapositions of tapestries. I did not understand the shape and scale of things: yellow cranes flying among pale purple maple leaves much larger than their wingspan, perfectly groomed pine trees painted in nature scenes, rain falling as unbroken diagonal lines across a river scene. These details, I thought, were deliberately artificial, ornate. At the same time, in floral paintings, there were often a few insect-eaten leaves or buds, supposedly to enhance the beauty of the perfect blooms. I did not understand this mixture of what I considered to be fantasy and superrealism. I knew that the words I used in my head—fantasy, realism, scale, perspective—were all useless terms for looking at this art, but they were the only concepts I had. I had grown up looking at Western art. I could only be lost in what I was seeing now.

My feeling of being lost was strongest in the last city I visited, Kurashiki, at a large museum known for its Asian collection. The collection was housed in a restored *kura,* a Japanese-style wooden storage building in which rich samurai families used to keep their treasures. As soon as I entered the building, before my eyes adjusted to the semidark, I could hear a clinking sound coming at twenty- or thirty-second intervals inside the crowded kura. I began to make my way among a group of older tourists to view the huge wooden statues of bodhisattvas. When I got close to the first statue, I realized what the sound had been: all around the pedestal of the statue, hundred-yen coins were scattered about. I looked around. The men and the women moved through the room in hushed reverence; dressed mostly in black, they must have been in their fifties or sixties. Some women were wearing their best black kimonos with family crests on them. At the head of this procession was the tour guide, a young woman carrying a yellow flag with the name of the tour group printed on it. Now and then, someone bowed to the statue in front of her or him and tossed another coin. I wasn't sure what I was supposed to think or feel about the whole thing—whether to be amused or irritated or moved. I wanted to be back at the Art Institute in Chicago where, in the Asian collection, my footsteps had triggered the lights as I moved through the deserted room of bodhisattvas. It was hot and close inside the kura. I felt terribly tired of moving among men and women who traveled in large groups and never did anything alone. Even the bodhisattvas made me feel like an outsider. There was something generic about them to what must be my Western sensibility. One bodhisattva looked pretty much like another, in a way that Van Gogh's poppies and irises never looked like Georgia O'Keeffe's. I know nothing, I thought, about art that is an expression of universal enlightenment instead of personal vision. Its beauty will always remain foreign to me.

Leaving that last city and boarding the train to Kobe, I wondered if my remaining three weeks might still offer some kind of homecoming, a double homecoming since I would be returning from my four-week trip as well as from my years in the States. Now, as the cab climbs the last leg of the uphill route, I cannot decide how I feel, lost or at home.

The front door of Sylvia's house is locked. The key chain I pull out of my backpack still has my keys from Green Bay: the house key, the car key, the keys to my office and the building in which I teach.

The foyer is dark as I unlock the door and step in. Putting down my suitcase, I kneel to take off my scuffed-up white Reeboks and reach toward the low wooden shelves. Next to the empty space where I put mine, there are two more pairs of Reeboks. The white pair looks almost identical to mine, only a little newer and perhaps a size smaller; the black hightops could be my own pair, which I have left in my closet in Green Bay. Half crouched in the entryway, I glance through the shelves and find other shoes that could be my own: Nike running shoes, Keds, oxfords, a few pairs of flat pumps. My white Reeboks look completely normal here.

When I look up, Cadine is coming around the corner from the kitchen. She stops, her face flushed, and puts her palm flat against her chest.

"I'm sorry," I apologize, standing up. "I didn't mean to scare you."

She lets her hand drop to her side. "I thought you were Hashimoto-san, the cleaning lady. I was alone. I was hoping it wasn't her."

"Why not?"

"I can't talk to her. She only speaks Japanese."

We stand in the hallway for a while.

"My school's out now," Cadine adds. "But Mom's still working." The Japanese colleges, where Sylvia teaches English, are in session for another week, though the International School Cadine goes to is out because it runs on an American schedule. "So how was your trip?"

"All right, but it's good to be back." As soon as I say it, I realize how true that is. "Hey, it's nice to see you." I smile, and I'm pleased to see Cadine smile back.

We go upstairs, where I put down my suitcase and open up the shades. The rain has stopped for now, but the view looks hazy beyond the porch, white mist hanging heavy over the city.

After unpacking my suitcase, I go into the shower, which consists of two rooms separated by a door: a wood-paneled changing room with a sink and a linen closet, a tiled room with a Japanese-style deep tub and a shower rigged in the corner. When I enter the changing room, one of the cats, Ophelia, jumps out of the closet where she has been sleeping on top of the towels. I undress, go into the other room, and turn on the shower. The water pressure is good and strong. I step under the steady hot stream. Then, squinting my eyes from the spray, I reach out for the shampoo bottle. My wet fingers close on a famil-iar bottle of Mills Farms Swedish Formula Jojoba shampoo. It's the same sixteen-ounce bottle I buy at the health food store in Green Bay. But this one is from the health food store downtown where Vince and I had lunch a month ago. Pasted over the bottle, there's a small tag that spells out the name, Jojoba shampoo, in the phonetic *katakana* script used for foreign words. I squeeze a half inch of the pink shampoo onto my palm and close my eyes. The familiar scent brings me back, momentarily, to the locker room at the YMCA where I swam twice a week all last year.

On Mondays and Wednesdays, I had my office hours from eleven to half past twelve and then drove to the Y to swim two-thirds of a mile after the lunch-hour crowd was gone. Sometimes there was no one else in the pool. I would get out just in time to shower and drive back to teach my two-o'clock class, eating my egg salad or tempeh sandwich as I walked from my car to the building. My hair would be wet or frozen as I sat down at the long seminar table and looked around at my students. "Let's see who's here today," I would say as I quickly checked off the absences in my grade book. It was a small class. I didn't have to call their names. Though I took attendance, everyone knew that I wasn't a big disciplinarian, that they didn't have to lie to me about why they had missed class.

As the water washes the lather off my hair onto my back, I squeeze my eyes tighter and remember who I have grown up to be.

Cadine is sitting in the living room when I come out of the shower. "The cleaning lady never came," she says. "Maybe my mom was wrong about when she's coming. My mom's Japanese isn't so good, either. She just keeps saying *hai, hai,* 'yes, yes,' even when she doesn't really understand."

"I'll call her later if your mother wants," I offer. "I'll ask her when she's coming."

I get a book from upstairs and sit down in the living room with Cadine. Outside in the yard, the orange trees are blooming and their other cat, Nietzsche, is stalking sparrows. I am glad to be back where I can talk or not talk, by choice. Now that the trip is over, I realize what a burden my solitude and silence have been, what a relief it is to be back here. Perhaps I can feel at home, not only in this house but also in the city of Kobe, with its familiar neighborhoods, the downtown shops, the mountains, and the sea.

Walking or running in various cities in the last month, I began to think that Kobe was indeed nothing like the other places in Japan.

Nobody ever visits Kobe to see traditional Japanese culture. All the points of interest mentioned in guidebooks about my hometown are foreign: the Victorian houses built by the British and Americans at the turn of the century, the cable car that goes up the mountainside, the big Western-style hotels, herb and rose gardens, the Indian restaurants downtown. It's no wonder, having grown up here, that I don't think of woodblock prints and Yuzen tapestries as my heritage, that I don't look for my "roots" in the traditional places and arts of Japan. Before my trip, I had assumed that my foreignness was a result of my years in the States and my particular family circumstance: I don't come from a "normal" Japanese family. But I wonder now if growing up in Kobe didn't have a lot to do with it—I might not have turned out traditionally Japanese even if my mother hadn't chosen to die; my foreignness isn't simply a result of tragedy or deprivation but a part of my Kobe upbringing.

I want to spend a few days thinking about that possibility, getting to know the city again, feeling at home here. It will be easier to see my family, to face the particular and personal things that made me "different," if I know that these were not the only important factors in making me who I am. So I decide to give myself some extra time before calling my father or my grandmother—even though, as soon as I come to that decision, I begin to suspect that I am simply giving myself an excuse, stalling and procrastinating.

The next morning, the rain stops as I get off the commuter train downtown and walk to the bus stop. When the bus for central Kobe pulls up to the curb, I climb on and give my token to the driver. "Could you let me know when we get to the Tsuyuno-cho stop?" I ask him. The bus goes through downtown and heads northwest, back toward the mountain ridge. Soon the driver is looking back and nodding at me. I stand up and get off at the next stop.

The area is almost exactly as I remember it. Across the street from the bus stop, there still is an *ichiba,* a roofed-over arcade of small stores where people shop for groceries, going from the greengrocer's to the fish store, the rice shop, the bakery, or the butcher's. Even thirteen years ago, when I was leaving the country, these ichibas had been disappearing because they couldn't compete with supermarkets. But this one is thriving. Women with baskets on their arms are coming in and out, some of them with small children tagging along. My mother and I used to shop here. This is the neighborhood where I was born.

I walk east toward the river, past the small hospital with a sign that says "Doi Gynecological Hospital." The small print under the name reads: "the doctor is a woman." She has to be the same doctor who delivered my brother and me—she was about my mother's age. If I knew how to introduce myself without awkwardness, I would stop in. But I continue on to the river, across the bridge, and then head north. This street, which borders the river, is the one our old house is on. Already I can see the steep hill in the back. Across from the low wall that separates the street from the river, I pass the corner store where my uncles used to buy me candy. The place looks unchanged, with a cloth hung in the doorway, instead of a wooden door, to make it look more inviting.

As I approach our old block—the last block before the mountains—something looks wrong. The green of the mountains looks too vivid, too close. Crossing the last street onto the block, I realize why. There is nothing obstructing the view; there are no houses. The gray concrete of a parking lot covers the space where the houses used to be: ours and two others, all of them wooden two-story buildings. Only a few cars are parked in the lot. The middle part, where our house was located, is empty. I go to stand where the small pond used to be in our yard. My uncles Shiro and Kenichi, who were living in this house with my parents back then, planted a mountain ash tree beside the pond when I was born. There is no trace of the pond, the tree, or the downstairs room where my mother and my aunt Keiko used to sew.

The house had been occupied by people in my mother's family from the Second World War until a few years ago, when one of my

younger cousins graduated from college and moved to Kyushu for a job. My grandmother had told me in a letter about the house being sold, but no one had said anything about it being torn down.

Another car is pulling into the lot. I walk out into the street. The low wall along the river is marked with children's drawings in red and yellow chalk: flowers, trees, stick-figure people. My uncles and I used to draw here. They were always teaching me to try complicated things like airplanes, ships, cars. Heading north, I climb the steep hill toward the reservoir we hiked to back then. Shiro and Kenichi took me walking every day because a doctor had told my mother it was important for me to get exercise and strengthen my legs. I was born with dislocated hips and spent my first sixteen months with my legs in a cast. After the cast came off and I learned to walk, the doctor warned my mother that if I didn't strengthen my legs, I might limp for the rest of my life. Climbing the last steep stretch now, I'm not sure if I remember walking up here with Shiro and Kenichi back then, or if I just remember being here at some later time with them.

Where the path levels off at the top, the reservoir comes into view quite suddenly, larger than I remember. The blue water looks deep and calm, divided from the path by a wire fence. There is nobody in sight. I linger by the water for a while and then walk along the fence to the ledge overlooking the western part of downtown, about two miles away. Tall white buildings cluster along the coast, and beyond them, the sea stretches dark blue. Right after World War II, my mother used to climb this same hill to look out at the sea because it was blue and calm just as it had been before the war, before miles of rubble stretched between this hill and downtown. My grandparents and their younger children had moved back to the countryside, leaving my mother and Shiro in town because they were still in high school. The year she climbed this hill to look at the sea beyond the rubble of downtown, she would have been seventeen, half the age I am now. She and Shiro had escaped the firebombs that destroyed most of Kobe because the house was too close to the mountains for the bombers to fly over. Neighborhoods only a mile to the south had burned down. Years later, my mother still had dreams about her house burning while she and Shiro ran up the hill to this reservoir to escape. Standing here almost fifty years later, I am inside her dreams of fire and water, dreams of destruction and narrow escape. Still, I cannot quite imagine what the downtown had looked like, reduced to rubble, any more than my mother as a young woman could have predicted this very moment: her daughter standing on this ledge after her death, after the destruction of her house in peacetime, and missing her with all the force of history.

As I get off the train near Sylvia's house, something begins to bother me. The trip to the old neighborhood has taken only an hour and a half each way. The two places where I lived with my father after my mother's death were both within five miles of Sylvia's house and therefore not significantly farther from the old house where Keiko and Kenichi were living. I could easily have gone to see them on my own. If my father had ever asked, my friends would have lied for me and said I had been with them. Why didn't I think of that back then? Was I so afraid of my father that I couldn't think of this simple way to disobey him?

I saw my mother's family only a few times between her death and my departure from the country. My brother and I were allowed to visit our grandparents twice together—for the third anniversary of our mother's death and for the fiftieth anniversary of our grandparents' wedding. Then, in the last week before I left Japan in 1977, I went alone to visit my grandparents in their village, and also Kenichi, who had gotten married a few years earlier and was living in our old house with his family. My father never knew. I pretended that I had gone with my friends to a cabin that belonged to one of their parents. By then, I knew better than to tell him.

Two years before that, I had been in Tokyo overnight for a school forensics competition. I called my uncle Shiro from the hotel when we checked in before the competition. He and his family came to hear my speech; afterward, they took me out to dinner. The next day, when my train was about to leave, Shiro and his wife came running onto the platform to see me off. They had been so happy to see me, they said, and they were proud of me for being in a national competition. As soon as I got home, I told my father about seeing Shiro. I made a point of being "honest," I suppose, because I was feeling self-righteous and angry in the way I often felt back then and still do sometimes, when I feel compelled to tell offensive or unpopular "truths," no matter what the consequences. My father hit me in the face and said he would never again allow me to go on overnight trips for school activities. He said it was no use allowing me to represent my school anyway, since I didn't win the competition.

I took no chances after that. Especially when I had only a week left before my escape to the States, I wasn't going to tell my father anything that might send him into a rage. Every night, I slept in my clothes and tennis shoes, with a big chair pushed against my door, ready in case he came in the middle of the night to kill me with my stepmother's butcher knife, something he had threatened several times to do. Maybe he would think this was his last chance and finally carry out his threat. I didn't want anything to happen so close to my freedom.

Walking up the long hill to Sylvia's house, I remember the urgency I felt back then about escaping his house with my life. This is why I haven't wanted to visit Kobe for so long: I didn't want to see him; I didn't even want to be in the same city with him. My reluctance to see him has kept me from seeing anyone else, and it continues to do so.

I know that I cannot contact anyone in my family without first fulfilling my duty toward my father and stepmother. My maternal grandmother, uncles, aunts; my father's sister, Akiko, and her daughter, Kazumi—all of them would feel awkward if I called them up and asked to visit them without first seeing my father, my stepmother, and my paternal grandfather, Tatsuo. Blood relationships are a webwork of obligations I cannot understand. Whether I like it or not, I have to honor their intricate restrictions so no one else will be forced into a bad position.

Coming into Sylvia's house, I am almost ready to pick up the phone and call my father's house, to get the thing over with. My stepmother is probably home, though my father must be working. Maybe Michiko still cleans the house every day—taking whole mornings to sweep, mop, polish every piece of furniture. Last year, when I saw the two of them in New York where they spent a weekend as part of their group tour, she asked me if I washed my socks and underwear every night rather than letting my laundry pile up for a week the way she had heard American women did. I told her I did my laundry every other week. She said she was happy that I hadn't gotten married and settled down in Japan, because she would have been embarrassed in front of her in-laws about what a terrible housekeeper I was. Though I was in New York that whole weekend staying with my friend Henri, I saw my parents just for one afternoon. That was the only time I saw them in the last thirteen years. I would be happy not to see them again for another thirteen years, or more.

All the same, I get my address book and go to the phone. I can't keep stalling forever, waiting to feel comfortable or ready, because I am never going to feel comfortable or ready. I have to call my father, so I can call everyone else. I remember what he looked like in New York: he had lost weight and his hair had turned gray. He is an old man now. I will never again have to fear for my life, not from him. Though I tell myself all these things, I cannot dial the number. Not today.

I dial my friend Miya's number instead. I have been calling her off and on since my first week in Japan and have never gotten an answer. The phone keeps ringing without an answer. Maybe she never got my letter. We might never be able to see each other. Still, I have enough things I want to do.

Three days later, Saturday, I get off the commuter train in Ashiya. The drizzle has stopped. The sky looks more blue than gray. People are staring at me because I am wearing my running shorts, tank top, and the heavily cushioned Brooks shoes I use for long-distance running. It's midmorning. Women are shopping in the boutiques around the station.

I stretch my legs against the wall and then start running east back into Kobe. After a mile, I head north up a hill. The last block before the house, which used to be gravel, is now paved. The brown dog that used to bark at me is of course gone. I speed up and sprint the last fifty yards. But when I stop and look up, the house my mother died in is no longer there. It has been torn down and the lot divided. Two new houses have been built, one of them with a shiny blue roof. The other house, with traditional ink-black *kawara* tiles, is situated where my mother's garden used to be, where her lettuce grew faster that last summer than we could eat it. But the same oaks and cherries in the back of the lot are casting shadows on the blue house. It was always cold and dark in the kitchen where my mother sat thinking about what a failure her life had become. I imagine someone else, a woman my age, sitting in the kitchen there. I want to go in and warn her. "My mother died here. Be careful. Get out while you can."

Retracing my steps back toward Ashiya, I pass the houses of my grade-school friends. From the names on the mailboxes, I know that the same families live here now: the Hondas, Yamanakas, Tanabes. Their fathers or brothers must still own the houses. I wish I could stop to ask after my friends, but most likely they have married and moved away; even their last names would be different. Whoever is in the house, their mothers or their sisters-in-law, would be puzzled to see a strange woman in a jogging outfit, sweaty and urgent with nostalgia. They would only feel awkward or embarrassed. So I don't stop, except once in front of a roadside shrine that was always here on my way to school. Inside what looks like a wooden cage the size of a refrigerator, several stone buddhas, called *jizos,* are seated on pillows.

Their faces worn down almost to nothing, the statues look more like piles of simple stones. Still, people have been bringing flowers and incense sticks. My grandmother used to pray to a roadside buddha like these on the road between her house and the river. For all I know, she still does—wishing her children and grandchildren success and prosperity.

In less than thirty minutes, I am approaching the seaside neighborhood in Ashiya where my family lived for five years, between when I was in kindergarten and in fourth grade. We were one of the twenty-four families living in a four-story apartment complex that belonged to Kawasaki Steel, the company my father worked for. My mother was happy there, surrounded by women her age who came over every day to drink tea and knit or sew together. When we moved to the house on the hill, she used to cry every night, saying that she missed her friends, she was so lonely. I want to stand in front of the apartment complex where she was happy and remember our time together.

In just a few minutes, I'm running in front of the post office where my mother and I mailed our letters to my grandparents every week. I turn the corner onto our street and stop.

In front of me stretches a thick barbed wire fence. Our building, twenty yards away inside the fence, is marked with yellow signs posted every ten yards or so: DANGER, DO NOT ENTER, CONSTRUC-TION AREA: HARD HATS REQUIRED. There are no curtains in the windows; the building has not been painted in a long time.

I walk slowly along the fence until I am directly in front of the ground-floor unit where we lived. Inside the north-facing bedroom where my mother and I used to sleep, the air seems tinted yellow as in old photographs. I know this is actually because the window is dirty; still, everything looks as if I were already remembering it rather than seeing it right now. Somehow the whole building looks smaller, reduced. The only thing that looks real is the loquat tree in front of the apartment that used to belong to the Kuzuha family. Gone wild, it's still bearing fruit the color of sulfur-pink sunsets. Everywhere else, grass is growing long in the large yard where I used to play with the neighborhood children every afternoon.

I jog around the building to the south side and stand before the balcony from which my mother used to call me when it was time to come in. Especially in the summer, I stayed out past dusk, until I was one of the last kids left playing. When I heard my name, I would sprint across the yard, push open the front door, kick off my shoes, and run into the kitchen where she was making supper. Sometimes, coming so suddenly into the bright light of the house, I would feel dizzy. I might even knock into the bookcase or the door before my eyes adjusted. Or else I would start talking very fast as soon as I entered the kitchen, even before my mother had turned her full attention toward me. "Slow down," she would say, laughing. "You're always in such a hurry. There's no reason to rush. We'll be here all night." But even as she told me to slow down, I knew that she was amused by my rushing, that my quickness was something I inherited from her. Standing in front of this fenced-off building now, I still hope that I made her happy back then, even though it wasn't enough to keep her alive till old age.

I turn away from the building and begin running south toward the embankment, following the way we used to walk to the beach to collect seashells. My mother and I walked up and down the tide line trying to find the few pink oyster shells and scallops that had come through the breakwater without being shattered.

At the bottom of the embankment that separates the road from the sand beach, I stop and climb the stairs. What I find, when I get to the top, is not the sand or water but tall buildings rising out of what used to be the sea. As far as I can see, there is nothing but land.

I had heard that a mile-wide landfill had been added to the old shoreline. But when I looked at the city from Sylvia's house, I couldn't tell where the curve of the shore had changed. From the old embankment, the buildings look new, with white concrete facades.

To my right, there is a park with red-clay tennis courts. For the last thirteen years, I have often dreamed of walking in the places of my childhood and finding the sea where the land used to be: right outside our old apartment complex, between the park and the bus stop, outside the second-story window of my elementary school. In the dreams, I am never surprised or afraid. "Oh, the sea has moved," I think. "Maybe I'll have to swim or row a boat to school." I wake up feeling almost happy about all that blue salt water everywhere. What I'm looking at now, as I stand on this old embankment, is just like that, only the directions are reversed: rather than the sea moving toward the land to submerge my childhood landscape, the land has moved into the sea.

The buildings on the landfill must be condominiums and office spaces. They are too tall to be anything else. Cars are parked beside the tennis courts where people in white shirts are hitting balls on the red clay. They are playing tennis beyond the boundaries of my past, swinging their rackets on the old sea. Though the houses in which I have lived have been torn down, time has added to the larger landscape of possibilities. Slowly, I climb down the embankment to stand on the ground, on a new paved road, and begin to run. Fifty yards down, past the old sand beach and the cement breakwater, I am stepping on what used to be waves. The shapes of the land and the sea have changed since I last lived here. I continue to run south, deeper into the old water.

Happiness

On the telephone, my grandmother Fuku calls me by my childhood name. "Kyo-chan," she says. "It's been such a long time."

I am upstairs in Sylvia's house, using the phone by the porch. The sky has cleared since this morning when I went running.

"Grandmother, how is your health?"

"So-so," she replies.

"I'm in Kobe now."

"At your father's house?"

"No. At a friend's house near Mikage, up on the hill."

She doesn't say anything. Beyond our blue roof, the neighbor's orange trees look glossy from the humidity.

"I'd like to come and see you," I say. "When would be a good time for a visit?"

"It doesn't matter when. I have nowhere to go. I'm always home."

"How about next weekend then? I can come on Friday or Saturday."

"I'm not able to do much for guests now. But if you don't mind that, please stay overnight."

"Of course." I always assumed that I would stay. It's a half day's trip just to get out there. "I'll come on Saturday, a week from now."

"Did you call your uncles and aunts?"

"No, not yet."

"Your uncle Yasuo and aunt Sayo will want to see you here while you are visiting me."

"I'll call them. I'm looking forward to seeing everyone."

She doesn't say anything more. She was never much for phone conversations. My mother used to write to her every week rather than call her.

"It'll be good to see you," I tell her. "Good-bye till then."

Hanging up the phone, I look toward the sea and trace the shore-line toward Ashiya. Now that I have been on the landfill, I can see exactly where it is: a thin strip of land beyond the green line of pines planted along the old shoreline. The late afternoon sun reflects off the tall white buildings with glass windows. Standing by the porch, I proceed to call my uncles and aunts so I can see them in the two weeks left of my stay.

It's early evening when I reach Kenichi, my youngest uncle.

"Ken Nichan," I say, "it's Kyoko."

"Kyo-chan. Your grandmother said you were coming to Japan. She was so happy to get your letter."

"I called her this afternoon. I'm going to see her next weekend."

"That's good. She's very anxious to see you."

"How is her health?"

"Very good."

"Really? She said her health was only so-so and she was too old to do much for guests. I was worried she might be sick."

"No," he laughs. "That's just the way she talks. Don't you remember? She always sounds pessimistic."

"Maybe that's true. How about you? And your family?"

"Everyone's well here. Asako was just a little kid when you left. She is in high school now. Then there's Jiro. He's in ninth grade."

"I don't remember him all that much. He was just a baby."

"So you've been in Kobe for a while now?"

"Yes. I'm staying at a friend's house. I traveled around for four weeks first. When I got back to town, I went to see our old house."

"You did?"

"Sure. But it was torn down, of course."

"You must have been surprised."

"I was. I walked up to the reservoir, though. That looked the same. The corner store is still there, and the ichiba and Dr. Doi's hospital."

"You remember a lot about the old neighborhood."

"Of course I remember." I pause, happy that Kenichi seems pleased by my remembering. "I want to come and see you soon. I only have two weeks left."

"How about Monday? I'll be back from school at three. You can take the commuter train to Itami. I'll come and pick you up in my car. We'll have dinner, and you can stay overnight."

"That sounds very good."

"Did you see your father yet?" he asks me.

"No. Not on this visit. I saw him in New York last year."

"I ran into him the other day. I had dinner downtown with some other teachers from our school. We were just leaving when your father walked in with his friends. He looked right at me but said nothing, so I didn't say anything either. I noticed he looked kind of old." Kenichi laughs as though satisfied. "Your father. He's an old man now. Imagine that."

"I haven't called him yet. Our visit in New York was terrible. I don't want to see him, at least not yet."

"You're grown up now," Kenichi says. "You can do what you want."

After we hang up, I wish I had told Kenichi about running in Ashiya this morning, how I felt the old obligations fall away as my feet pounded what used to be the sea. Even the land and the sea had changed their shapes. I knew then that the old roles were no longer relevant; I was free to call my mother's family first, without contacting my father. I wanted to explain these thoughts to Kenichi, but I couldn't say what I meant in Japanese. Because my thoughts involve too much feeling or intuition, not step-by-step logic, it's almost impossible to express them in Japanese, a language that encourages, even prizes, vagueness in referring to feelings. In Japanese, one discusses only what is logical and leaves the feelings unsaid, subtly, ambiguously implied. To do otherwise—to launch into discussions of one's own feelings—is considered rude, intrusive, selfish. But even when I lived in Japan and was speaking Japanese every day, I could never think without referring back to feelings and intuitions. The perceptions and observations I wanted to express were not based on rigid logic, even back then. It's no surprise that after thirteen years away, most of my immediate thoughts come to me only in English, without proper translation.

At Kenichi's house on Monday, my cousins, Asako and Jiro, excuse themselves soon after dinner and go up to their rooms to study for upcoming tests in their classes. Because they attend public schools, their school year is a series of examinations meant to prepare them for more examinations next year. Each year of schooling is designed to train them for the university entrance examinations they will take at the end of their high school senior year. *Juken jigoku*, "examination hell," is the phrase often used to describe this system.

One of the last decisions my mother and I made together was for me to avoid spending my teenage years in that examination hell. In January of what was to be our final year together, I applied to Kobe Jogakuin. If I got into its junior high school, by taking a series of examinations in February, I would be guaranteed a place in its college. "This way," my mother said, "you only have to take exams once, for two days. When you go to school afterward, you will really be learning something rather than cramming for more exams." Kobe Jogakuin, founded by two American women in the 1870s, had a reputation for emphasizing the arts and languages and also giving students a lot of freedom; while other schools, public or private, had military-looking uniforms, Jogakuin had no uniforms and not much of a dress code. My mother and I both thought that I would be happier there. Her death came two weeks after we had found out the results of the exams: I was one of the 150 girls who had been admitted out of 500.

As we sit in the living room talking after dinner, Kenichi's wife, Mariko, says that I was lucky to go to Jogakuin and avoid the examination hell.

"Poor Asako," she sighs. "She's a senior this year. She has to take the exams in March. I should have sent her to a private school."

Sitting in the chairs across the coffee table from me, Kenichi and Mariko tell me about the problems Asako has had at school. Her teachers are disappointed in her because she studies only what interests her. She might spend days writing an essay on a subject she likes and then almost fail an examination in another subject because she spent all her time writing the essay. That was how I was as a student, but my teachers at Kobe Jogakuin never treated me with the kind of harsh disapproval Asako has received from hers. "An intelligent person like you could do better than that," my geometry teacher said every semester, sounding a lot like my mother, who used to say, "You think everything is funny." They both wished that I would improve my conduct somehow, but, basically, they were resigned to the way I was. Most of

my teachers were like that. When I kept failing multiple-choice examinations in a history class because I always marked "none of the above"
or else wrote in my own answers, my history teacher allowed me to
write papers instead. The algebra teacher let me make up my failing
grade by constructing a diamond-shaped die, devising a board game,
and writing a paper about probability studies based on my game. I
would never have been given the same flexibility at a public school.
Having me apply to Kobe Jogakuin was another thing my mother had
done for me. She had left me a legacy of tolerance rather than the
oppression of the examination hell whose essence is that everybody
must do the exact same thing in the exact same way.

"Maybe Asako will go to college in the States," Mariko says. "She
says she doesn't care if she can't get into any of the Japanese colleges
next April. She doesn't want to be part of the system, she says."

"Asako can come and stay with me in Wisconsin if she wants to,"
I suggest.

At ten, Mariko decides to go to bed so she can get up early to do
some woodworking. She made the coffee table, the bookcase, and the
chairs in the living room, all of them with ornate flower-and-leaf patterns. We say good night, promising to go for a walk after breakfast to
a park where the trees are covered with white egrets.

"Mariko Neisan is very nice," I say to Kenichi. Because he and
Mariko got married a few years after my mother's death, I have met
her only once before, when I came to their house to say good-bye
before leaving for the States.

"She used to work at your father's company," Kenichi says. "She
was a secretary there for five years."

"Did she know him?"

"Not personally. They weren't in the same department. All she
ever heard about him was that he was *shigoto no oni*." *Shigoto no oni*
means, literally, "a monster of work" and therefore a person aggres-

sively dedicated to his or her job. Sometimes the expression is meant as a compliment, other times not. It's hard to say how my father's co-workers might have meant it.

"I haven't called my father," I tell Kenichi. "I have to do it eventually, though, because I want to get in touch with Aunt Akiko and Kazumi at my grandfather's house."

Kenichi shakes his head. With his square face and small, round eyes, he looks remarkably like my maternal grandfather, Takeo. He has gained some weight and no longer looks skinny in his white polo shirt and blue twill pants.

"When we saw each other in New York last year," I add, "my father criticized me for not making enough money and not having gotten a degree from a Japanese university. My stepmother said that my mother didn't raise me right. He didn't seem offended by that. It was as if he completely agreed."

"I never thought much of your stepmother," Kenichi says. "She was a very abrasive person. You could see she wasn't very educated or cultured."

"My father had the same complaint about her once. The first time I left home to go to Arizona for a year in high school, he wrote to me and said he wasn't very satisfied with Michiko. He wanted to marry someone more genteel and feminine, more refined. He said I could write back to him and tell him what I thought. Only, he wanted me to write to him at his office, not at home."

Kenichi leans forward and raises his eyebrows. "So did you write to him?"

"Yes. I said I didn't have any opinions about who he was married to. That was his business, not mine. But if he and Michiko got a divorce and he couldn't remarry, he shouldn't expect me to keep house for him. I was planning to come back to the States to go to college or graduate school, so I wouldn't be there for him."

"I didn't realize you were so grown up at sixteen. That was a very mature thing to say."

"He didn't think so. He wrote back and said that he was appalled by my selfishness. Here he was thinking of a big change for our family, he said, and I could only think of how it was going to affect me. He had decided to stay with Michiko after all and warned me never to mention his previous letter to anyone."

Kenichi frowns, his shoulders hunched. "Your father had no right to say you were selfish. He is the most selfish person I've ever met."

"I know that now. But at the time, I didn't understand what was going on. Maybe he was seeing another woman while being married to Michiko. When he said he wanted to marry someone more genteel and cultured, maybe he had someone specific in mind. I never found out."

"I'm sure he had someone in mind," Kenichi says. "He was up to his old tricks. That's all."

We look at each other. I know what Kenichi is thinking about, but I ask him anyway. "Do you mean the way he married Michiko so soon after my mother's death?"

He nods.

I look down at the rose-leaf pattern Mariko carved into the coffee table and trace the leaves and the flowers with my eyes. "I stayed at some minshuku when I was traveling around the country earlier this month. I imagined what it might have been like for my father visiting the minshuku Michiko's mother was running. I know what was going on."

Kenichi nods but doesn't comment. Michiko's mother's minshuku was in Shimonoseki, a city my father visited often on business. Like the men I saw this summer, he must have come back from his meetings, taken off his shoes in the foyer, and called to the room where Michiko and her mother were sitting. Maybe both of them came running out with a pair of slippers for his feet; or more likely, the older woman brought the slippers and chatted with him in the hallway. Then later, Michiko served him dinner and sake in his room and stayed on talking and flirting. Soon he was going to Shimonoseki to stay with Michiko whether he had business or not. To my brother and me, my father pretended that he had only known her slightly, that someone else had recommended her as a possible second wife for him. "My friend from work suggested this woman in Shimonoseki whose mother runs a minshuku," he said. "I knew the woman and her mother because I myself have stayed there a few times. They seemed like suitable people."

Kenichi suddenly gets up and goes to the kitchen. He returns with a big amber bottle of beer and two glasses, pours the beer into the glasses, hands me one; then he sits back down in his chair. After taking a drink, he says, "I know something about your father I should tell you about."

I put down my glass on the coffee table, careful to place it on the coaster so it will not leave a stain.

"I told your grandparents some of it, but not everything."

I nod so he will keep talking.

"Remember when I was staying at your father's house to burn incense for your mother's soul?" he asks.

"Yes. I remember."

"Those couple of weeks after you and your brother moved to your grandfather's house, your father came home late, drunk, almost every night. He made a lot of noise stumbling around, so I usually got up and went downstairs to see if he was all right." Kenichi takes another drink of his beer and grimaces. "He was my brother-in-law after all. I didn't want him to get hurt. Every night when he saw me, he said, 'Sit down. Let's have some scotch.'"

"Really? He wanted to drink with you?"

"I guess he was lonely. What was I supposed to do? I accepted since it was his house and he was trying to be hospitable. Besides, I felt like drinking anyway. Your mother's death was hard on me." He sighs.

"I know."

"So your father and I used to sit at the kitchen table drinking scotch for a couple of hours. Your father is a sentimental guy when he drinks. He always cried after a couple of shots."

"No."

"Yes. He shed big tears. He even said, 'It's all my fault. Poor Takako. If I had been a better husband, she would never have chosen to die.' "

I pick up the beer and put it down without drinking. "I can't believe he said anything like that."

"Oh, he said it every night we drank together. I began to feel sorry for him. It was the only time I almost felt close to your father. You know I never liked him before, even when we were younger and lived together."

Kenichi doesn't say anything more for a while. I take a drink. The beer is stronger, more bitter, than the American beer I'm used to drinking. I put the glass down wondering why Kenichi is telling me this story.

Kenichi clears his throat and continues. "Then one night during the last week, everything changed. We were drinking as usual, and he was crying about how your mother's death was all his fault. It was past midnight. All of a sudden, he poured himself another shot, gulped it down, and said, 'Ken-chan, I have a woman in Shimonoseki. I've been seeing her for a few years now. We're in love. How long should I wait till I can have her move in with me?' " Kenichi pauses and looks into my face, maybe to make sure that I am not too shocked or hurt. I look back at him. I want him to know that I am all right. He continues. "I didn't know what to say. I was drunk. For a second, I thought maybe I didn't hear him right. Your father started crying about your mother again and then said, 'But I'm in love with this other woman. What am I supposed to do?' "

"He had no right to ask you that."

"I know," he shakes his head. "In the end, I had to tell him, 'It's none of my business. I'm the wrong person to ask. Do whatever you think you should.' That was the last time he asked me to drink with him. I only had four or five days left to stay at his house after that anyway. But the last couple of nights, I heard your father talking to someone on the phone late at night when he thought I was sleeping. You remember the phone was downstairs in the hallway and I slept upstairs in your brother's room. So I couldn't hear what he was saying, but I could hear his voice. He talked for a long time."

"You think he was talking to Michiko."

"That's right."

We drink our beer without speaking. Upstairs, everyone must be sleeping. The house is quiet.

"One evening, a few weeks after that," Kenichi adds, "your father showed up at our house in Kobe with some boxes and suitcases. I was home alone because your aunt Keiko and her family were having dinner at her in-laws' house. When I came downstairs to answer the door, your father was already putting the boxes and the suitcases in the foyer. His cab was waiting outside; I could hear the engine running. Your father said, 'These are Takako's things. I can't keep them because my woman's coming to live with me tomorrow. You and Keiko can do whatever you want with them.' He was gone before I could say anything to him." Kenichi sighs. "I sat down in the foyer looking at all that luggage. It was as if he packed your mother's things to divorce her, to send her back to her parents' house—except what happened was much worse than that; she was dead."

I imagine Kenichi sitting alone in the dark with my mother's things. He would have been only thirty at the time, younger than I am now.

"Your grandmother still has some of the things he brought that night. Keiko and I sent them to her to keep for you. We didn't know how long it would be before you could get them. Soon after your father came to our house, he said that none of us should ever try to see you and Jumpei." Kenichi pauses.

Looking at his face across the coffee table, I want to say, "I didn't know how much my father hurt you back then. I'm so sorry," but that seems too direct and intrusive in Japanese. I'm not sure what I can say instead to indicate that feeling without directly saying it.

"Did you ever wonder why your grandparents gave up so easily?" Kenichi asks me. "When your father told them that they couldn't see you anymore, they didn't come and visit you against his wishes. They didn't even write to you until you were in the States because he told them they couldn't write to you as long as you lived with him. Did you wonder why they didn't tell him he was wrong?"

I think about it for a while. "No," I reply. "I guess I understood that my grandparents had to do what my father said."

"Well," Kenichi says. "Your grandfather didn't accept it right away. He went to see a lawyer."

"He did?"

"He wanted to take your father to court so you could come and live with him and your grandmother out in the country. He didn't think your father would give up your brother because he was the only son, but he thought maybe your father would let you go."

My life would have been completely different if my grandfather had gone through with his plans. I would have grown up in the country with my mother's family.

"But in the end, he gave up the idea," Kenichi says.

"Why?"

"For one thing, the lawyer told him that his chances were very slim. Things could get ugly. You would be asked to testify in court and state whom you preferred to live with and why. Then, too, your grandfather started thinking that maybe you would prefer to live with your father in the city anyway. You had just gotten into Kobe Jogakuin. Your grandparents had no money to keep sending you to a private school, especially since you'd have to live in the dorm during the school year. If they had custody, you would have had to attend a public school in the country. They didn't think your mother would have wanted that. She was so proud of how smart you were. She would have been sad to see you go to a country school. So in the end, your grandparents decided you would be better off with your father and stepmother. All the same, your grandfather was never sure if he had done the right thing. He talked about you and missed you all his life. He was talking about you right up till his death."

I don't speak for a long time. I don't know what I would have chosen back then, living with my grandparents in the country or staying in the city to attend the school my mother and I had decided on. In my grandparents' village, I would have missed not only the school but the museums, theaters, bookstores—the places and things my mother had taught me to appreciate. Even though I had enjoyed my summer visits in the country, I would have been afraid of being stuck there year round, going to school with rough farm kids who didn't speak like my friends in the city. It is possible that, in the end, I would have thought the same thing my grandfather did and chosen to stay in the city. Perhaps I was lucky not to have had to make such a difficult choice at twelve or thirteen.

"You aren't mad at Grandfather and Grandmother, are you?" Kenichi asks. "You don't think they let you go because they didn't care for you, do you?"

"Of course not," I assure him. "Grandfather and Grandmother had no idea how bad things were at my father's house. I'm not surprised they thought I'd be better off there. My father had more money and lived in the city. I understand." My grandparents had given me up because they believed I would be better off in the city, even though they could no longer see me then—just as my mother had given me up so she could die alone and I could go on living. They gave me up, I know, because they loved me and it was the only thing they could do for me. In many ways, they were right. The choices they made, in the end, allowed me to escape the small world in which my mother had been so unhappy.

But Kenichi doesn't seem all that convinced. He's still looking at me with a wrinkle between his eyebrows.

"I wrote to my grandparents every week," I add. "I never told them how bad things were at home. I only wrote about school or friends because I didn't want to write anything that would worry them. To them, I must have sounded like a typical teenager. They must have thought I was happy. They could see I enjoyed going to Kobe Jogakuin. And it was important for me to go there."

Kenichi suddenly leans forward and looks me in the eye. "But I should have known better," he says. "I knew more than anyone because of that time I had spent with your father. He wasn't the kind of person a young girl should have to grow up with. How could I leave you with him and a woman he was seeing behind your mother's back? I must have been out of my mind. I should have done everything I could to get you out of there and still make him pay for your education. I'm so sorry I didn't. You have to forgive me."

I want to get up, walk over to Kenichi, and give him a hug. But in Japan, only women hug each other; if I tried to hug Kenichi, he would be embarrassed. He would think that I have become a foreigner in spite of our mutual past. I try to smile instead. "Ken Nichan," I say as calmly as possible, "it isn't your fault. There's nothing to forgive." That April when my father started beating me, I never told Kenichi, though I saw him every day for a while. Even he didn't know everything.

Kenichi tilts his head, smiles back, and says, "It turned out all right in the end, didn't it? You're *kofuku* now."

Kofuku means both "happiness" and "good fortune." The Japanese concept of happiness is both unspecific and absolute. It doesn't allow for the gap between the way things turn out (good fortune) and the way one feels about them (happiness), or the way some things turn out well and others do not. You are either kofuku or not; there is no room for small dissatisfactions. This is not how I think of happiness or good fortune. They are not the same in my mind. I am often happy about one thing and unhappy about another. Sometimes things turn out all right, but I am in no way happy about them because I feel embittered by the process. How can I make a blanket statement about being kofuku? Worst of all, I don't even know how to explain my thoughts in Japanese. In a tired, late-night sort of way, I am sad about having thoughts I cannot explain to Kenichi. I want to reassure him, to say something positive without being insincere.

"Of course I'm happy," I tell him. "I'm talking to you right now. That gives me happiness."

Kenichi nods and smiles. "Yes," he says. "*Natsukashii*." It's been a long time.

By now, it's one o'clock in the morning, time to go to bed. While I am taking out my contact lenses at the downstairs sink, Kenichi brings a big colander and puts it over the drain.

"I'm not going to drop my lenses." I laugh because the colander is big enough to serve spaghetti to a dozen people. "I'm not that clumsy."

"Well, just in case," he says, and shrugs.

It's the kind of thing my mother might have done. On windy days, she braided and pinned up my hair so the loose strands would not get caught in any machinery and cause me injury. It made no difference that there were no machines at school or at home where my hair might get caught. Even cars never passed very close by. She had instructed me to walk on the crown on the sidewalk facing the traffic so that I would not be run over, kidnapped, or splashed with mud. "Just in case," she would have said, too.

"Thanks," I say to Kenichi. "I'll be careful."

He goes upstairs to his bedroom.

Washing my face at the sink downstairs, I remember how he taught me to use soap when he, Shiro, and Keiko lived with my family in Kobe. My mother bought soap that came in small paper-thin sheets of pink, blue, and green, all of them almost transparent. Kenichi used to stand behind me at the sink while I poured water over my hands. Then, after he gave me a sheet of soap, I would close my palms and stick my hands under the water again.

"Keep rubbing your hands together until all the slippery stuff comes off the soap onto your palms," he would say.

I rubbed my hands until I could open them and show him that the soap was gone.

"Look at that," he would exclaim. "Where did the soap go?"

"I don't know," I would reply. The almost-transparent pink or green had turned into nothing, leaving a faint scent of flowers and leaves.

Lying down in the guest room upstairs, I think of my grandmother Fuku, who had two older sisters named Masu and Ko. When you said all three names together, you came up with *masu kofuku,* which means "increasing happiness and good fortune." My mother told me once that my grandmother's name had not come true, that Fuku was not kofuku since her family had been reduced to poverty after the Second World War through the Land Reform. At that time, Fuku and Takeo were forced to give up almost all the land they had inherited from Takeo's father, so that the government could redistribute it among their sharecroppers. They were allowed to keep only a few paddies for their own use, though they knew nothing about farming.

Fuku and Takeo had spent their adult lives in Kobe: Fuku, who was a pharmacist, cared for their children and ran a small drugstore out of their home; Takeo became a schoolteacher because teaching was considered a good genteel occupation for a landowner's son who would eventually live off his land, on the rent he collected from his sharecroppers. Until my great-grandfather's death in the last year of the war, Fuku and Takeo had only visited the countryside in the summers to vacation, not to work. Now, left with a few paddies, my grandparents didn't know how to make a profit. Takeo applied for a teaching job at the village school so he would have a steady source of modest income. Fuku worked outside from morning to night, while he taught during the day and came home to help her. They made barely enough money to raise the three children still living with them. By the time I was born, my grandparents always looked tired, even though my mother and her siblings sent them money to help out so they were better off than right after the war. Stooped and sunburned, they didn't look like people who were kofuku.

My grandfather Takeo has been dead for twelve years now. My grandmother, the only one left of the three good-fortune sisters, lives alone in the house in the country, surrounded by the land she and my grandfather lost. She must feel lonely. She must wish that my mother were alive to comfort her in her old age, to take care of her garden and sew her clothes and tell stories to make her laugh.

"Poor Takako," my father had said to Kenichi. "If I had been a better husband she would never have chosen to die."

How could he have said that and then invited Michiko to live with him only a few weeks later? If he had felt that way once, even drunk, why did he sit there and say nothing in the hotel room in New York last year, when Michiko went on about how my mother hadn't raised me right? Instead of showing remorse after my mother's death, he had added to my grandmother's unhappiness by forbidding her to see my brother and me. He had gone to Kenichi's house with my mother's things, without an apology or an explanation, and left him alone to sit in the dark and feel terrible.

I cannot believe that my father could have acted with such insensitivity if he had really felt guilty about my mother's death. But at the same time, nothing Kenichi told me surprises me: for years, decades, I have expected only the worst from my father. The thing is, I can never reconcile these two ways I feel about him. Seeing him in New York last year or hearing about him from Kenichi tonight, I am amazed at his insensitivity and yet not even slightly surprised. That's what bothers me about him. Even though no one can make me as angry as he can, he always seems slightly unreal to me. He is like somebody I have imagined, somebody I don't want to think about if I want to get to sleep. I can never be completely happy or even at peace so long as I have to think of him, much less plan to see him in the near future.

So, trying to sleep, I remember the early summer mornings at my grandparents' house when I was a child. Every morning when I got up, I went to collect the eggs from the hen house and brought them to the kitchen where my grandparents were having tea. Inside the basket I carried, the eggs were white and still warm. The three of us would hold them up to the bulb one by one and watch them flood with light and become clear spheres. "Yes, that's a good one," we would nod to one another as we put the eggs back into the basket, as though each good egg were a special accomplishment, a small perfection that might add up, in spite of everything, to a larger happiness.

Hunger

The coffee shop, called Marco Polo, is a block from the commuter train station in Nishinomiya, the suburb my school was in. My aunt Keiko is waiting in front of the door in a green dress with large yellow flowers printed all over. She starts waving as soon as she spots me walking across the street toward her.

"I'm so glad to see you," she says, reaching out to hold both my hands in hers. Her black leather purse slides off her shoulder and bumps against my arm. "You've grown taller." She smiles and lets go of my hands.

"It's good to see you, too, Neine." We haven't seen each other since my grandparents' fiftieth wedding anniversary, seventeen years ago.

"So I'm still your Neine at fifty-two." She laughs.

I started calling her Neine when she and my uncles lived with my family and I was too young to be able to say *Neisan,* "Big Sister."

We are standing next to a glass case that displays wax models of the food served inside. Dust covers the stiff white spirals of the ice cream. The noodles in the spaghetti dish are too yellow, as if uncooked. The toast placed on the edge of a saucer is brown, and thick as a book.

"Let's go in." Keiko puts her hand on my back and nudges me toward the door. I walk in ahead.

With gold-and-red damask curtains in the windows, the interior is dark, though it's three in the afternoon. The only light comes from the dim overhead lamps. The four large tables are occupied by young men and women, students at nearby colleges. A few couples and pairs of older women are sitting at the small glass-top tables. Because this place was only one stop away from our school on the train, my friends and I used to come here on our way home and spend afternoons drinking coffee and talking. We smoked Dunhill cigarettes and listened to jazz records. The decor looks about the same now, but there is no music coming from the speakers.

While Keiko and I wait to be seated, the young women at the nearest table glance up at us and then turn back to their conversation. They are wearing tailored suits in taupe, charcoal gray, light blue, mauve—the colors my friends wore in the last years of high school and in college, when they were moving away from the bright reds and yellows of childhood into the more sophisticated shades of young womanhood. In my blue jeans and tie-dyed shirts, I must have looked completely miscast among them.

"I wonder what's taking them so long to seat us," Keiko whispers a little too loudly behind me.

The young women look up at us again, one of them frowning slightly. Keiko and I make a strange pair: me in my shorts and red

T-shirt, a gym bag slung over my shoulder for swimming later; Keiko in a dress much brighter than usual for her age. She shifts her purse from one shoulder to the other and stares back at the women. More than likely, her purse is stuffed with the religious tracts she passes out in front of train stations and at shopping centers. She wanted to meet me at Marco Polo because she would be at the station "teaching" about her religion.

A waiter in a black uniform comes up to us and bows. We follow him to one of the glass-top tables and sit down while he goes to get our menus and water.

"I'm glad you are free today," Keiko says, setting her purse on the floor and leaning toward me. She has her hair cut like my mother's: a few inches below the ears, parted in the middle, and permed. "I'll be going with you to Grandmother's this weekend," she adds. "But I want to see you alone first. A lot of important things have happened to me since I last saw you. I want to tell you about them."

The waiter comes back and hands us the menus. He sets the water glasses on the table and leaves.

"I'm walking the path of faith," Keiko declares.

I pick up my glass and look at her in silence while I sip the water.

She tilts her head a little and smiles, her lips outlined in bright red. My mother didn't wear much makeup. Other than that, they look a lot alike. Even their voices sound the same: clear and high. "Maybe Kenichi told you," Keiko says. "He doesn't understand. It's my way of trying to help your mother's soul."

I have known about Keiko's religion for some time. When my brother, Jumpei, visited me in Wisconsin two years ago, he told me that Keiko had invited him to a shrine and tried to convert him to a religion called *hirameki-san*. She had burned incense, prayed, and asked Jumpei to notice the divine spirits and ancestral souls floating in the air around them. The world is full of spiritual power, she had told him. "I don't care what she believes," my brother said. "But her religion is notorious for being like the Moonies. Keiko and her husband

already gave up almost everything they own, and they still make con-
tributions every month. Of course, I wanted to have nothing to do
with that religion." Mariko and Kenichi, too, warned me yesterday.
They predicted Keiko would ask me to go to a shrine with her to
pray. I'm supposed to decline as firmly as possible.

"I never forgot your mother," Keiko says. "Not a day goes by
without my thinking about her."

The waiter has come back and is standing next to the table.

"Are you hungry?" Keiko asks me.

"No. I'm meeting a friend at six to swim at his health club. I can't
eat now."

We both order iced coffee, which is brought to us in thick glass
mugs with a thumb-sized pitcher of cream for each. I pour all my
cream into the mug and watch it filter through the ice cubes before I
take a sip through the straw. The coffee is cold, bitter, and sweet at
once; it's one of the tastes I associate with being in Japan because
almost everybody here drinks a lot of it in the summer.

Keiko doesn't immediately return to the subject of her religion.
For about half an hour, we talk about family news: which of my
cousins have graduated from college, gotten jobs, or married; how
my grandmother manages alone, who helps her with various chores.
I tell Keiko about my job in the States, about my sabbatical project.

Keiko says abruptly, "I'm so glad you have gotten married after
all." She stirs her coffee with the straw.

I pick up my mug, which is heavier than it looks because of the
thick glass. I'm irritated by the way she keeps smiling. Like most
women her age, Keiko must value my marriage above everything
else I have done since we last saw each other; to her, my having married is my real accomplishment, the thing that made my life turn out
all right.

But that isn't what I think of my life or my marriage. I resent the
idea that an unmarried woman is flawed, unfortunate, inferior. I'd
like to think that my happiness does not have to depend on any one

person. If I had not gotten married, my life would be different, not worse or better, certainly not incomplete. Why should I expect any-one—even my husband—to make my life all right, as though, alone, I would find myself lacking and inadequate? There are tasks in my life—this very trip, for instance—that I must accomplish alone. No friend, family, or husband can help me come to terms with the sor-row or pain contained in my past. Even my mother could not protect me from the unhappiness that destroyed her life. There is a limit to what other people can do for me, regardless of their relationship to me. I want to explain this to Keiko, but no words come to me.

"I was worried for you because I believe in karma," she says. "My religion teaches about it. There's personal karma, and then there's family karma. Your mother was unhappy in her marriage. I don't want you to repeat her unhappiness."

Putting down my mug, I snap back, "My mother was unhappy because my father neglected her. She was lonely. My marriage would never be like that. My happiness doesn't depend completely on my husband."

At the next table, a man and a woman, about my age, are drink-ing tea and talking in low voices. The woman glances in my direc-tion because I've raised my voice; she quickly looks away when our eyes meet.

"I don't believe anyone can *make* me happy," I say in a quieter voice. "Marriage didn't make my life better—just different."

"Is that good?" Keiko asks.

"Of course it is. But none of this has to do with karma, unless you mean my mother should have married someone else. I've always thought that myself."

Keiko shakes her head. "Don't say that. You wouldn't be here if she hadn't married your father. It's bad luck to talk against your own life."

"Regardless, I wish my mother had married someone else and been happier. I would be glad not to have been born, just for that."

Keiko looks into my face, her hands curled around the glass mug. I try to laugh because what I have said is absurd, but it isn't funny, either.

"Your parents were very happy together once," she says.

"When was that? I don't remember anything like that."

She sighs. "It was a few years before you were born, when they were first married and lived with Shiro, Kenichi, and me."

I cannot contradict her about a time before I was born. All the same, I ask, "What makes you think they were happy? Maybe they were pretending because you were around. My father was always good at that. He could really put up a front."

"No. This wasn't like that. Back then, your father was different. He was very considerate. He spent a lot of time at home with your mother. He didn't stay out late with his work friends or go out with them on weekends. He even made us breakfast. You remember how your mother was always tired in the mornings. She was such a heavy sleeper."

I nod.

"Your father wanted her to sleep in and take it easy, so he got up early enough to make everyone bag lunches. After that, he ironed his own shirt and then my blouse for work, which he would hang up on my door so it wouldn't get wrinkled. When everyone was up except your mother, he started cooking breakfast. He was a good cook; he could make beautiful omelettes. He went to wake up your mother just in time for her to eat with us before we all left for work."

The couple at the next table get up to leave. The man puts money on the table and waits for the woman to pick up her purse and put on her lacy white cardigan. As they open the door, I can see the sunlight outside.

Keiko says, "Your parents seemed like an ideal couple. You know I wasn't married then. I used to think, 'I hope my marriage turns out to be just like theirs.' "

"I can't believe that. They were never like that when I was around."

"I know. But it isn't so strange after all. Your parents married for love. There had to be a time when they were happy together."

My parents had met on the job at Kawasaki Steel, where my mother worked as a secretary to support herself and Shiro, and my father was employed as an engineer. She turned down an arranged marriage offer and got engaged to my father instead. Soon after, he came down with tuberculosis. For the next three years, while he was in a sanatorium, my mother quit her job and took in piecework. She sat at his bedside sewing neckties and knitting socks every day. Even his parents advised her to break off the engagement and marry someone else. The doctors didn't think he had much chance of recovering.

"I always knew how much my mother once wanted to marry him," I tell Keiko. "She told me about nursing him when he had tuberculosis. I could never put it together, though, with how they were when I knew them."

Keiko draws her lips into a resigned half smile. "It's the way your mother's karma worked out. Her happiness wasn't meant to last."

"I don't think it's karma."

"It is. When your parents had been married three years, everything changed suddenly. Your father got promoted at the office and became very ambitious about his work. He scarcely came home anymore. He was either working late or drinking with work friends, which he insisted was part of his work. The same year, your mother had her first miscarriage, and then another one the year after. Suddenly, there was a big gap between them. Your father felt that his life was going very well since good things were happening to him at work, while your mother felt that her life was full of misfortune. See, something came between them and divided them."

"What came between them wasn't karma," I insist. "They shouldn't have felt divided like that. Why didn't they think that everything that happened happened to them both?" When I pick up the mug again, there is a ring of water on the table. I put a paper napkin over it. "I can see how my mother wasn't very happy about his promotion because it took him away just when she needed him most. No wonder she felt like the good things at work were happening only to him rather than to both of them. But what about him? How could he feel as if the miscarriages were happening only to her and not to them? That's weird, isn't it? They were—or would have been—his children, too."

Keiko shakes her head. "You know your father. He doesn't know how to comfort people. He always walks away if someone's unhappy or sick. He doesn't have much patience. That part of him was the same."

I don't say anything, though I wonder how my mother could ever have loved someone like that.

"You shouldn't blame your father," Keiko says. "He can't help being who he is. Besides, he was under a lot of pressure at work. He had to put in long hours to get ahead."

"Come on, Neine. That's just an excuse."

"Maybe it is. Still, your mother was suddenly burdened with misfortune from then on. She had been healthy all her life, but now she had the miscarriages and then you were born with dislocated hips and your brother's neck was twisted. There had to be some bad karma. Don't you see?"

"No." I put down my mug and shake my head. "I don't think people's health problems are caused by karma. Besides, Jumpei and I got well. There's nothing wrong with us now."

"Her bad luck didn't stop there, though. Just when both you and Jumpei were beginning to be healthy, your father decided to move your family to Ashiya to live with his father. She was so unhappy there."

"That's because my grandfather was mean to her and my father didn't help her out."

Keiko stirs her coffee with her straw several times, though it's more than half gone. The two women who got seated at the next table are smoking. The smoke drifts slowly toward us.

"I'm not denying that she was unhappy," I admit. "I just think it was more my father's fault than karma. I know my grandfather was always overcritical of my mother and they couldn't get along. Instead of trying to smooth things out between them, my father started taking long trips to avoid being home. How could he do that? He should have helped her out."

Keiko doesn't answer.

"Even if she was unhappy at my grandfather's house, that lasted only for a year. We moved to the seaside apartment. I think she was happy there, for five years. That's a long time, isn't it? So you can't say that my mother's life was nothing but a series of misfortune and bad karma. I think she *was* happy sometimes."

Keiko lightly touches my hand. "Of course. I didn't mean to imply she was unhappy all the time. How could she be? She had you and Jumpei. She loved you."

"She also had a lot of friends," I add.

"I know," Keiko smiles. "One of them told me something. She said, 'Whenever your sister walks into any gathering, she brings extra cheerfulness. The room seems brighter and warmer with her in it.' I always wanted to tell you that."

I remember my mother sitting in our small living room with a dozen other women to whom she was teaching embroidery. Making up her own designs from pictures in art books, she embroidered landscapes on wall hangings, butterflies and violets on my blouses. She had stitched roses and ferns on a cloth draped over the top of my upright piano so that, during my daily practice, I could look at pink and red petals in satin stitches. On weekends, she invited her friends and their children to go on picnics and hikes. We walked all over the mountains that bordered Kobe to the north. Though my mother had maps, we often got lost and ended up going longer than planned. She had a terrible sense of direction and the rest of us knew it, but we always expected her to lead the way because she was so cheerful and confident. Though we didn't trust her not to get lost, we completely trusted her to find our way again, to have everything turn out for the better. "If we hadn't gotten lost," she would point out later, "we would never have seen that patch of hydrangea."

My father never came along on any outing my mother planned. I can't picture the two of them together laughing or talking or even just sitting side by side at home, watching television.

"I guess she was happy because she had us and good friends," I tell Keiko. "But my father wasn't around even then."

"I know. Your mother used to say that she and your father just went their separate ways. She said it was hard to remember how the two of them had such a big romance before they were married. She had friends who were in arranged marriages. They and their husbands did more things together and seemed warmer toward each other. She tried to laugh it off, though. She kept saying it was all right the way things worked out."

"Do you think she really meant it?"

"I don't know, but later on, the same thing bothered her, after you moved to that house on the hill."

"I ran by that house the other day, but it was torn down and two new houses were there instead. The place looked the same anyway—it was shady and gloomy."

"Your mother had a bad feeling about that house from the start," Keiko remembers. "The day after she went to see it, she called me. She said she wasn't sure about the house, even though there was nothing wrong with it. She just felt depressed as soon as she stepped inside. She should never have moved there." Keiko pauses. "You, too. It's important to trust your feelings. Don't ever move to a place if you don't feel good about it. It doesn't matter how good the location is or how reasonable the rent is. Don't repeat your mother's mistake in this." She looks me right in the eye as if to emphasize this point.

"The house didn't ruin my mother's life," I point out. "Her marriage was bad even when she thought she was happy at that apartment house. It's just that moving to a new place and having no friends forced her to see that."

"The problems in their marriage weren't your father's fault only," Keiko says. "By the time they moved, your mother must have known about his affair. Instead of confronting him about it, she stopped sleeping with him herself. Your grandfather was worried that last year. He'd stayed at your house and found out that your parents didn't even sleep in the same room."

"They never did. My parents always slept separately at the apartment house, too. Grandfather didn't know because he had only visited us there when Hiroshi was gone."

"So you think your father had affairs all along?"

"I don't know. But he was seeing Michiko for a few years before my mother's death. I know that."

Keiko picks up and puts down her iced coffee, which is completely watered down. The two women next to us are getting ready to leave, gathering up their purses and summer jackets. "I used to wonder how much you knew," Keiko says. "I wasn't sure if you were old enough back then."

"I didn't figure everything out at the time, but soon afterward. Ken Nichan told me some things, too, yesterday."

"Men are often unfaithful," Keiko grimaces and then forces a smile. "You must understand that for yourself. You can't expect them not to fall in love and flirt with someone else. You shouldn't think it is a crisis every time they have an affair. Affairs aren't always serious." She shrugs. "There's not much you can do about some flaws in human nature. You shouldn't judge your father too harshly. He's not the first man to be unfaithful to his wife." She nods as if to say, *We all understand this.*

Wait a minute, I want to say. *His being a man has nothing to do with it.* But I am stuck. I have never learned this kind of adult talk in Japanese. I don't know how to be indirect about sensitive subjects and still get my points across—by being politely vague but not too vague, clear but not too embarrassingly clear, insinuating and talking around the issues a lot. I notice how other people do it, but I don't know where or how to begin.

"Your mother must have known about Michiko for a long time," Keiko goes on. "A woman always knows."

Every time my mother referred to the future in her journal the winter before her death, she wrote that my father would no doubt remarry. She must have suspected that he had someone specific in mind, but it wasn't because "a woman always knows." A generic statement like that reduces my mother's particular situation to a trite principle. But I know that my aunt does not mean to trivialize my mother's suffering, so I say nothing.

"Your mother could have handled the situation differently," Keiko adds. "If I had been in her position, I would have cried and complained or thrown and broken all the dishes in the house and begged my husband not to leave me. I would have won him back by showing him that I couldn't live without him. But your mother was too proud. She pretended that she didn't care what he did. She was a perfectionist. She couldn't admit that he had failed her in this way. She didn't understand that maybe he had been attracted to Michiko in the first place because Michiko wasn't as smart as she was. You see, your father could relax in front of Michiko. She treated him as the smartest, greatest person in the world. He could never relax in front of your mother, who outdid him in everything. She didn't laugh at his stories; she told more amusing stories than he did. Rather than praising his hard work at the office, she tried to match it with her hard work at home. Maybe that's how she thought she was showing her appreciation, but that's not what he wanted. He wanted someone to admire him, not compete with him and make him feel inferior. Your mother didn't do any of this on purpose. But you must remember he was unhappy, too."

Keiko stops just as the waiter comes toward our table. Though we sit in silence, he must see that we are in the middle of a serious conversation. Instead of stopping to ask if we need anything, he walks by very slowly so that it will be up to us to flag him down. We don't. He passes the table, looks back, and bows slightly. His restraint is so typically Japanese I'm suddenly annoyed, almost angry: everyone here is supposed to know his or her part without being told or asked. But what if you somehow missed an important cue so that everything you did after that was completely out of sync, inappropriate? Is that what Keiko is saying about my parents—they missed each other's cues? What marriage doesn't have a few missed cues?

Keiko is waiting for me to say something.

"I don't blame my father for being unhappy with my mother or making her unhappy," I offer. "I don't even blame him for having an affair. You're right. He's not the first man to be unhappy or to have an affair. But I can't forgive him for having refused to talk to my mother those last times she asked him to come home early so they could talk. He called from some place drunk and didn't come home for days. I don't forgive him for what he did to me after her death. He kept me away from you and Ken Nichan and everyone who loved me. He tried to make me forget my mother."

Keiko leans forward. "If you don't forgive him, you'll be stuck in the same bad karma your mother had. Things turned out all right in the end for you. There's no reason to keep holding a grudge."

I take a deep breath. "But he's still the same. Last year, when I saw him in New York, he let Michiko say terrible things about my mother. He showed no interest in what I was doing. He said he was disappointed in me because I had gotten my Ph.D. in English literature but I knew nothing about Japanese literature. As soon as we sat down the first time, after twelve years of not seeing me, he asked me how much money I made. That's all he wanted to know. How could I forgive someone like that?"

Keiko sighs and looks into her empty glass.

"I should be calling him soon, but I keep postponing it. I'm leaving in less than two weeks. I wouldn't even bother calling him at all if Akiko and Kazumi didn't live with my grandfather." I look away from Keiko toward the clock. It's almost five-thirty.

"Your mother loved your father," Keiko says. "She was very happy with him once. When he had tuberculosis and she was nursing him, people were worried that she might catch the disease herself. She told them she didn't care; she said if Hiroshi died, she wanted to die, too, and be put in the same coffin. Because she loved him like that, you need to forgive him."

"That makes no sense. It's more the reason not to forgive him. How could he treat her the way he did after that?"

"You won't help her soul by holding a grudge against him. Any grudge you hold comes back to you. You won't be able to get out of her bad karma unless you forgive him. Don't repeat her fate in your life." Keiko reaches out across the table as if to take my hand, but I pull away.

"Her fate is part of my life whether I forgive him or not," I insist. "I want it to affect my life. She was my mother. Why shouldn't her fate affect mine?" I stop, feeling dizzy and cold. "Besides," I add, "it isn't just what he did to her. I don't forgive him for what he and Michiko did to me and keep doing to me."

In New York, he said that Keiko was a religious fanatic, that her obsession with religion was another manifestation of the mental defect in my mother's family. The only member of my mother's family he could stand, he told me, was Shiro, who had become a distinguished professor of microbiology at the Hiroshima National University. Sitting across the table from Keiko now, I can't help being angry at him for saying these things, no matter how much Keiko wants me to forgive him.

That afternoon in New York, after eight hours of walking with Hiroshi and Michiko in midtown, I left to have dinner with Henri, the friend I was staying with. As soon as we sat down, I proceeded to tell him about my afternoon. I thought I was being more ironic than angry, making fun of my parents' pettiness and insensitivity. Hiroshi and Michiko were no worse than I had expected them to be; I wasn't surprised. I told Henri that Michiko had criticized the way I held chopsticks at the Chinese restaurant where we had lunch. To her, it was another occasion to say that my mother had not raised me right.

Henri interrupted my story and said, "Listen. I want you to remember something. You left their house twelve years ago and went

to Illinois, where you didn't know anyone. That was a very coura-
geous thing to do. I want you to remember that everything you've
done with your life since then has been remarkable."

I looked at him, a little stunned by what seemed like a non
sequitur, and then suddenly I was on the verge of tears. Henri was
trying to comfort me, I realized, because I was hurt and angry. He
was reassuring me because I needed to be reassured. Hiroshi and
Michiko had gotten to me even though I had told myself that they
could no longer hurt me. I blinked hard to stop the tears and smiled
at Henri. I wasn't sure if I was crying more because I was touched by
his kindness or because I was hurt by my parents' insensitivity. That
moment was only the beginning of my realization. I still went back to
Green Bay thinking our visit was not as bad as it might have been. It
took me two, three months to fully understand how terrible our
afternoon together had been, how angry I was.

"There's so much I can teach you," Keiko says. "Just once, come
to the *hirameki* shrine with me. I've been doing a lot of teaching there
and in the streets. I want to tell you about my faith. It's all about forgiveness and letting go. It won't hurt you to hear it, will it?"

I look away from her earnest gaze. "It won't do me any good," I
say. "I'm not interested in forgiving or letting go."

We sit in silence for a while.

"I'm sorry, but I need to leave," I tell her. "I'm meeting my friend
in twenty minutes."

"You're sure you don't want to eat something before you go? You
were always too thin."

"You know I never eat before I go swimming."

Tilting her head sideways, Keiko smiles. She must be remembering all the arguments we used to have at my grandparents' house in
the summer. Keiko, my grandmother, and my mother wanted me to
eat lunch before swimming in the river at one or two, and I refused
because I thought the food would make me heavier and cause me to
drown. In the end, I always got my way about not eating, as well as
about most other things.

One afternoon when I was ten, I even sneaked out of the house to go swimming alone in the rain while everyone else was taking a nap. As I walked down the path among the rice paddies to the river, the sky to the west began to look silver rather than black. It was a sign that everyone else had been wrong to say that I couldn't swim: the rain was clearing up, and there would be no lightning.

When I got to the river, I waded in and started swimming toward the deep water. I already knew the breaststroke and the sidestroke. My mother had been teaching me freestyle all that summer. While I was practicing that alone—trying to kick my legs and turn my head to the side—I swallowed water, splashed in panic to the shallows, and stood up, pressing my left foot onto a piece of glass. For a second, I thought I had been bitten by a water snake. I would faint any minute from the poison and drown. But once I lifted my foot and saw the piece of glass, I got out and started hopping my way home. The path through the rice paddies was muddy. I hopped all the way to keep my bleeding foot clean so I would not get tetanus. When I was halfway home, my foot began to throb. I was dizzy by the time I was across the street from the house and saw Keiko standing next to the hydrangea bushes by the gate. "Where have you been?" she called to me. "Your mother's gone to the school grounds looking for you." Feeling faint, I didn't answer. I wanted to save my breath. Keiko frowned as I hopped across the street. She must have thought I was doing it as a joke.

"I'm wet because I went swimming," I said, "not because it was raining. You were all wrong. It didn't thunder, but I cut my foot."

As soon as she saw my cut, Keiko lifted me in her arms, carried me inside, washed and bandaged my foot. She didn't talk the whole time. I didn't cry or flinch though she disinfected my foot with peroxide. I wasn't going to give her the satisfaction. I wouldn't give anyone reason to say, "Didn't we tell you not to swim alone? Didn't we say it was dangerous?"

Now Keiko is signaling the waiter. When he comes, she pays the bill. We get up and walk out the door without speaking and head toward the station. Keiko stands behind me while I put my coins in the machine to get a token.

"It was good to see you," she smiles.

"I didn't mean to be rude," I tell her, "about going to the shrine and about karma. I don't believe those things. I can't. But I shouldn't have spoken the way I did."

She puts her hand on my elbow. "It's all right. You weren't rude." She squeezes my shoulder lightly when we say good-bye. "See you on Saturday," she says as I put the token into the slot and the electronic arms swing open.

Walking down the stairs to the platform, I can't get over the feeling that I have somehow let her down. I want to run back up the stairs to find her, to apologize once again, but it's too late.

When I get off the train two stops to the west, in a residential area on the western edge of Nishinomiya, Vince is already waiting. We walk out into the street, which is crowded with people coming home from work.

At the health club, a few blocks away, Vince registers me as his guest and pays the fee.

"Thanks."

He just smiles.

He knows that I don't have much money left. I don't protest or thank him too dramatically. His generosity is one of the basic facts of my life. I take it for granted because he wants me to.

"See you in the pool." I head toward the women's locker room, which is much more posh than the one at the Y in Green Bay. The floor here is covered with a pink carpet. Small bottles of shampoo, conditioner, soap, and skin lotion are lined up on the shelves by the mirror. In the shower area, the tiles are green and blue. I change quickly and walk to the pool.

It must be suppertime for most people. The pool isn't crowded at all. I jump into one of the middle lanes. Vince is already swimming two lanes away, alternating laps of breaststroke and freestyle. I envy how easily he can glide along. Swimming has never been a natural sport for me, though I've learned to be an adequate swimmer. I don't float very easily. I get cold in the water. This water is already colder than I would like. Still, I begin my mile in freestyle, flutter-kicking and moving my arms, trying to keep my knees straight. At first, I breathe every two beats and then, after I warm up, every four beats.

Somewhere between the quarter mile and the half mile, I think of the way Keiko frowned and drew her lips into a straight line while she bandaged my foot on the afternoon I swam alone. She frowned the same way this afternoon when I mentioned my unwillingness to forgive. She must have been frustrated by my stubbornness, but her reaction had nothing to do with anger or self-righteousness. I had been too proud to cry in front of her, both times, afraid to show any weakness. But I had no reason to feel that way: if I had cried, she would simply have comforted me. Unlike my father, she would never have told me where I had gone wrong, how she had been right all along. When we argued, she wasn't trying to prove herself right in the way he always did. She wanted me to see her point of view only because she thought she could make me happy.

Vince and I get to the wall at the same time, nod, and then dive back under the surface. After a few strokes, I pass him because this is his breaststroke lap. As I continue to kick and breathe, I think of what Keiko said about karma: the same bad things happening over and over in our lives. But the reverse has been true in my life. The bad things are balanced by the good.

One of the worst things in my life has been the way my father used money to threaten me. At least once every month during my high school years, he said, "You know, I've been thinking it's a waste of my money to send you to Kobe Jogakuin. Why am I paying such a high tuition for you to go to a private school when you can go to a public school for free? I don't think you're getting a very good education there. Your teachers must be stressing too many American ideas and not enough respect. Maybe you'll benefit from the discipline you'll get at a public school. It'll be good for your character. Besides, sending you to Jogakuin was never my idea." This was one of the things he said to reduce me to cold sweat and tears. I had to beg him to continue sending me to Jogakuin because I could not possibly go to a public school where I would have to take exams every day and wear a navy blue military-looking uniform. If I had to do that, I would have to become a totally different person. My father never let me forget that my life could be destroyed by some simple action on his part because he had complete financial and legal control over me.

But this particular bad thing has not continued in my life. I have not been financially connected to my father since I received a scholarship to transfer to Rockford College at twenty. More than that, other people have been generous to me. Even this summer, Vince keeps giving me money and wanting me to downplay my gratitude; Sylvia never wants me to pay her back for anything we both use. It never occurs to my friends that they are doing me a favor.

No bad thing has happened in my life without there being a balancing good thing. Keiko, who believes in karma, is herself part of the good. Like my mother and the rest of her family, Keiko wants to influence my views only to do me good, not to prove herself right. Unlike my father, she isn't motivated by concerns about how my behavior would embarrass or vindicate her. She wants her religion—whose name means a holy flash of light—to light up my life and make everything clear to me so I can feel peace and happiness. Even though I cannot agree with her about religion or forgiveness, her concern—her earnestness about my happiness—is still a gift. I should have thanked her rather than tried to argue.

A few laps past the half mile, I am cold, my toes are cramping up, but I keep thinking about Keiko. You can't expect any man to be faithful, she said, as though that were an accepted fact. Had she been in my mother's position, she would have cried, complained, broken all the dishes in her house to make her husband see how much she needed him. Did anything like that ever happen in her own life, and if so, did she win back her husband in the way she described? Or does Keiko know so much about my mother's loneliness and pride because she feels the same way?

Keiko's smile is the same big frank smile my mother had. Most Japanese women their age don't smile so openly, any more than they wear the bright yellow flower print Keiko was wearing today or the brown coat my mother lined with red-and-green tartan when she was forty. Unlike Keiko, they don't talk about love, *aijo*. The other women are, or at least pretend to be, content to have years of hard work pay off. They make jokes about their husbands' indifference, insensitivity, or even infidelity, so long as the men are financially responsible. For them, love is for novels and movies, not for life. But my mother chose to die because she no longer felt her marriage had love. She wasn't able to say to herself, "Well, at least my life is financially secure and I have good children."

My mother had never been content just to live and be comfortable. She always wanted something more—some form of beauty. She and I started going to art exhibits together when I was in the second grade. The old masters were my immediate favorites. In their portraits, a little light from a candle flickered across the sitter's eyes in an otherwise dark room. In their still lifes, the skin of each fruit shimmered against white cloth. I liked their dark canvases with just enough light to see by. My mother, on the other hand, loved the impressionists, who blinded you with their light. I was sure they had been nearsighted to see the world in huge blurs of bright colors. One day when I was in third grade, we saw a Rembrandt show in the morning and a Pierre Bonnard show after lunch. I didn't understand why she was moved by the trees that melted like fireworks seen through wet glass. I didn't understand what longing for love or beauty had motivated her to take a nine-year-old daughter to two art exhibits in one day.

My mother wanted to be surrounded by beauty and warmth. She filled our apartment with embroidery, planted the small garden plots with sweetpeas and poppies and petunias, and baked cakes and pies almost every night in the winter because it was cold outside. She must have been trying to fill the emptiness of her house, just as Keiko is clothing herself daily in the holy light of her religion now. Their longing is like hunger, the recurring theme of their stories about the wartime.

In the third summer of the war, they once told me, when food became scarce in the city, their family planted some pumpkin seeds they had saved from the year before. The plants grew well and bore huge pumpkins. My grandmother cooked all the pumpkins, then the leaves, the stems, even the roots cut up and mixed into rice. As I continue to kick my legs in the cold water, I imagine my mother and Keiko as young girls. I see them eating the tooth-edged leaves and hairy stems of the pumpkin vines, the small springs of tendrils, all that green like sharp points of light.

Getting to the wall, I kick and turn. I am in the last quarter mile now. The black line at the bottom keeps me going straight. I start wondering how much distance I have covered underwater or on the road running alone, how many hours of my life I have spent on other seemingly monotonous activities like weaving, spinning, knitting, needlework. I have inherited this restlessness from my mother; living isn't enough. I run and swim so I can feel I am getting somewhere that is more than an actual place. Knitting or weaving, I like to feel my fingers making something that is more than useful. Everything I do is a passion—like my mother and Keiko, I don't do things halfway. Choosing to be a writer, weaver, spinner, I want to take what could only be an afternoon's entertainment for my mother and make a life out of it. I want to be immersed in what she could not have enough of.

Another lap done, I kick the wall and glide. Though the water is cold and I am dizzy from not having eaten all afternoon, I am finally swimming easily, as effortlessly as in my recurring dreams of water. There are very few people left in the pool now—just Vince and me and two others in the far lanes. The room seems very brightly lit. Every time I turn my head to breathe, my eyes catch the shine on the water from the overhead lamps. It spreads a white glimmer on the surface all around me like the fragile skin of loneliness we try and try to shed. My arm reaching up into the air as I breathe, I break through that surface momentarily and then glide back beneath it.

The Philosopher's Path

I wake up the next morning with the sun coming through the large windows of the porch and immersing the telephone stand in a column of light. It's seven o'clock. My father must be getting up just about now. Soon he will sit down to breakfast while my stepmother, who has gotten up earlier to cook, will go to dress and put on makeup so she can drive him to work.

I try to count how many days I have left in Kobe after today, Wednesday. I'll be gone Saturday and Sunday to my grandmother's house, Monday through Wednesday next week to my uncle Shiro's in

Hiroshima. That leaves only five full days before my departure, two Sundays from now. If I don't call my father today, I may not have time to see him.

Right now, he must be at home, in the kitchen, shoving hot rice and miso soup into his mouth, the newspaper spread open on the business page. My stepmother, in another room, must be blackening her eyelids with the dark liner she has always worn. She will put on a dress, nylons, and high heels to drive my father to work, because that is how a proper woman dresses in public, at least in her own country where she knows people who "will talk."

When I met them in New York last year, Hiroshi and Michiko were wearing baggy jeans and navy blue polo shirts. Almost everyone in their tour group was dressed in the same way: with the studied casualness of affluent Japanese people on vacation in a foreign city. Away from home, there was no pressure to dress up, nobody worth impressing.

Hiroshi and Michiko hated New York. The streets were dirty, they complained; the whole city was full of Mexicans, Koreans, Middle Easterners. Hiroshi kept telling me he had seven hundred dollars in his wallet. Michiko gawked at the porters at their hotel and called them *kurombo,* a derogatory term for African Americans. Both she and Hiroshi called the homeless *kojiki,* "beggars," and warned each other that these kojiki were sure to be pickpockets and alcoholics.

For a few weeks after the visit, I thought more about their general pettiness and racism than about their repeated personal criticism of me. "I finally see my father and stepmother for what they are," I told friends. "They are narrow-minded and petty people. I shouldn't have taken everything so personally before. I shouldn't have expected them to be nice and decent toward me when they have never been nice or decent toward anyone."

Our meeting had been in early May. It was June or even July before I fully realized that what I was saying made no sense. People shouldn't be excused for one kind of meanness because they are also guilty of another. Why should I forgive Hiroshi and Michiko for insulting me constantly because they also made derogatory comments about people they didn't know? What kind of logic was that—the meaner and more narrow-minded someone is, the more I should accept it?

Even now, I'm angry at the way the two of them judged me: no matter what I did, I didn't make enough money, I didn't know the right people or the right things, my mother hadn't raised me right. At the same time, my father had been eager to introduce me to their friends from the tour group. He told them I was a college professor. He had me escort his friend to a pharmacy to get aspirin so the man could hear me speak English. This is what I cannot forgive: my father wants it both ways. He wants my achievements to reflect well on him in front of other people while he himself never acknowledges these same achievements.

My father always wanted things both ways. When I lived with him, he wanted to influence every aspect of my life—even the time I came home from my part-time jobs—so that our neighbors would not gossip about us; and at the same time, he showed no interest in anything I did at school or the books I was reading at home or the friends I made. He wanted to know nothing out of affection or interest. If he had wanted to control me, to interfere in my life because he loved me and was being overprotective in the way my mother might have been, I would have come to understand, to tolerate and forgive. But he was only worried about what people would say. Until I was able to go abroad on a scholarship, he would not let me move out of the house on my own. My moving out, he said, would make him and his wife look bad: a young woman from a good family simply did not live on her own; people would think that something was wrong with our family if I didn't live at home. While he would not give me permission to move out, he kept reminding me that I was "living in his house" as if it were a privilege I had asked for. Contradiction is a basic element in his character. He has not changed. Right after my mother's death, he shed big tears in front of my uncle Kenichi and said that her death was all his fault; at the same time, he was planning to have Michiko move in as soon as possible. He has never stopped to question his contradictions and double standards. If I go to see him today, he will behave in exactly the same way.

I don't want to spend the few days I have left being angry at him. I didn't come all the way here to feel bitter and hurt. I get up and dress to go running.

Returning an hour later, I go to the phone and dial my friend Miya's number. I have been calling her almost every day in the last week and have never gotten an answer. This time, somebody picks up the phone and says *moshi moshi,* "hello."

"This is Kyoko," I say. "I'm trying to reach Miya Ueda."

"Kyoko. It's me. Miya."

"Oh. Did I wake you up? I'm sorry."

"No." Miya coughs. "But I have tonsilitis. I was lying down."

"Are you all right?"

"I will be, in a few days. I'm glad you called. I was worried we'd never get in touch."

"Me, too. You must have been out of town."

"Back in May, my father-in-law got sick, so my husband and I had to move into their house to help my mother-in-law. My husband is an only child."

"So he had to take care of his father?"

Miya laughs and coughs at the same time. "No. He didn't do anything. He went to work as usual. I took over the housework so my mother-in-law could concentrate on taking care of her husband. They live in Osaka, so I drove back here some nights to clean the apartment and to see my students. I told you in my letter last year, didn't I? I tutor high school kids."

"Yes."

"Anyway, by the time we had to move, it was too late to write to you. I was hoping you would happen to call on the nights I was here.

But my father-in-law's better now, so we came back here last night, and then I started running a fever in the middle of the night."

"I should have given you my number at Sylvia's house. I'm sorry."

"It's okay. I'd like to see you as soon as I get better."

We agree to get together next week, after I come back from Hiroshima. I hang up the phone and continue to sit there, wondering if I should call my father's house after all. I don't have any plans for today or tonight. But the sun is shining outside. It's a perfect day to go to Kyoto, which is only a ninety-minute train ride. If I leave now, I can be there before noon.

When I get off the train in Kyoto, the weather has changed. The sky is overcast and the streets are wet. Taking Cadine's red fold-out umbrella out of my backpack and holding it over my head, I begin to walk along the Philosopher's Path, a riverside route that winds around small temples and shrines. In the drizzle that starts and stops, the cedars along the path are wet and dense as water grass. I notice again how various and textured the trees are in Japan: cedars, bamboo, pines, spruces, persimmons, cherries. On the mountains that surround Kyoto, they make a collage of blunt and sharp edges like pins scattered on a patchwork quilt. Because the mountains are in every direction in Kyoto—unlike in Kobe, where *yamate,* "mountain-direction," is synonymous with *kita,* "north"—I am always slightly lost here.

Coming up a hill, I stop in front of the wooden gate of a small temple. Its name is written on a plaque above the gate, but the characters are the old forms no longer taught in school. The temple isn't marked on the map I got at the tourist information booth, unless I'm mistaken about where I am. It doesn't matter since the path will eventually wind back to some major road. I decide to go in through the gate.

The grounds are deserted. After crossing a footbridge over a lotus pond, I follow a flagstone path to the main building and stand before a small altar. The bodhisattva on a wooden pedestal is taller than I am.

Circles of heartwood mark his forehead and cheeks. Like every bod-hisattva, he looks gaunt and sad. At his feet on a small wooden table, yellow summer oranges are stacked up into a perfect pyramid on a sil-ver platter, and a notebook lies open with a pen next to it, for visitors to write their names and remarks. On the left-hand page, there are a few signatures and dates followed by brief comments. The entry at the bottom, dated today, two hours ago, was signed by two women with the same family name: "A beautiful quiet temple. My daughter is twenty. This is our first trip together, just the two of us." Below this line is an empty space the width of my palm. The whole right-hand page is still blank.

Instead of writing my name, I turn away and walk back toward the lotus pond. As I step on the white stone bridge, the sun comes out momentarily through the drizzle, throwing a dappled shadow of a ginkgo tree at my feet like a sudden sentence I am too slow to catch before it fades away. My mother and I will never be able to take trips together; we will never write a remark and sign it together. On the other side of the pond, to my left, white pebbles have been raked to form two mandalas, the lines shimmering like water. I walk out the gate into the shade of cedars.

Somehow, it isn't the gate through which I first entered the tem-ple. I'm in another—adjoining—temple with its own building and altar. In the far corner beyond a moss garden, there is a pond where an old woman stands on a stepping stone. As I approach, I can see she is feeding the red and black carp, the big fish called koi, whose name puns with the word for romantic love. *Koi* also means "Come here," an informal command of the word *kuru*. "Koi, koi, koi," my mother and I used to call at temple gardens as the fish rose to the water's sur-face in a sinewy tangle of hunger, mouthing hard at the bread crumbs falling from our fingers.

The woman doesn't seem to mind the drizzle. Without an umbrella, she stands feeding the carp. Across the pond, beyond the low fence, a tall white *kannon,* "bodhisattva of mercy," is placed on a pedestal overlooking a small family cemetery. She is a *yakuji kannon,* "medicine-bearing bodhisattva." One of her hands is curled in a gesture of meditation; the other holds out a small jar of salve toward the grave markers—as if the dead still need consolation.

Walking back to the gate, I think of my cousin Kazumi, who used to play hide-and-seek with my brother, Jumpei, and me in our family cemetery. On his visit to Wisconsin, Jumpei said he would rather die than be stuck living with our grandfather Tatsuo, the way Kazumi was. Kazumi had no way out: she was too old to marry unless a match could be arranged with a widower, and because she was a woman from a good family, she could not move out on her own to find work. For a few years after college, Kazumi worked as a secretary at our grandfather's paint company, but he never considered training her as his successor because she wasn't a man. Instead, he tried to arrange a match for her with a man who could be his heir. But none of the prospects worked out, even when Kazumi was still in her twenties. She struck the men as being too intelligent and self-assured. She had an economics degree from one of the better universities in our area. Our grandfather was mad at her, Jumpei said, for not having gone to a junior college instead and gotten a two-year degree in something "more feminine" like home economics or child development. "It's so sad," Jumpei shook his head. "What a terrible life."

Even Jumpei—who was a man, after all, and was allowed to move out of the house to go to college as soon as he was eighteen—seemed to sense the terrible restrictions of being a woman from a "good" Japanese family. If I hadn't left, I would be living at home just like my cousin. I might have had a slightly easier time finding a job because of my English. But that would have been the only difference. No one would have wanted to marry me. If Kazumi—who was always much more mild mannered than I—had struck the men as too self-assured, I would have come across as plain arrogant. I might have tried to marry all the same, because that would have been my only way out of my father's house. But in a culture that doesn't value intelligence in women, how would I have found a husband who wasn't, in the end, just like my father and my paternal grandfather? So I would have had only two bad choices: to live with my father or to live with someone like him. "You're right," I said to my brother. "I would rather be dead, too."

I stop at the gate of the temple and look back. The woman is still feeding the carp; she has not even noticed me. Stepping outside the gate, I am back on the path. The gray wall I am walking away from reminds me of the walls that surround our family cemetery in Osaka, where I imagine some ghostly versions of us playing hide-and-seek. In our thirties, Kazumi, Jumpei, and I are still the only three children of our family. None of us is likely to change that. Whatever family legacy we have stops with us. My brother and I, having escaped that small world of stones, can say that we would rather die than be stuck there. We have left Kazumi alone to care for a grandfather whose cold eyes reminded us of fish eyes, who locked us in his dark drawing room for hours as punishment for talking too loudly or running down the hallway of his house, instead of walking quietly.

Long ago, Kazumi and her mother, Akiko, went hiking in the mountains with my mother, brother, and me to see the red maples in the fall, the cherries and azaleas in the spring. I cannot come this close and not see them. I have to call them, even if that means calling Hiroshi and Michiko first—and of course, it would mean that; otherwise, I would embarrass Kazumi and Akiko. So, walking in what I hope is the correct direction on the Philosopher's Path, I know the time has come, or almost. It's only one o'clock. I have the whole afternoon and half of this path left before I must head back to Kobe to make the phone call.

Back in Kobe, Sylvia is in the kitchen cooking supper.

"How was Kyoto?" she asks, stirring a pot of soup.

"I went to the Philosopher's Path. It was nice." I sit down at the table. "I decided to call my father."

She puts down her spoon and looks back at me. "It's hot. Can I make you a drink?"

"Sure. Thanks."

She mixes a gin and tonic, squeezing a slice of lime over the glass.

"Are you going to call him now, or would you like to have supper with us first?" she asks, handing me the drink. "We can eat in fifteen minutes."

"I'll eat first. I don't want to call him on an empty stomach."

"Okay." She goes back to the sink to peel some cucumbers.

In the dining room, where I go to set the table, Cadine is reading a magazine. "Look," she points to the glass jar on the windowsill. "The caterpillars turned green."

Last night, when Cadine and I found them on the orange tree, the caterpillars were gray. Sylvia said they looked like bird droppings. Now both of them are bright green, their backs marked with black spots.

"I know what they are," I tell Cadine, remembering. "They're swallowtail larvae. My mother and I used to find them on our Japanese pepper tree. I didn't recognize them last night because they were gray."

"So they're not moths?"

"No. Butterflies. We used to keep them in jars, too."

Cadine gets up and brushes her long hair away from her face. "There are some messages on the machine. One of them is for you. Let's go hear them."

I follow her into the study, where she pushes the button on the answering machine by the doorway. Immediately, a woman's voice comes on, loud and high, enunciating every word.

"Sylvia, this is Cindy Seton. How are you? Listen, my husband has some antiques you and Jacques might be interested in. Here are the times we'll be home so you can come and look at them. . . ." The machine cuts her off while she's mentioning the times.

"She sounds exactly the same," I tell Cadine, who is standing in the doorway next to me. "Very perky." Mrs. Seton used to teach at Kobe Jogakuin, but I never took classes with her.

"Sylvia," the next voice starts, equally loud, but very low. "This is to tell you that Mike and I can't come over for dinner on Saturday because we've already been invited to the Stephans' that night. So we're busy. Maybe another time."

That's all. She doesn't thank Sylvia or express regret.

"Mrs. Peterson." Cadine wrinkles her nose. "*Sylvia*," she mimicks in a nasal tone. "*Mike and I can't have dinner with you because we're so busy. We're so popular everyone else invites us to dinner.*"

I start laughing. She rolls her eyes.

The machine beeps one more time and then Vince's voice comes on. He is talking so softly that I have to strain to hear him. He sounds half-asleep.

"So the movie's at seven every night." He says the name of the theater, but I can't catch it. "Call me and let me know when you want to go. I'll come and pick you up. Don't forget to call that guy Peter about your meeting with the writers' group tomorrow. He'll give you directions."

"Everybody sounds so weird," Cadine says after Vince's message is over. "What's wrong with Vince? You can't hear half the stuff he says."

"He kind of mumbles, I guess."

"Maybe he spends too much time having to speak Japanese," Cadine says. "You know how you don't open your mouth very much when you speak Japanese? Vince does that with English, too, so you can't hear him."

Cadine pushes the button again and replays the messages. Halfway through, we burst out laughing and can't stop. She's right; everyone sounds weird. They sound like caricatures of themselves: extra perky, extra rude, extra low-key.

"We live with some weird gaijin people," Cadine shrugs. We play the messages a third time so we can laugh more.

As I sit down by the phone upstairs after dinner, the sun is low over the Rokko Mountains to the west. Birds are swooping down outside, their wings almost grazing the eaves. They must be swallows going after insects. I close my eyes and listen to the phone ringing on the other end.

My stepmother, Michiko, answers on the third ring. "Mori residence," she says, businesslike.

"Hello. This is Kyoko. I'm in Kobe, as I said in the letter I sent Father."

She doesn't say a word. I watch the swallows flying diagonally across the windows.

"You should have called sooner," she says finally, her voice shrill and accusatory. "I'm going to Hokkaido tomorrow. When I come home next week, your father is going into the hospital."

For a moment, I am relieved. There won't be time to see much of them. Then I understand that my father must be having a health problem.

"What's he going to the hospital for? Is he sick?"

"Nothing serious. He has some polyps on his intestines. He's having them taken out. They could be cancer, but most likely not."

According to my watch, it's a little past seven. "Maybe I should come and see you tonight," I suggest. "I'm going to visit my grandmother on Saturday. Then I'll be going to Hiroshima to see my uncle Shiro. After that, I only have a few days before I leave. I don't have much time."

She doesn't answer.

"Is that inconvenient?" I ask.

"You can come if you like. Your father's here. He got home about an hour ago, and we had dinner. Did you eat?"

"Yes."

"You can come and have some coffee, then."

"Okay. Tell me how to get to your place."

"Wait a minute. Let me ask your father first and make sure he wants to see you tonight." She covers the receiver to talk to him. The voices are muffled. She comes back on and asks, "Are you anywhere near the commuter train? See, we don't even know where you've been staying all this time."

"I can get to the train."

"Take it to Ashiya and wait for me a block south. That way, I won't have to park the car. Your father says you can just take a cab, but I think I should come and meet you in my car."

"All right. I'll be at the station in about half an hour."

"I'll be waiting in my car."

After I hang up the phone, I grab my backpack and run downstairs. Sylvia and Cadine are doing the dishes. Cadine has cut off the tops of some carrots and put them in a dish of water to see if they will grow leaves.

"I'm going to see them right now. I want to get this over with."

"Good luck," Sylvia says.

"I'll tell you about it when I get back, if you're still up." I get my shoes and go out the back door.

In Ashiya, I walk a block south from the train station and look around. Michiko isn't here. None of the cars driving up and down the riverside street seems to be slowing down to stop. The sky is still light with the afterglow of the sunset. I stand waiting for ten, fifteen minutes before Michiko comes walking across the street in a green pantsuit.

She stops a few feet away from me. "I almost didn't see you," she says frowning. "This isn't the block I meant. I was looking for you on the other side of the station. I thought you'd be able to figure out which side I meant, since I'd be coming from the north."

"I'm sorry. I didn't know exactly where you live now, so I wasn't sure which way you might be coming."

"I guess you've never had a very good sense of direction." She turns around and crosses the street to a white Mazda parked by the curb with the flashing lights on. She opens the door and sits down. "Get in. The door's unlocked."

As soon as I sit down and close the door, she starts driving.

"Did you go to your grandfather's house already?" she asks a few seconds later. She is squinting at me as though she expected me to say yes so she could add this to the list of things I have done wrong.

"No. I thought it more proper to contact you and Father first."

"You don't know then." She squints back into the rearview mirror.

"Don't know what?"

"Your aunt Akiko's in the hospital. She had to have a major operation on her liver."

"Is she okay?"

"I hear she is. But she's not seeing anyone but Kazumi, so you won't be able to see her."

"She's not fully recovered?"

"I don't know the details. The operation was almost a month ago, so she must be doing pretty well. Maybe she doesn't want any intrusion. Receiving visitors takes a lot out of you when you're sick. Believe me. I know it from all my operations on the ulcers. You're not her immediate family. You haven't seen her for so long. She must think it'll be too awkward and exhausting to see you. You're almost a stranger to her now."

We are going up the hill above the grade school Kazumi, Jumpei, and I once attended. When we had schoolwide concerts and athletic events, my mother and Akiko came together and sat side by side in the audience. They met us afterward and took us out for ice cream. Our teachers always thought that the two of them were sisters, not sisters-in-law.

"Poor Akiko," my stepmother says. "She's been through so much misfortune. Her husband doesn't come home anymore. He's taken an apartment near Osaka and lives with another woman. Kazumi asked him to proceed with an official divorce since he and Akiko are married in name only. He wouldn't do it. Maybe he's interested in your grandfather's money or his company. I don't know."

I close my eyes. The uphill movement of the car makes me feel as if I'm falling backward. When I open my eyes, I can see the sky has begun to darken. No one has told me, till now, about Akiko's husband living with a girlfriend. I'm not surprised by the secrecy. Women from good families never talk about divorce. A woman in my aunt's situation would usually pretend that her husband had to move away because of his job. Only after years of separation might she admit, "We haven't lived together for so long, and now that the children are grown, we have nothing in common." Even then, the woman would not initiate a divorce and call attention to her single status.

"It's all your grandfather's fault," Michiko continues, grimacing. "He supports Akiko and Kazumi with his money so they don't need her husband. No wonder he left. He felt inferior."

"I sure hope Aunt Akiko is okay. I really wanted to see her and Kazumi."

"You might not be able to see Kazumi, either. She's very busy taking care of her mother. She's gone all day, and she has a lot on her mind. If she can't see you, you shouldn't take it personally. But if you do see her, don't mention what I told you. It's none of your business. You shouldn't be intrusive. Don't say you heard anything from me."

We come to a large condominium building, where she drives the car into an underground garage. The white lights in the garage turn her green suit ashen blue.

We get out of the car and climb the stairs. "When Akiko went into the hospital," Michiko says, walking ahead of me, "I gave your grandfather a million yen to express your father's and my good wishes. I figured they needed help. He took the money and said, 'It's good to have relatives in our times of need. We can help each other so much.' What a joke. He never gave us anything when I was sick."

We are at the top of three flights of stairs. She stands in front of the door, puts the key in the lock, and turns it.

"Words are cheap," she says as she opens the door to her place.

My father, Hiroshi, is drinking tea in the dining room, which has large windows facing south. Though the air conditioner is on, he doesn't have a shirt on over his shorts. On his chest, I can see the dark red scars from the surgery he had for tuberculosis. They curve around his nipples and disappear under black hair.

Hiroshi doesn't get up or say anything. He just sits there looking in my direction. I don't take a step toward him, smile, or say hello.

"Shouldn't you put on a shirt?" Michiko asks. "You don't want to embarrass her."

"She's my daughter. I don't have to stand on ceremony." He nods toward the chair across the table from him. I sit down while Michiko goes to the kitchen to make coffee. The windows of the dining room overlook the city. It's basically the same view I have from my room at Sylvia's house, though his house is a few miles to the east. Soon the curve of the bay near downtown Kobe will be lit up by the neon signs.

"Good evening," I greet him, putting on my stiff and formal voice as though we were strangers. "I hope you are well." I stare directly at his bare chest, narrowing my eyes a little into what I hope is a clear expression of disapproval.

My father ignores both my greeting and my expression. "What's the phone number at your friend's house where you're staying?" he asks.

Because I haven't memorized the number, I have to look for the notebook I carry in my backpack.

"Why would you need that number?" Michiko asks from the kitchen. "She won't be there much. She's already made all her plans. She's busy seeing everyone but us. We don't want to call and bother her friends in her absence. They probably don't even speak Japanese."

"That's true," he says. "Forget it. We don't have much time anyway."

I put the notebook away. Michiko brings the coffee and sits down next to me. After a while, she says to Hiroshi, "There's not enough time for all of us to go out to dinner before she leaves, but at least you should take her out once while I'm out of town."

"No. You should take her the night I go to the hospital. Ask Kazumi, too. Try that Chinese restaurant near the station. I've heard good things about it."

Michiko frowns. "How can I go out to eat while you're in the hospital? You'll need me there. I'm supposed to be there."

"They won't do much the first night, except prepare me for surgery and ask me a lot of questions. I won't need you then. Go ahead and make a reservation." He lights a cigarette and immediately flicks it over the ashtray, which is already full.

"But you're her father. You should go while I'm in Hokkaido."

"I don't have time for that. I have a lot of work to do before I go to the hospital."

"Maybe she doesn't have time anyway," Michiko says. "She's already made plans with everyone else. I wouldn't be surprised if she has no time left for you."

They both turn to me.

"You don't have to take me to dinner if you're busy," I say. "But I don't have all my plans made. I would still like to see Akiko and Kazumi. Maybe I should call Kazumi. You mentioned asking her out to dinner."

"She's very busy. I told you in the car," Michiko says.

"Call her now," Hiroshi suggests. "She should be home by now. The phone's right over here." He points to the shelf behind him.

"Your father might be sleeping," Michiko says to him.

"No. He stays up late." Hiroshi gets up, takes the phone off the hook, and hands me the receiver. He is already dialing the number. The phone begins to ring on the other end.

Kazumi answers right away. "This is the Mori residence." She sounds just like Aunt Akiko.

"Kazumi. This is Kyoko. I'm calling from my parents' house. How are you?"

"Your father mentioned you were coming in June." She pauses. "Did you call to speak with Grandfather?"

"No. Why would I want to talk to him? I called to talk to you."

Michiko is staring at my face, her lips drawn tight.

Kazumi starts laughing. "You sound just the same," she says. "It's been a long time."

"Is Aunt Akiko all right? I heard about her surgery. Can I see her?"

"Of course. She's eager to see you. We knew you were coming because your father told us, so we already talked to the doctor. The doctor said she should wait another week before seeing anyone except me. She's doing well, but he's afraid of her getting too excited and having a setback. So can you come next week?"

"Of course. I don't want to leave without seeing Aunt Akiko."

"She'll be happy to hear that. I'll tell her tomorrow when I go to see her. She talks about you every day."

"So it's not as though she doesn't want to see me."

"Why wouldn't she want to see you? She misses you a lot."

I glance at Michiko. She gets up and goes into the kitchen.

"What are your plans?" I ask Kazumi. "Can I see you soon? I don't have to wait till next week to see you, do I?"

"I'll be here tomorrow morning," she says. "I don't go to the hospital till the afternoon. You should come and pay a visit to Grandfather, you know," she reminds me.

"I'll come tomorrow morning then. He doesn't work till the afternoon, right? I can pay my official visit to him and still see you. Is he the same as he used to be?"

"Yes."

"Too bad. But I guess I do have to see him."

Michiko comes back with a pot of tea and sits down. She pours the tea for Hiroshi. They are both listening to my end of the conversation. "Listen," I say to Kazumi, "I want to visit my mother's grave in Osaka. Can you come with me some morning or afternoon soon? I don't remember the way to the temple. It's been a long time. But you know the way, don't you?"

"I can go with you anytime."

"How about the day after tomorrow? That's Friday. I'll be going to see my grandmother on Saturday. When I see her, I want to tell her that I visited my mother's grave in Osaka. She would be glad to hear me say that."

"I'll be happy to go with you."

"One more thing. My parents think one of them should take us out to dinner. What are your plans next week?"

"Whatever suits you and them is fine by me. I'm not working anymore, so my schedule is pretty flexible. I have a lot of time on my hands."

"Great." I glance at Michiko again. "I've been warned that you may be too busy to see me. I was afraid you'd have no time for me."

"I would never be too busy to see you. Don't be silly."

"I'll talk to my parents about dinner and tell you tomorrow. Tell Grandfather that I'll come to see him tomorrow morning, will you?"

"You don't want to tell him yourself? He's upstairs. I can get him."

"No. It's all right. You tell him."

She laughs.

"You know how it is. I'm never very eager to talk to him. But it'll be good to see you."

"It'll be good to see you, too."

When I hang up, Michiko is frowning at me from the immaculately polished dining table. Behind her, the white walls are spotless. In the glass-covered cabinet, not a dish is out of place. She must polish the glass panels and wash the walls every morning. When I lived with them, she cleaned the house at least once every day, twice if she saw some dust in the afternoon. I sit down and take a sip of the coffee, which is cold by now.

"So you're leaving a week from Sunday?" Hiroshi asks me.

"Yes. I'll be leaving in the morning."

He looks toward Michiko and then back to me. "Michiko will take you and Kazumi out to dinner on Friday night next week, then."

"Only if you're free," she adds.

"I don't have any plans."

"I won't be able to join you," Hiroshi says. "I'm going into the hospital that afternoon. They won't let me leave once I check in."

"No," Michiko interrupts. "They don't let you eat before surgery. I know from all those times I had to have surgery on my ulcers."

"If I have time next week while Michiko is gone to Hokkaido, I'll call Kazumi," Hiroshi continues, "and Kazumi can call you. Maybe we can go out then. But don't count on it. I'll be busy." He purses his lips and jerks his head up and down once, as if to say, *discussion closed*. It's as if we are planning a business meeting.

"I'll be busy, too," I announce. My voice sounds just as stiff as his. "I'm going to visit my grandmother and then Uncle Shiro. I won't be back till Wednesday night."

"Remember when Jumpei was going to see their grandmother?" Michiko asks Hiroshi and chuckles. "I was right there when he made the phone call." She turns sideways to address me. "This was about a year and a half ago. He was staying here a few weeks before going to South America. He called her and said he'd drive over to see her. Guess what she said."

I shrug.

"She said she wasn't feeling very well. It was in the middle of winter. She asked him not to come because she couldn't do much to entertain him anyway. You should have seen his face. His jaw dropped. He said, 'Fine then. Maybe I won't see you for a long time now. I'll be leaving the country soon.' He hung up in a big sulk." Michiko has to stop because she is laughing too hard. "Imagine being rejected by your own grandmother," she says between gasps of laughter. "I had to remind him that people get funny when they get old. They get so they don't want any intrusion."

"Maybe she was really sick," I suggest.

Neither Michiko nor Hiroshi answers.

"Jumpei said he didn't start seeing our mother's family till Grandfather's funeral," I say. "He was a junior in college then. I thought you were going to let him visit when he was eighteen."

I lean back in my chair and look at my father, who is still sitting bare-chested, sipping his tea. The afternoon he forbade Jumpei and me from seeing our mother's family, Hiroshi was wearing the suit he had worn to work and sitting bolt upright in his father's drawing room. I am amazed, suddenly, that all these years have passed and I am grown up. He is just a frail old man without a shirt; even his hands look bony and stained with age.

"Jumpei never asked to see those people," Michiko says. "He was pretty busy back then, going to school and working part-time."

Hiroshi drains his teacup in a gulp. He scrapes the chair legs against the floor as he stands up. "I'm going to lie down for a while," he says to Michiko. "Wake me up when you have to drive her back to Kobe. I'll go with you so you won't have to drive alone on the way back." He glances at me and then turns back to Michiko. "She doesn't seem sure about the directions. She has such a poor sense of direction, but I can figure out the way from the address."

"I don't know the way because I don't drive here." I pause, take a deep breath to keep my voice from sounding shrill and defensive. I need to sound calm and polite: I am a grown-up guest, not an upset child forced to live in their house. "You don't have to drive me back. I can take the train."

"How can I not give you a ride?" Michiko protests. "This is the only time you visited our house. I have to give you a ride. Otherwise, you'll say we did nothing for you."

Hiroshi is already walking toward the bedroom.

"Do you not feel well?" I ask him.

He stops, turns around. "Nothing is wrong," he declares. "I'm just tired from working late last night. I need some rest."

"Do you want me to leave now so you don't have to get up later?"

"No. You can stay." He goes into the bedroom and closes the door.

"You should have called a day ahead of time," Michiko says as she pours herself some tea. "He's not up to a visit."

"I didn't realize he would be sick."

"He is not sick. This has nothing to do with the surgery. Your father's not a very sociable person. It's not a good idea to visit him all of a sudden." She notices my empty cup. "Do you want some more coffee? I can make another pot."

"No. Thanks."

"You don't drink green tea, do you?"

"Not usually."

Michiko shakes her head. She pushes her chair back a little and turns sideways toward me. "I guess that's very American," she says.

"I never liked green tea. It has nothing to do with where I live."

Michiko changes the subject. "I'm surprised your grandmother only wants you to visit overnight. Why doesn't she ask you to stay longer after you've come all this way? But then you haven't seen her for so long. At her age, I suppose she's not ready to see anyone new."

"She's my grandmother. I'm scarcely someone new."

Michiko sips her tea. "You can't help losing touch with your relatives. You live so far away. But you and Jumpei are lucky to have ended up in foreign countries. You wouldn't fit in here. You didn't have a very good upbringing, even though I did everything I could. It was too late by then."

While she rambles on, I concentrate on staying silent and calm. Every time my mind forms devastating words I could say to interrupt her stupid talk, I push those words away and try not to think of any more. Regardless of what Michiko says about my upbringing, my mother didn't raise me to be a rude person. She taught me that dignity is important.

"Remember how you knew nothing about housework when I came? You would never have been good enough to marry here. You started too late. I would have been embarrassed in front of my in-laws. But in America, you don't have to worry about that. I heard about how American women don't do housework the way we do in Japan. Everyone probably does their laundry only once a week. I never forgot your telling me that in New York. I hope you don't get sick from the germs. But it's none of my business."

I won't even address her comments. Politely changing the subject, I ask her instead if she heard from my brother lately.

"He called last week from Quito," she replies. "Your father answered the phone. Jumpei didn't identify himself at first. When your father said I wasn't home, he said he'd call back another time. They didn't even talk. It's a pity. He's never been very close to your father. But at least he's close to me."

"Jumpei said he didn't talk to Father for two years while he was in college. Is that true?"

"They had a big fight during one of the vacations. Jumpei said he would never come back to our house for a visit. Your father told him he would stop sending money then—the allowance Jumpei needed to pay his tuition and the rent at his lodging house. The money he made working part-time was mostly for buying clothes and taking trips with his friends. He couldn't live on that. So I sent him the same amount he was getting from his father, every month."

"Did you try to talk Father into forgiving him?"

"No. We never discussed it. He didn't know what I was doing. Your father always expects me to manage our finances. He never asks how I spend our money. So I did the right thing by Jumpei. That's all I cared about. How the two of them felt about each other was none of my business."

"So how did they ever make up?"

Michiko grimaces. "Your Aunt Akiko invited the two of them to dinner and insisted that they forgive each other. She tricked them. Each of them thought he was having dinner with Akiko alone. If she had told them ahead of time, neither would have shown up."

"Did you know ahead of time?"

"Of course not. Your Aunt Akiko never tells me anything. She's pretty close and sly."

Outside, the neon signs have been lit in the distance.

"I think it's too bad you and Jumpei aren't close to your father," Michiko continues. "But that's perfectly understandable. He was never home when your mother was alive. You never got to know him. It's your mother's fault, too, for keeping him away. Still, he isn't naturally good with children. He's a great husband, but he's not suited to being a father. He should never have had you two, especially the way he felt about your mother. He might have been talked into spending more time at home if he'd had children with me, but even then, he probably wouldn't have been a very good father." She points at the lights outside. "See those white lights just down the hill? That's where the hospital is. I drove my mother there every afternoon for her treatments until they could admit her. We had to wait a month for a bed to become available."

She finishes her tea and pours another cup.

"I used to hate my mother," she says, "when I was young. She wasn't happy in her marriage. My parents fought every day, so when my father died, I thought it was all her fault. I was only twenty. But I'm glad I took good care of her when she had cancer. She was very grateful to me at the end. I think she finally understood how wrong she had been to favor my brother over me. She saw the truth. As they say, people learn a lot from painful experiences. Of course, I had no help from my brother or his wife. My mother still left her money to them. I don't mind. My brother's a good-for-nothing. He needs everything he can get. And it is my mother's fault in a way, for having spoiled him when he was young. So everything turned out the way it should. It always does, you know."

She stops and looks toward the doorway. My father has come out of the bedroom and is standing there in a polo shirt and gray pants. "Are you about ready to take her home?" he asks Michiko.

"Yes," I say, getting up and grabbing my backpack. "I'm ready to leave."

Downstairs in the parking garage, Hiroshi opens the door on the passenger's side and gets into the front seat, leaving me to sit in the back. Michiko starts the car, and we proceed down the hill.

"Don't take the highway," Hiroshi says as we approach the commuter train station. "That takes you out of your way. Here, turn west on this street."

The street he points out is the one that cuts through our old neighborhood. In a few minutes, we are driving only a few blocks from the house where Michiko came to live with us the spring after my mother's death.

"This is near where we used to live," I say. "I ran here the other day. The house is gone. Did you know that? They poured concrete over that next lot where my mother had the vegetable garden and built another house there."

Ahead, the headlights of a car appear around a bend in the road. Where our two cars come together, the road is too narrow. Michiko waits for the other car to back up. When it doesn't, she sighs and puts hers in reverse, steps hard on the gas. We zoom backward to the corner where the road widens.

"I used to walk here in the rain," she says, tapping her fingers on the wheel, "with groceries in my basket to make you food."

"So did my mother," I say. "She hated it." The other car approaches slowly. We are at the same corner where Hiroshi long ago told me that he would remarry because I could not be expected to keep house for him. I look out the window at the dim yellow light of the lamppost and remember my mother with her basket of oranges, loaves of bread, bouquets of carnations and roses she bought in the winter when our garden was bare. I wish that at least her shadow could cross the headlight fanning out from Michiko's car and be seen, even for a moment. It is unfair that she has no voice, not even mine, to make a protest: how can Michiko, who got what should have been my mother's—the house, my father's and my brother's affection—claim the past as well? *You only took care of us because it was my father's excuse for marrying you,* I want to say. *You didn't do it because you loved me. I owe you nothing.* But of course, I refrain and, in silence, watch the other car come closer and then maneuver around us. Michiko jerks her gear into drive and steps on the gas. We don't talk the rest of the way.

In front of Sylvia's house, Hiroshi turns in the front seat and sticks his hand toward me. He is holding three thousand-yen bills.

"I don't need any money."

"Take it. You can always use money."

His hand is not moving. His bones and veins stick out from beneath the skin.

I reach out to take the bills, careful not to touch his fingers. "Thank you," I say. To myself, I think, *The money doesn't make any difference now. I can take it because I don't need it.* "If I don't see you before I leave, good luck on your surgery."

He nods and says *ja mata,* "Well, another time."

"Thank you for the coffee," I say to my stepmother, "and for bringing me back in your car."

She doesn't answer.

"Good-bye," I say and get out.

Immediately, they drive away. My friends both in Japan and in the States would wait in the car till they had seen me enter the house. It would be a small gesture of courtesy: making sure I got home all right. I cannot remember my father or stepmother ever making such gestures of courtesy or consideration. When they did anything for me, whether it was giving me money, taking me to dinner, or driving me somewhere, they made a big production out of it. Each time, they wanted me to observe how meticulously they fulfilled their obligation toward me. Nothing they did had to do with courtesy or affection. This time has been no different.

I take my shoes off in the foyer and go in. Sylvia and Cadine are sitting on the couch in the living room. Cadine has brought the jar of caterpillars and put it on the coffee table. There are new leaves inside. One of the cats, Ophelia, is sleeping on the floor.

"So how was your visit?" Sylvia asks me as I sit on the floor next to the cat.

"About what I expected," I reply. "They argued a long time about which one of them should take me out to dinner because they were both busy. My father got up from the table and went to lie down because he had worked late last night and he was tired."

"He went to sleep?" Cadine asks, her eyes rounded in surprise.

The look on her face makes me realize, truly, how unbelievably rude my father has been. Still, I try to keep my tone light. I shrug. "I don't know if he really fell asleep or not. But he was gone for half an hour. He came back out and asked my stepmother if she was ready to drive me home. He wanted to come with her because I was so bad with directions."

The cat sniffs my hand and goes back to sleep. Her whiskers twitch. Nobody says anything.

"I guess that's a weird thing to do," I add. "I mean my father's taking a nap. Most people wouldn't do that in the middle of a visit, especially after you haven't seen them much in the last thirteen years."

"No, they wouldn't," Sylvia says.

"If my father were a normal person, he wouldn't do that regardless of what I did or said to him."

"You could say that."

"I don't know why I need to ask you that. My father always has this effect on me. I want people to confirm that he's weird, that I'm not just imagining his behavior."

"I understand," Sylvia smiles a little.

"He's supposed to have surgery in a week and a half to remove some intestinal polyps. My stepmother's leaving town on vacation tomorrow and coming back in time for the surgery. So I won't be seeing much of them again. I guess that's the best part."

"Are you worried about him?" Sylvia asks.

I think about it and have to say, "No. Maybe I'd feel different if his condition were life-threatening. But they both made like it was nothing." As I say this, I know I wouldn't be worried even if my father had been more seriously ill. Unsettled, maybe, but not worried or concerned the way I am about Aunt Akiko.

We don't talk for a while. Inside the jar, the caterpillars are eating the leaves they are perched on. By morning, all will be gone except a few stems too short to crawl on. Every night, the caterpillars are bringing down their own house, eating their way toward flight.

"I'm still glad I went to their house tonight," I tell Sylvia and Cadine. "I talked to my cousin Kazumi on the phone from there. Her mother, my aunt Akiko, is in the hospital recovering from surgery. I made plans to see them both."

"You have cousins?" Cadine asks.

"I have lots of cousins. Only one on my father's side, but lots on my mother's."

"That's neat," she says. "I don't really know my cousins."

Cadine's cousins would be in Ohio, where Sylvia is from, and in France, where her father, Jacques, grew up. Cadine sees them once every summer, if that.

Lying in bed a little later in my room, I think of how isolated Cadine and Sylvia must feel, stuck in the small community of gaijin in and around Kobe. In that small group, people tend to get eccentric. One of my old teachers from Kobe Jogakuin, Paul Bennett, and Cadine's father, Jacques, have a three-year-old feud going on because Paul once had people over to watch a Joan Crawford movie and Jacques made fun of her acting. The two men haven't said a word to each other since that evening. I wasn't surprised when Sylvia told me that. Nor was I surprised, exactly, at Mrs. Peterson's abrupt and rude message on Sylvia's machine. People can lose touch with something when they are constantly outsiders—some sense of moderation or balance. They get extra bossy, extra sensitive, extra blunt. Isolation takes its toll on people. I know Sylvia worries about herself and Cadine because of it. She's told me that she never feels at home, either in the States or in Japan. Though I have known Sylvia only for a few weeks now, I know we share something important: we are both outsiders no matter where we go; isolation is a fact of our lives.

But we didn't become outsiders by moving to a foreign country: we have never felt at home anywhere in the first place. It was the same way with my mother and Aunt Keiko. They didn't have to be foreigners to feel that they never fit in, that they were isolated and lonely. If my mother had survived the period in her life when that loneliness seemed unbearable, she might have come to accept it and make the best of her quiet life surrounded by her garden flowers and all the beautiful things she made; or she might have tried to overcome her isolation by reconnecting with the friends she had at our apartment house. Either way, she would have been someone I could have talked to about my own feelings of not fitting in, not being home anywhere. This is how it is for me, seeing my father and stepmother: always, after seeing them, I miss my mother terribly.

If I had come to visit my mother, she wouldn't have left me in the middle of the conversation to take a nap. She wouldn't have gone on about how she was too busy to take me out to dinner. She would never be so rude to anyone under any circumstance.

I sit up in bed, suddenly too angry to keep lying down. My father didn't even get dressed to greet me in the first place. He sat at the table with no shirt on so I had to see his hairy chest and his scar. Then he insisted that he didn't have to stand on ceremony because I was his daughter, as though there was some closeness between us that did away with the visit's awkwardness. Actually, when he said that I was his daughter, he meant that I was a person not deserving of a guest's special treatment or respect. He didn't mean that he loved me or that we were close in any way. Because he was my father, he implied, he had every right to embarrass me with his bare chest, his scars.

I hold my knees to my chest. Above me, shadows of trees are swaying on the ceiling. The cats are running up and down the hallway. Even though I had expected every bit of my father's behavior, I still cannot believe how rude he was, how hurtful. The message Mrs. Peterson left on Sylvia's machine this afternoon was nothing by comparison—nor Paul kicking Jacques out of his house in the middle of the movie and telling him, in front of everyone, never to set foot there again. Their actions were simply thoughtless or eccentric. My father is in a league of his own when it comes to rude, insensitive, and strange behavior. My stepmother, too, acted with plain malice—

saying hurtful things about my mother, my grandmother, how nobody would want to see me after all these years.

If anyone else had behaved in the way Hiroshi and Michiko did, I would have been outraged on the spot, not later. I would have protested and defended myself. I would even have said some ugly things in return, expressing my anger right away. But with Hiroshi and Michiko, it's different. What happened tonight is a repeat of our visit in New York. When I am with them, I don't fully realize how angry I am. I get stunned into politeness, an icy, stiff kind of politeness that enables me, at least, to keep my dignity. I make inquiries about their health, thank them for their trouble, wish them well at parting even though I couldn't care less about their well-being. When I talked to Kazumi on the phone, I was talking like family, without that stiff politeness. I knew that Hiroshi and Michiko were listening. I wanted them to hear the difference. That was how I was getting back at them, trying to be hurtful in my own way: I wanted Hiroshi and Michiko to know that they would never be family to me in the way Kazumi, Akiko, and my maternal relatives were.

It's possible, then, that I acted no better toward my father than he did toward me. I did nothing to hide my reluctance about visiting his house. When I got there, I immediately started talking like a stranger. I didn't insist that he take my phone number over my stepmother's objection. I did little to make conversation. More than likely, my barely masked indifference contributed to the bad feeling between us. Perhaps, rather than remaining icily dignified, I should have confronted him and said, "What is wrong with you? Why won't you take me out to dinner? Why must you talk about me as if I were nothing more than an unpleasant obligation? You are supposed to be my father. You have no right to behave this way." If I had said something like that, we would have been openly angry at each other. We would have been forced to be honest. There might then have been a chance, however small, of further discussions. If not, I would still have the consolation of having acted with honesty.

My aunt Keiko told me yesterday that my mother's problem was her retreat into silence: she should have confronted Hiroshi about his affair, his indifference, his reluctance to spend time at home. My mother had been too proud, too concerned about her dignity, to break the dishes in her house, cry, and protest. What I did tonight was no different. Maybe I was just repeating my mother's mistake, her karma as Keiko would put it.

In some crazy way, my father might even have been trying to establish a casual atmosphere, the mood of a family visit. When I arrived, he didn't return my stiff greeting and instead asked for my phone number. He sat there exposing his tuberculosis scars to me. Even his taking a nap later could be interpreted as a gesture of casualness: since we were all family, he might have been trying to indicate, he could go lie down if he was tired. My insistence on formality, then, was the greatest insult I could have given.

Still, I simply cannot make myself regret my behavior. How dare my father make these bizarre gestures of familiarity when, five minutes into my visit, he and Michiko were arguing about which one of them should take me out to dinner because neither wanted to? Every time we discussed the possibility of getting together, he mentioned how busy he was, as though seeing me were just business, a boring obligation. When he got up from the nap, he made it clear that he was riding with us only to help Michiko, not because he wanted to see me safely back to Sylvia's house. He didn't say it was good to see me; he didn't even ask me how I was. So how could I take his "not standing on ceremony" as a gesture of true intimacy or affection? It's just another manifestation of his wanting things both ways. Even though my father himself acts without warmth or affection toward me, he wants me, when it suits him, to act like family. He wants to pretend that we are a normal family who can be casual with one another. That's just his version of not confronting the truth. I cannot accept that. Why should I blame myself for not wanting to behave like his daughter when he doesn't treat me like his daughter in any real way?

I have to keep remembering that I am a stranger to him now, that I have gone to live in a foreign country. In the life I have chosen for myself, I will never have to see him again, much less forgive him. My father is irrelevant to my life in the present and the future; forgiving him is not important. Why should it be up to me to force a confrontation with him that might, someday, lead to reconciliation when he keeps pretending that he never wronged me in the past?

Perhaps I would have felt differently if I believed in a doctrine of forgiveness as Keiko does. Along the Philosopher's Path this afternoon, countless bodhisattvas have stood over me, extending their many arms in consolation or forgiveness as the gold clouds of transcendence swirled at their feet. At least for a while, they made me long for the all-encompassing forgiveness that goes beyond personal pain or grudges. But in the end, the quietness of the bodhisattvas, their gray-stone halos and carved jars of salve, are foreign to me. I cannot enter that gray world of stone and learn impersonal peace.

Exhausted by my thoughts, I lie back down and try to sleep, thinking of the swallowtail caterpillars eating in the dark. *If you are very quiet,* my mother might have said in one of the bedtime stories she told to help my brother and me fall asleep, *you can hear them eating, impatient to grow, bringing down their green house every night with their hunger.* I wonder what other images my mother might have had as we lay on our futons, our heads half covered with quilts, eyes slightly open to see her face as she read or spoke, peeking at her even though she kept telling us: *Close your eyes now. It's time for sleep.*

Purple
Orchids

There used to be a cherry tree in front of my grandfather Tatsuo's house. Though the tree was outside the concrete walls that surrounded the house, its pale pink petals and red stamens shed on the patio inside. In April, my aunt Akiko had to sweep twice a day because Tatsuo could not stand the clutter of petals. Tatsuo wanted everything spotless. Once, in front of me, he told my stepmother that he had avoided our house during my mother's life because my mother did not sweep the floor properly: the hems of his pants got dirty from the accumulated dust. Michiko repeated this remark to me whenever she had the chance, in case I had forgotten.

The tree has been cut down, leaving a knee-high stump. Everything else is the same: the walls with jagged pieces of glass stuck on top, the heavy wooden door painted dark brown, my grandfather's name on the plaque above the door. When I ring the bell, a dog starts barking inside. Though my brother told me about the dog, I cannot believe that Tatsuo actually allowed it into his house. When my brother and I lived here after our mother's death, Tatsuo often threatened to take our dog Riki to the pound. Every afternoon when I came home, I was afraid that the dog might be gone. Riki *was* lost, though it was a year after my brother and I had moved back to our father's house. My stepmother used to take him off the chain at night to run loose, so he wouldn't bark and bother my father. Our house wasn't fenced in. One night he ran away and did not come back. My brother and I never wanted a dog again.

I can hear footsteps on the other side of the wall.

"Ran-chan, be quiet," Kazumi is saying. "Come here. I have to tie you up." The chain rattles. She must be putting it around the dog's collar. Kazumi opens the door and stands behind it, smiling, wearing a white apron over her green T-shirt and black pants. Her hair is shoulder length, just as it was when we were younger. She used to be a little taller than I, but we are almost exactly the same height now. Behind her, the dog rears up and is pulled back by the chain.

"Come in. It's good to see you. Don't mind the dog. He just barks."

"It's good to see you, too." I step into the patio.

"You'd better go see Grandfather right away. He's waiting in the drawing room."

I follow her into the house, through the kitchen, down the hallway, into the drawing room where Tatsuo used to scold me and lock me up afterward. As before, the room has a long couch, a glass-top table, and two stuffed chairs. I am not sure if the couch and the chairs are the same old ones or their replacements.

Tatsuo is sitting in one of the stuffed chairs, a black cane between his knees. He raises one of his hands from the handle and points at the couch. Kazumi goes back to the kitchen.

"Have a seat," he says to me.

I sit down. Across the glass-top table, Tatsuo looks much smaller than I remember. He used to be one of those old men who tended to be fat, whose balding head was shiny with grease. Now his body shrinks away from the starched white shirt and gray dress pants, especially around the collar and the waist. It's as though someone had let out the air from a balloon.

"How is your health?" I ask.

"Ever since that heart attack," he replies, touching his chest as if I might not know where his heart is located, "my health has been very delicate. But I am doing my best to hang on."

I nod. The last heart attack he suffered was seven years ago. He was taken to the emergency room where the doctor on duty called a heart specialist. That specialist happened to be one of my mother's cousins—the older brother of Takeshi, whose suicide two years before my mother's had led my father and Tatsuo to believe that my mother's family was mentally unstable. Keiko told me these details. It's one of the things she attributes to karma.

Kazumi comes in, carrying two glasses of iced tea on a tray. She sets down the glasses on the table, mine first and then Tatsuo's, treating me like an important guest. Tatsuo doesn't thank her or even glance in her direction. She turns to go.

"Kai-chan," I call her back, using her childhood name. "Sit down with me."

She looks toward Tatsuo, who still says nothing.

"I'm sure Grandfather doesn't mind." I move over on the couch to give her room.

"It's a hard time for our family," Tatsuo says as Kazumi sits down. "Your aunt is in the hospital. Her health has never been the same since that afternoon she and I went looking all over Hiroshima for her brother Tsuyoshi. It was only a day after they dropped the atomic bomb. We didn't know there was radiation left in the ground. What a misfortune. We had no idea the bomb would affect all of our health for years to come."

"My mother's doing very well," Kazumi whispers. "Don't worry."

Tatsuo ignores her and goes on. "At least your father was healthy. He wasn't affected by the bomb, having been in Kyoto. But now he has intestinal tumors. He'll be in the hospital for nine weeks."

"I didn't realize it was such a big operation," I say, a little surprised. "He acted like it was nothing. He didn't say he would be staying so long."

Tatsuo sighs. "Hiroshi has no appreciation or gratitude. He takes his health for granted. He showed no concern when I had that heart attack."

Again he lays his hand over his chest. He talks on and on about the medications he is taking, the shortness of breath he experiences. When he stops, nobody talks for a while. Soon Tatsuo dozes off while sitting straight up, his fingers clasped over the cane.

Kazumi turns to me and shrugs.

"I was in Kyoto yesterday," I tell her. "I thought of you at a temple. Remember playing hide-and-seek in the cemetery in Osaka?"

"Yes. My mother still talks about it when we go there. She laughs about that stone you broke when you were pretending to be a ninja."

Kazumi is talking about the year I climbed on another family's memorial stone while the adults were inside the temple, attending a service to honor our family dead. As I jumped down to attack my brother, the stone toppled over and cracked. Tatsuo had to pay to replace it.

"He was pretty mad." I tilt my head slightly toward Tatsuo. "He said maybe something bad would happen to me as punishment. That family whose stone I broke—maybe their ancestors would cause me to be hit by a car or fall and break my leg."

"Yes. That made your mother mad at him for trying to scare us. She told us not to be scared of dead people for they meant no harm. She said the family's ancestors would be happy that none of us got hurt."

I take a sip of my tea. It tastes like lemon.

"I'm glad you want to go to the cemetery," Kazumi continues. "My mother and I brought flowers once a month until she got sick. We started doing that when I was in college. We like to remember your mother."

"Do you remember her very much, from when she was alive?"

"Your mother? Of course."

"What do you remember about her?"

"Beauty," she says right away. "Everything she did was beautiful. Her embroidery, her flowers, even the food she cooked. When she made cold noodles in the summer, she cut the eggs and cucumbers and tomatoes into very thin threads and arranged them on top. When my mother made the same dish, she cut the vegetables any old way, sprinkled them on the noodles, and poured soy sauce over the whole thing. Your mother's noodles were much prettier."

From the corner of my eyes, I can see Tatsuo still sleeping, his mouth slightly open.

"Your mother was also considerate," Kazumi adds. "When I came over to your birthday parties, she reminded you to pay special attention to me so I wouldn't feel left out. The other girls were your friends from school. They were a year ahead of me, so I didn't know them."

"My mother liked you a lot," I tell Kazumi. "When our families got together, she always told me to follow your example and stay out of trouble. 'Watch what Kai-chan does and do the same,' she used to say. But I made you follow me instead and get into trouble. Later, my mother would ask, 'Why are you so restless? Why can't you be good like Kai-chan?' "

"My mother always said I should be smart and quick like you. She wanted me to be more lively. I was too quiet and boring compared with you."

We laugh.

"You always bragged about your mother," Kazumi continues. "You said, 'I'm a lot like my mother, so I'll grow up to be smart and beautiful. I'm lucky.' You said that a lot."

Tatsuo taps his cane on the floor. He is staring straight ahead. I can't tell how long he has been awake.

"How many years?" he mumbles. "How many years since Takako's death?"

"Twenty-one," I tell him.

"Hmm," he says. "Poor Takako. She was a gentle person. She was a much better daughter-in-law than your stepmother." He closes his eyes and dozes off again.

"What was that about?" I ask Kazumi. I'm sitting in the same spot where he and my father told me that I could no longer see my mother's family. A few months after that, Tatsuo said that my mother had tainted his bloodline with her mental instability and suicide. "She brought in bad blood" was how he put it. "I should never have allowed Hiroshi to marry her."

"Grandfather is old," Kazumi says. "He only remembers what's convenient to remember."

Behind the chair where he is sleeping through my visit—just as my father did—the glass cabinet still holds his Ming vase, white Imari plates, purple crystal goblets. He has always collected expensive breakable things. The afternoon of my mother's death, he did not rush over to our house, though Aunt Akiko was there twenty minutes after my call. Tatsuo came a few hours later, neatly dressed in a black suit. Getting out of the taxi, he did not say, "Poor Takako." Instead, he looked me in the face and croaked, "Your mother has done a terrible thing." So I feel a momentary urge to say to Kazumi, "His age has nothing to do with it. Grandfather was selfish and mean all his life." But I refrain because Kazumi is the one who must live with him. I can only criticize him as much as she wants to, not more. If she wants to pretend or even believe that his thoughtlessness is due to his age, if that is what makes it possible for her to put up with living with him, then I have to respect that pretense or belief. To do otherwise, to embarrass her with what I consider to be "the truth," would be rude and inconsiderate. I want to be polite to my cousin—not in the superficial way I was polite to my father but in a true sense—by being considerate and sparing her feelings. I smile and sip the iced tea. "This is delicious," I tell her.

It's eleven o'clock. I have to leave for Kyoto to meet with a writers' group Vince knows. He gave me money for the train fare and put me in touch with Peter, the American man at whose house we are to meet.

"I'm going to a meeting in Kyoto" is all I tell Kazumi. How can I explain to her that I am meeting with four men I don't even know, to talk about poetry? It's like the rest of my life in the States. I don't know how or where to begin the explanation. What I do now is so different from her daily life, from the life I would have led had I stayed here.

"I'll walk to the station with you." Kazumi takes off her apron and gets up. "I'm going to Osaka to see my mother. We can take the same train part of the way."

"Wait," Tatsuo says, blinking himself awake. From a porcelain box placed on the glass-top table, he takes out a newspaper clipping and pushes it toward me. "Here, this is for you. I wanted to give you something."

It's a one-column article, a thought for the day with quotations from several Taoist philosophers on the meaning of wisdom and obligations. Most of the quotations are in the old literary language I never mastered. I fold up the article and put it in the pocket of my shorts.

"Thank you. Take care of your health, Grandfather," I say in my formal greeting voice.

He nods and remains seated in his chair. I'm not sure if I will see him again, but I just get up and leave. I'm happy to be walking away from his house, the dog barking after us.

"It looks like rain," Kazumi says.

The half mile from the house to the train station still has the stores and restaurants I recognize. In front of the flower shop where a dog once ran out and bit my leg, a black van passes us, its loudspeakers playing the national anthem.

"What's that?" I ask.

She shrugs. "Some political announcement."

"Is it the right-wing party?" I have read in the newspapers, in the States, about the resurgence of militant nationalists in Japan. They are partially funded by the *yakuza,* the Japanese Mafia. In several cities I traveled to earlier, I saw vans and trucks with big posters announcing the upcoming coronation ceremony for the new emperor. I have heard that the liberals who protest against the ceremony have been harassed by the yakuza. But Kazumi seems unconcerned.

"I don't know," she says. "They always play the anthem, or else the song about unfurling the flag."

"That's kind of right-wing, isn't it? Do they broadcast nationalist slogans?"

"I'm not sure. I don't listen. They're a nuisance."

The music fades away in the distance. Halfway to the station, we pass several Chinese restaurants, some of them new.

"My stepmother's going to take us to dinner on Friday next week," I tell Kazumi. "She wants to go to one of these Chinese restaurants around here. I hope you're free then."

"I am."

"Good. I don't want to go unless you can come. I don't want to have dinner with her alone."

"You and she never got along," Kazumi says matter-of-factly. "She's not at all like Aunt Takako. I never warmed up to Michiko, either, even though she and your father visit us."

"My father says he might take us out, too, if he's not too busy working. He'll call you so you can call me."

Kazumi tilts her head slightly.

"He has to call you because he didn't take down my phone number. He didn't seem at all happy to see me. He went to lie down while I was visiting, soon after I called you."

She doesn't say anything. Maybe my father's behavior is too bizarre for commentary, or maybe she's being polite, just as I was being polite in not commenting on our grandfather's selfish character. Kazumi doesn't want to embarrass me or hurt my feelings by speaking ill of my father. The truth is, I would be relieved to hear her say that my father is a completely thoughtless and selfish person. But I know she would never say that. A statement like that is never a declaration of a simple fact. It's too tinged with feelings, and her upbringing—our upbringing—doesn't allow us to mention anything that might invoke feelings of anger and hurt. All our lives we have been taught to discuss only the facts in a polite, levelheaded tone, to leave the feelings unsaid so as to spare each other embarrassment and pain. So we walk on in silence. Of course she knows how poor my father's behavior was, how hurt I must feel. She doesn't have to say it.

At the station, we buy our tickets and climb the stairs to the platform. The train is already waiting. We sit side by side.

"I don't know if my father will call you," I say. "He told me not to count on it. He has a lot of work to do."

"He'll call."

"How do you know?"

"Well, he's your father."

"That doesn't mean anything."

"Besides, he seemed excited when he first told me that you were coming. He sounded like he would be happy to see you."

The train starts moving.

"That's impossible," I tell Kazumi. "He scarcely talked to me the whole time I was visiting him." I stop, afraid that I have allowed myself to sound too bitter, but Kazumi nods as though what I said were completely normal.

"I understand. My father and I are the same way. I see him only once a year, if that. When I call him on the phone, he sounds happy to hear from me, but when I go to see him, he has nothing to say. I don't even feel related to him. He hasn't lived with my mother for the last seven years, you know." She tilts her head slightly with no expression at all except for a slight downturn of her lips.

Now it's my turn not to comment on how appalling the situation is. "I heard that," I say in my most level voice, "from my stepmother. Of course, she told me not to let on."

Kazumi grimaces. "That's just like her. She always talks behind people's backs."

"I know."

We are in Osaka already. The train is slowing down. I give Kazumi my phone number at Sylvia's.

"I'll meet you at the main gate of this station tomorrow," Kazumi says, standing up. "You still want to go to the temple, don't you?"

"Of course."

After she gets out, the train moves on past downtown Osaka, the residential areas, and then into the countryside. I take out my notebook and look over the directions I got over the phone from Peter. He told me to get off at the main Kyoto station and take the number 21 bus. "Getting off the bus is the tricky part," he said. "Our actual stop has no landmarks, so the easiest thing to do is to look for the next stop, which has a big Kentucky Fried Chicken on the left side and a gas station on the right with a Bridgestone sign. Then you have to walk back a stop." "Wait a minute," I said. "I don't want to walk if it's pouring rain. Tell me the name of your stop. I'll look for it on the map or else ask the driver to let me off there." "Do you speak Japanese?" he asked. "I was born here," I replied. "Well," he said, "I didn't know. You sound American."

So it wasn't just my clothes or shoes or long straight hair. It's the way I sound on the phone, the way I talk and think. Going from my cousin's house to the house of people I have never met, I know that I can tell these people about my job or my writing in a way I could never tell Kazumi. My life in the States is something she can't begin to imagine—the mundane everyday texture of it such as my running and swimming and eating my sandwich in the parking lot on the way to my class because I don't like to drive and eat, much less my being a writer, or my being a woman teaching at a college in a small midwestern town. But how can this be when all of my present life actually stems from the one she and I once shared? How can I not tell her about my writing when she remembers the very things that motivate it—my mother's love of beauty, her cold noodles with thread-thin cucumbers? I want to find a way to tell her what is important to me now, but I don't know how.

Getting off the train in Kyoto, I stick my hand in my pocket for the ticket. Along with it, I find the folded newspaper clipping from Tatsuo. I crumple it up into a ball and toss it into the trashcan. Taoists, wisdom, and obligations have nothing to do with my past or present. I can't believe that Tatsuo really handed me a newspaper clipping as a gift after not seeing me for thirteen years.

When I get to the main entrance of the Osaka station on Friday afternoon, Kazumi is waiting in a black skirt and a black top with tiny red dots. We always wore dark colors to go to the family cemetery. Today I am wearing a navy blue T-shirt over my black shorts.

"Grandfather gave me money for the tickets and the flowers." Kazumi hands me the train ticket she already bought for me.

We walk toward the tracks, past the regular lines and into the subway area. I wouldn't have found the right line on my own. The subways in Osaka run in intersecting loops.

"How's Aunt Akiko?" I ask as we sit down in an air-conditioned train.

"She's recovering faster than the doctors thought. She is very eager to see you."

"My stepmother made it seem like Aunt Akiko scarcely wanted to see me. She said you might be too busy, too."

Kazumi frowns.

"She even tried to stop me from calling you from their house. She said Grandfather might be sleeping, but my father dialed the number anyway."

"Actually," Kazumi says, "your stepmother told me that you might be too busy to see my mother and me this summer. She said you had a lot of things planned."

"When did she say that?"

"About a month ago, when your father got your letter. She and your father came over one night to visit Grandfather. She took me aside and told me that she wanted to apologize for you ahead of time because you wouldn't have much time to spend with me or my mother."

"That's crazy. I didn't say anything in my letter about how busy I was going to be or what other plans I had. I certainly didn't say anything about being too busy to see you."

"I thought it was strange, what she said."

"What else did she say?"

Kazumi hesitates a moment. "She said I shouldn't take it personally if you didn't spend time with me. You were always too independent-minded. You never understood your obligations toward your relatives. It couldn't be helped, she said. You live in a foreign country. It was natural for you and me to lose touch."

For a moment, I am too astonished and angry to speak. Outside the window, the high-rise apartments and office buildings of downtown are gone. We are passing old neighborhoods with black-slated roofs. The streets are narrower.

"My stepmother said the same things to me." I try to speak calmly, but my voice sounds shaky. "She said you would be too busy to see me, I shouldn't take it personally, and it couldn't be helped that I'm not close to you anymore."

Kazumi touches my hand for a moment and then looks at me, try-ing to smile. It's the same look she used to give me when she found me sitting in the dark in our room after my father's visits. She is wor-ried about me because I'm upset, she wants to make sure I'm all right, but she doesn't know what to say. As we look at each other in silence, I realize what I have always known: there is nothing she *can* say, now or back then, to change or even explain the bad things that happened to me; she can only offer me something different—a gesture of con-solation, a silent reassurance that she cares about me.

I try to calm down. "I'm sorry you had to hear lies about me from my stepmother. None of them is true."

"Of course I know that."

Looking at the narrow, curvy streets outside, I remember the anecdote my stepmother finds so amusing—how my grandmother had been too sick one year to see my brother so she asked him not to visit. "Imagine being rejected by your own grandmother," she told me, laughing and gasping for breath. She takes pleasure in telling these anecdotes; she is always repeating how my brother and I are not close to our father, how Jumpei didn't even identify himself on the phone when Hiroshi answered, how I told Jumpei—I was in junior high school at the time—that I was embarrassed to be seen with him. Divide and conquer is her strategy. She kept sending Jumpei money when he and Hiroshi weren't speaking to each other. She did noth-ing to bring about peace. In fact, by sending the money in secret, she took away any incentive the two men had to contact each other. I realize that there is something I need to ask Kazumi.

"Remember when we were in junior high school?" I ask her. "I used to come over to see you and Aunt Akiko every Sunday. Did Aunt Akiko ever say that I was bothering her, that I should spend more time at my own house rather than hanging out at yours all day?"

Kazumi narrows her eyes in surprise. "No. Why would my mother say a thing like that?"

"You're sure?"

"Of course. She used to cry every Sunday after you went home. She felt so sorry about your mother's death. She said she wished you could have gone on living with us. She wanted you back."

I take a deep breath and say, "I stopped coming to your house because my stepmother suggested I was bothering Aunt Akiko. She said Aunt Akiko wanted to spend her Sundays alone with you, since you were her daughter and I was only a niece. I was intruding on the two of you, she claimed."

Kazumi covers her mouth with her hand and says nothing. It's as if she's holding back ugly, angry words. Finally, she calms down enough to say, "My mother had no idea. She was lonely for you every Sunday after you stopped coming."

The train is lurching to a stop. Kazumi and I silently look at each other. I am relieved and angry both: relieved to finally come to this truth—my aunt never wanted to avoid my company—and angry at my stepmother for her lies. *She is a truly evil person,* I think, but don't say. The reason for not stating embarrassing or painful truths, we were taught, is that these things need not be said, everyone already understands. In a way, that is true. Kazumi knows. We all know.

"One more stop," she says, patting my hand. "We can get off then."

Where we get off is an old section of town. We walk through a roofed-over arcade, ichiba, like the one I saw in my old neighborhood in Kobe where my family used to live with my uncles and Aunt Keiko. The small stores here look as though they haven't changed in fifty years: groceries, fruit stands, bakeries, fish stores, cloth and notion stores.

"You remember the way to the temple?" Kazumi asks.

"No. I'm afraid not." When we went to the temple for the annual reading of the sutras for our grandmother, Kiku, I never paid much attention to the way. Those were the only times I ever went to the temple or practiced any Buddhist ritual with my father's family. Hiroshi didn't hold ceremonies for Takako at the temple after her death. We never visited the family grave after her name was carved on it.

Kazumi stops in front of a store at the end of the arcade.

"Here's the flower shop," she says.

The store we go into is nothing like the flower shops in downtown Kobe that have big glass windows and bright white lights. This place is dark. An old man in a gray apron is seated behind a plain wooden counter. There are buckets of cut flowers on the floor. The flowers have no tags explaining their names, the suggested occasions; no ribbons, tinsel, or greeting cards. The cut flowers are tall. The sharp scent of cedars and chrysanthemum leaves hangs in the air. I know what this place is. It's where one gets flowers for visiting the dead.

"I ordered some flowers for the temple visit," Kazumi says to the man. "Do you have them ready?"

He goes to the back room and returns with two bunches of flowers completely covered with newspaper. Kazumi gives him Tatsuo's money and hands me one of the bunches. It's heavier than any bouquet I have ever carried.

A block past the end of the arcade, we stand at the temple gate. Kazumi opens the sliding wooden door. Carefully, we step over the stone slab at the bottom of the gate. It's a bad omen if your foot touches this slab as you enter temples and shrines. Anyone who grew up in Japan would almost unconsciously lift his or her foot a few inches higher to make sure. It's like seeing a hearse. Your hands automatically go into loose fists with thumbs tucked inside, because otherwise, your parents will die young. A few years ago, when I saw a hearse in Chinatown in Chicago and my hands did that, I wondered how many Japanese men and women make the same gesture, long into adulthood, well past the death of their parents.

"I seldom stop to see the priest." Kazumi points to the small house to our right where the priest lives. The path to the cemetery is to the left, behind the main temple building. "If it's the anniversary of someone's death, he comes to visit the grave with us and talks a little. But we can stop if you want to see him."

I shake my head. I wouldn't recognize the priest if I saw him. I only remember his shaved head, black robe, and the sing-songy way he read the sutras. I used to think that the sutras were written in some foreign language, like Sanskrit or Chinese, or a made-up language only the dead could understand.

Kazumi and I follow the path to the back of the building, around the mountain of jizos—dwarf stone gods that protect the souls of children. There must be at least thirty of them here, stacked on top of one another like children in a school photograph. As we pass them and enter the cemetery, everything looks vaguely familiar, but I couldn't have found our memorial stone by myself. At least fifty other families have their graves here.

"It's getting so crowded," Kazumi says, leading the way on the narrow path between the stones. "My mother often loses her balance and almost bumps into another family's gravestone. Then she says, 'Excuse me,' as if she has stepped on someone's foot at a train station. I used to laugh at her, but now I'm beginning to do it, too."

The path is covered with moss. My mother did not want to be memorialized here. She did not like this temple because it was damp and gloomy. In the letter she left for my father, she asked that her ashes be buried with those of her own family, her name carved on their stone. My father did not allow that arrangement because it would have made him look bad. People would wonder why she did not want to be remembered as his wife. Still, my mother's family wanted her wishes honored. As a compromise, her ashes were divided, and her name carved on both stones.

"My mother cries for Aunt Takako every time we come here," Kazumi says as we approach our family's stone.

She stops at the faucet against the wall and fills up the bucket kept there. Taking the ladle that hangs on the wall, she goes to our stone and pours water over it. The basins at the foot have two withered bouquets. Kazumi pulls them out and takes them to the wastebasket by the faucet. There isn't much more cleaning to do. The rain washes the stone almost every night. It was raining just this morning.

"I'm glad it cleared up." She turns back to face me. The sky is silver, full of hazy light. My eyes hurt when I look up.

Kneeling down, we begin to unwrap the flowers from layers and layers of newspaper.

"I hope they gave us something bright and pretty like I asked," Kazumi says. "Aunt Takako was still young and pretty, not like most of the people remembered here." She waves her hand vaguely around her, indicating the various family stones. For a fleeting moment, I picture my mother sitting among the gray figures of old men and women. She is still beautiful at forty-one, dressed in a dark purple kimono with patterns of maple leaves. In ten years, Kazumi and I will be older than she ever was. Under the newspaper, my fingers uncover purple and pink petals. Kazumi is already taking out her flowers, holding them carefully the way we used to pick up the dolls people gave us when we were young—we lifted them gently out of the boxes so that their ruffled dresses and long hair would not get crumpled and tangled up.

The two bunches are identical. Each has one long spray of purple orchid, a few tiger lilies, pink poker flowers, asters, purple statice, snapdragons, and sprigs of cedar. We put them in the basins.

"Do you remember her spirit-name?" she asks.

I shake my head.

"Look." She points to the names carved on the side. Our grandmother, Kiku, her son Tsuyoshi who died in Hiroshima, and my mother, Takako, are remembered on the same stone by their names in this life, the dates of their birth and death, and the nine-character names given to their spirits after their souls completed the forty-nine-day journey into paradise. I read Takako's spirit-name and remember what it means: "the sister who walked the path of reverence and mercy."

From her purse, Kazumi takes out some matches and incense sticks wrapped in plastic.

"This is just like before," I say. "You're prepared. You know exactly what to do. My mother can see I'm still following your example as she wanted me to."

Kazumi strikes the match and holds it to the handful of incense she has unwrapped. Small flames go up on the ends like sparklers we used to light on summer nights. She waits for the flames to go out, leaving the orange glow at each tip. White smoke starts to rise as she places the incense in the small bowl under the carved names.

"You visit first." She gets up and steps away. "Stay as long as you want to."

I move sideways till I am kneeling directly in front of the grave. Kazumi is standing by the wall, but I can't see her because the stone is in the way. The silver gray sky stretches over the rows of graves. There is nobody in the cemetery except the two of us and the dead.

I close my eyes and put my hands, palms together, in front of my face. Even with my eyes closed, I can feel the hazy gray light around me. A few cars drive by on the other side of the high wall. I think of my mother, this time in one of the dresses she liked best, a white cotton A-line with blue flowers she had embroidered. She must have been in her late thirties when she sewed that dress—only a few years older than Kazumi and I. It seems strange for us to have grown so old.

How can I talk to you? I think. *Are you really here?*

The cemetery is absolutely quiet now. I want to talk to her, even though it's possible that no part of her lingers, even here.

Wherever you are, I love you always. No one can take your place. Remember me wherever you are.

I don't tell her, *Rest in peace.* How can she rest in peace as though I were a long ago dream she has forgotten? She wouldn't want that. I don't want that. So I keep saying, *Remember me. I never will forget you. Be with me.*

After what seems like a long time, I open my eyes on the purple orchid, its petals flying from the long stem like a leap of faith. The incense keeps rising in wispy white columns. Getting up, I feel dazed by the hazy light.

Kazumi puts her hand on my arm when I reach the wall where she is waiting. "Are you okay?"

I nod. She goes to kneel before the stone. Even from here, I can smell the incense and the cedar sprigs, their crisp fragrances mixing with the damp smell of moss. I imagine Kazumi and Akiko walking through this cemetery excusing themselves as through a crowd at a train station.

Before long, Kazumi comes walking toward me. Her face is wet with tears. I put my arms around her.

"I want you to be happy," she says, hugging me back. "Be happy for her."

I press my cheek against her shoulder.

"She should have lived to see us," I say. "She promised your mother. I miss her."

"I know."

We stand holding each other, both of us crying. Her shoulders shake. My tears are making a dark spot on her blouse. We walk back to the stone and kneel down together.

Look at us, I think to my mother. *We will always miss you.*

When we stand up, our knees are black. Kazumi hands me some tissue from her purse as we start walking through the crowded cemetery to the mountain of jizos. We stop for a while. Many of the jizos have been given handsewn or knitted red bibs to wear around their necks. Someone has hung a garland of origami birds around one jizo's hands folded in prayer. Looking back toward the cemetery, I notice the fresh flowers in front of several stones. There's a toy windmill stuck among some freesias in front of one grave. I try to take comfort in the flowers, the origami birds, the windmill, all the colors that dot the gray landscape like points of interest on a map. I want to believe that the soul's journey does not end in a pure, empty place. The path to enlightenment should be marked with reminders of joy from this life. The warmth of knitted bibs, the flight of cranes, and the beauty of flowers should be touchstones on our journey, not distractions to be renounced through endless meditation; then our final freedom would come not from forgetting but from remembering.

Kazumi and I proceed to the gate, where she stops and looks back toward me. "Are you all right?" she asks.

Nodding, I catch up with her so we are side by side as we lift our feet over the stone slab and walk into the city traffic. It's late afternoon. People are driving home from work or walking to the arcade with baskets on their arms. I put my hand on Kazumi's shoulder. My fingers connect the red dots on her blouse.

We walk on through the arcade, past grocery stores and bakeries. In the coming week inside the temple walls, our two identical bouquets will wither slowly where we used to play hide-and-seek. In our memory of that cemetery, I will always be seven years old, stomping on the stones, intent on shattering them, while Kazumi watches, forever trying to save me from trouble. In the end, it seems more a comfort than a source of grief to know that the past stays the same, that we are never completely free from it. Some part of us will always remain trapped in the past even as we walk side by side away from its pain into a summer afternoon with people coming home, preparing dinner. Kazumi is turning her face sideways toward me. She wants to know that I am all right, that the visit to the cemetery has not upset me too much. She smiles uncertainly. I shrug. Then I give her a big smile. Still smiling, I slide my hand off her shoulder and reach out for hers. For a few seconds, we swing our hands together; then we let go.

The Mansion
of Broken Dishes

On the old express train, which took three hours from Kobe to Himeji with several stops, my mother, brother, and I ate sandwiches while comparing the shades of green outside the window: the dark green of the mountain ridge to the north, the gold tints mixed into the bamboo groves, the bright squares of paddies. The scenery has not changed much, but it whips past me in double time. The new express train stops only once, at Akashi, in front of the planetarium we visited on Sundays; there the large clock on the observation tower still points to Japanese Standard Time. "Every watch or clock in Japan has to agree with that one," my mother used to say, flicking her wrist to see if hers did.

I am alone on the train because my aunt Keiko couldn't meet me in Kobe as planned. She called me at seven and said, "I have to do something at my shrine first. I'll be at Grandmother's house in the afternoon. Don't wait for me. She's anxious to see you."

As we approach Himeji, the countryside disappears and is replaced by factories and residential areas. The train begins to slow down. An announcement reminds us that this is our final stop, that we should be careful not to forget our luggage. I get off, cross the street to the bus terminal, and stand in line behind the sign for Yamasaki, the closest town to my grandmother's village. Ten minutes later, the bus rolls in, still painted orange on a cream-colored background. I remember to choose a seat near the front to avoid getting motion sickness. The bus is only half full.

For the first twenty minutes, the bus keeps stopping and starting in the heavy downtown traffic. The drive is anything but smooth. My brother and I used to feel queasy here. As the traffic thins, we pass the Himeji Castle and then an old samurai mansion with a sign in front that says *sara yashiki,* "Mansion of the Plates."

My mother told us the ghost story that made this mansion famous. Okiku, a maidservant here in feudal times, broke one of her master's twenty heirloom plates and was beheaded by him. Rather than giving her a proper burial, he threw her body into a well. From then on, her ghost crawled up from the well on rainy nights. Amid the gusts of wind and rain, her master heard her counting the plates and weeping because no matter how many times she counted, one was always missing. This story didn't make sense to me. Okiku's punishment reminded me of having to stay after school to make up some work I didn't do right—like memorizing the multiplication table or converting fractions into decimals. "Your story is unfair," I told my mother. "Poor Okiku had to count the plates even after she was dead. Her master only had to listen. I thought he was the villain. He should have had to do the counting every night." My mother laughed and said, "This was supposed to be a ghost story, not a joke."

Passing the samurai mansion this time, I think of what Keiko said—my mother should have broken some dishes, cried, and begged my father to spend more time with her, to love her. I wonder how many marriages are saved by such outbursts, held together by broken dishes. As the bus drives on, I imagine a huge empty house filled with shards of china, porcelain, stoneware. The image makes me sad for my mother, for Keiko, for all the women doomed to years of loneliness in their own houses.

Outside the city, the bus gets on the highway that cuts through the mountains. For a few minutes at a time, we pass through tunnels under orange lights that turn everything gray. Between the tunnels, we stop at small villages with terraced plots of rice and tea on hillsides. A few people get on or off, all of them old men and women in gray smocks and loose black pants that farmers wear. My grandparents dressed just like them when they worked outside.

The bus continues on through villages whose names I still remember. The countryside, I am sure, has not changed much since my mother was a young girl growing up in Kobe. Every summer she visited her grandparents at the same house where I am now going to see my grandmother. My mother never lived in that house—she and Shiro stayed on in Kobe during the war when her family moved there—but she considered my grandparents' village to be her home: *sato,* "the place one comes from." When she talked of our summer visits there, the word she used was *kaeru,* "return," rather than *iku,* "go."

Looking outside at the lush paddies and the mountains behind them, I think of how her life might have been had my grandparents not lost the land they inherited from my great-grandfather. My mother had been planning to go to college as soon as the war was over, to become a nurse or a pharmacist. After they lost the land, though, her parents had no money even for their daily expenses, let alone for her tuition, so my mother went to work at Kawasaki, where she eventually met my father. If her parents had been rich, she would have worked at a hospital as a nurse or pharmacist and married someone else. Even if she had wound up with a man like my father, she could have left her marriage without stigma.

Couples in my parents' generation seldom divorced. In the rare cases when they did, the woman left their home, and the children stayed with the man, who would marry again. The divorce was assumed to be the woman's fault. The man was "sending her away" or "sending her back to her parents" to replace her with a better wife for himself, a better mother for his children. If my mother had chosen to leave her marriage, she would have lost my brother and me; she would have become a burden to her parents.

But if my mother's parents had been landowners, her divorce would have been different. Wealth removes social stigma. Wealthy women, when divorced, can return to their parents with their children and live in prosperity. If that had been the case with my mother, my father would have been considered "not good enough for her." "She doesn't need him," people would have said. "She has her own family. They're rich. Her children are well provided for."

In reality, my mother could not return permanently to her home, her sato, except by having her ashes buried there, her name carved among members of her own family rather than my father's. She asked for that burial arrangement because she was divorcing my father by her death and returning to the land of her family. But during her life, my mother had preferred the city to the countryside. Though she looked forward to her summer returns, she was happy, at the end of August, to go back to the city, to our convenient life. Life in the countryside reminded her mostly of her parents' poverty. She used to try and get my grandmother to wear brighter colors and more cheerful styles of clothing. "I don't want you to look like a poor old woman from the countryside" was how she always put it. She could no more return to her sato than I could return to Japan to live.

But the countryside I'm passing now would have meant something different to my mother if her parents had been able to keep their land. Then they would have been able to dress and eat well, to visit the city for pleasure. They wouldn't have been poor, helpless, forced to pursue an occupation they weren't prepared for. If my mother, my brother, and I had come back to live with them under those circumstances, we would have taken this bus to visit Himeji and Kobe, to go to museums and concerts, to go shopping, to visit friends. I might have gone away to college and then returned to marry near home. My life, as well as my mother's, would have been totally different.

After an hour on the highway, the bus enters the town of Yamasaki and stops in front of a small terminal building. The dozen people left on board all get off. From inside the building, I call my uncle Yasuo's wholesale grocery store, which is on the other side of town. His wife, Sayo, answers.

"Hi, Aunt Sayo. I'm in Yamasaki. Aunt Keiko is coming later, so I'm alone."

"I'll come pick you up in my car," she says. "I'll drive you to your grandmother's house."

"Are you sure? I can take the bus. I remember which one."

"Don't be silly. I'll be there in five minutes."

Sooner than I expect, she pulls up to the terminal in her small green Toyota and walks over to where I am standing.

"Welcome back," she says, taking my backpack and putting it in her trunk. "It's good to see you."

"It's good to see you, too." We sit in the car, and Sayo starts the engine.

"Your uncle wanted to come, too, but some customers showed up before we could close the store. He was disappointed. We haven't seen you since your grandparents' fiftieth anniversary. How long ago was that?"

"Seventeen years."

Sayo shakes her head. "It's a very long time. Your uncle and I are old now."

"Well, you look the same," I tell her.

She laughs. "You don't have to flatter me."

"I'm not flattering. How are Akira and Toru?" I inquire after my cousins.

"Akira finished college this year. He lives in Osaka now. He wants to join the Self Defense Army."

"Really?"

"He has to get in shape first. Toru is still in college in Kyushu. He has another year. I'm sorry they weren't home. Your uncle wanted them to see you. He holds you up as an example to them."

"Me?"

"Don't be so modest. All your cousins know how smart you are. Your grandfather was always telling them."

We are driving on a country road between two small villages. The land my great-grandfather owned extended to these villages. He was one of the wealthiest landlords in our prefecture.

"I'm sorry," Sayo says. "You must miss your grandfather."

I nod. "It will be strange to visit their house and not see him."

On the right side of the road, I can see the river where I learned to swim; on the left, rice paddies extend all the way up to the foot of the mountains.

"How is Grandmother these days?"

"Her health is very good for her age. Her mind is clear, too." Sayo pauses and then adds, "She never forgets anything."

Soon we are in my grandmother's village, past the elementary school where my grandfather taught during the day before going home to work his land—though by the time I knew him, he was over fifty-five, the compulsory retirement age for public servants in Japan. He and my grandmother lived on his pension, the little they made from rice-farming, and the money my mother and her brothers sent them. The house is a few blocks down the road from the school. Sayo drives her car into the front yard and parks between the persimmon tree and where the hen house used to be. My grandmother must have given up her hens; there is no hen house.

Getting out of the car, I see that swallows are still making a nest over the front door. When I was young, I used to leave the door open on purpose so they would come flying into the house and swoop over the pots and pans in the kitchen. My grandmother, Keiko, Sayo, and Shiro's wife, Michiyo, covered their heads with their hands and screamed while my mother grabbed the broom, opened the back door, and chased the birds out.

My grandmother, Fuku, is in the front room with the TV on. She is sitting on the floor at a low table.

"Kyoko's here," Sayo announces.

I drop my backpack on the floor and sit down next to Fuku so she won't have to stand up to greet me. "Hi, Grandmother. It's good to see you." I take her hand. Her fingers are thin and cold.

She lets go of my hand and rubs at her eyes. "I'm so glad you came all this way to see me."

I can't get over how frail she looks, even though she has always been a small woman. My cousins and I became taller than she when we were only nine or ten. Back then, I used to run up to her, put my palm on top of her head to emphasize how much shorter she was than I, and grin. Now her white hair is so thin that I can see the exact shape of her skull underneath.

"I'm too old to do much," she continues. "I wanted to make you lunch, but I cook only for myself now. I would ask Sayo, but she's a busy woman. I don't want to impose on her."

"That's all right," I say quickly so Sayo won't have to offer. "I'm not hungry."

After Sayo goes back to the store for the afternoon's work, Fuku and I visit the *butsuma*, the room in which the Buddhist altar is kept.

The large black altar there is one of my earliest memories. The image of Amida glimmers in the back in gold leaf; on one of the shelves, six gold nameplates stand side by side. They are for my mother, her two older sisters who died of measles and dysentery before she was born, my great-grandparents Takehiko and Kayo, and my grandfather Takeo. Fuku and I each light an incense stick to put in the bowl in front of the nameplates. Then we close our eyes to address our family dead, who, Fuku always told me, watch over us night and day.

Grandfather, I pray silently. *I am home.* There is so much I want to say to him, but I can't concentrate. It feels too strange to address him as a spirit instead of having him next to me. The afternoon I learned about his death, I walked to the shore of Lake Michigan in Milwaukee and could not believe that there was so much water in the lake— so much water and not a drop of it touching any land he had ever walked on.

I open my eyes and see the garden pinks, the cups of tea and rice, and a plate of pink *manju* dumplings on the shelves.

"I went to visit my mother's spirit in Osaka," I tell Fuku, "at the family grave there. Kazumi went with me."

Fuku nods, her eyes red, but says nothing for a while. Finally, she starts getting up, slowly. She points to the plate of dumplings. "We'll take down the manju."

I pick up the plate and follow her back to the front room.

"The coffee's in the cupboard," she says as she sits down.

I get out the jar of instant coffee, two cups, and two spoons and go to the kitchen to boil some water. Her aluminum kettle is small and dented. From the ceiling, she has hung the old bamboo colanders she no longer uses. They look dusty. I know the kitchen doesn't look that different from when I was a child—my mother often complained about Fuku cooking in the same old pans instead of using the new ones her children had bought for her. My grandmother was always like that—frugal to a fault, saving things for special occasions that never came about. Still, I am struck by how meager and desolate the kitchen looks now.

"It's okay to give me strong coffee," Fuku says when I return with the steaming kettle. "The doctor says I can eat and drink anything I want. At my age, I should enjoy whatever I can since I won't be living very long no matter what I do."

I don't think this is exactly how her doctor put it, but I keep silent while I prepare two cups of medium-strength coffee, set them on the table, and sit down across from her on the floor, my legs stretched in front of me.

"We'll have the manju from the altar," Fuku says. "The plates are in that cupboard, too."

I get up again to serve the manju. They are balls of sticky pink rice with sweet bean paste inside, each dumpling wrapped in a pressed cherry leaf that wouldn't come off in one piece. I hate sweet bean paste. Still, I peel off the leaf in broken fragments and bite into the pink rice.

Fuku finishes her manju and takes a sip of coffee. "This is delicious," she smiles, holding the cup in both her hands. "Sayo makes my coffee too weak." She picks up another manju, peels it, and eats it slowly, chewing with her lips and gums because she is not wearing her dentures.

On TV is a special program being broadcast all day because the emperor's second son is getting married this afternoon. Right now, the camera is showing the town in which the bride's family lives. They are commoners who rent a small apartment. The camera goes inside. A man is interviewing the family members while the bride is in her room getting dressed. I cannot help being annoyed by the tone of the interviewer as he cuts away from the family and starts talking to another newscaster, back at the main studio. They seem to be saying that this woman is lucky to be chosen, that a great honor is being bestowed on her and her family.

I remember the van that Kazumi and I saw in Ashiya, its speakers blaring out the national anthem, the words to which mean "long live the emperor." I cannot believe that Kazumi was not bothered by the van, that my cousin Akira wants to join the Self Defense Army. I am struck, suddenly, by how politics separates me from my relatives. Like most Japanese people, they are not politically or environmentally conscientious. They see little or no connection between politics and their daily lives. I have spent my adult life in a different world, among friends who believe that even small individual actions can contribute to the public good or harm. As a result, I want to feel morally upright even in the choice of what I eat and wear. I cannot hear ignorant prejudiced remarks without feeling a rush of anger and resentment. Unlike my cousin, I cannot dismiss them as a "nuisance."

My grandmother keeps chewing her manju, her eyes on the screen. I can't believe that we are sitting here after all these years, watching the emperor's family on TV. There is so much I need to say to her, and, with the TV on, I don't know how to begin.

I drink my coffee in silence, telling myself to be patient. That was what my mother always told me—we had to be patient with our grandparents when they seemed stubborn or nagging. We should be polite to our elders, she said, even if we disagree with them; we must first show respect to them if we want to be treated with respect in return. She taught me that, especially among family members, disagreement shouldn't end in snide comments, unkind remarks, and other forms of rudeness.

I think back to my visit to Kenichi's house. I had decided, after all, to be frank about my vegetarianism because honesty seemed to be the only polite way—it would cause Kenichi's family awkwardness and embarrassment if they prepared food I could not eat—so I told them ahead of time. Mariko made mostly vegetarian dishes for our dinner, except for a few additional things in case my cousins wanted meat. Everyone seemed vaguely amused and puzzled by my choices; still, no one made fun of my eating habits or any of the other choices I made in life. I, on my part, felt no need to criticize them or to bring up my political agenda at every turn.

It's the same thing now. Sitting here with my grandmother, who seems to show a reverential interest in the imperial family, I don't need to tell her that she is wrong; I don't even need to hold silent judgments and resentments against her. It doesn't have to be the way it is with my father. When I felt angry at him for showing no sympathy toward the homeless in New York, for being so openly prejudiced, I was, in a sense, giving vent to my own personal resentment toward him. I was already feeling defensive because of the way he and Michiko had criticized me. I latched onto my anger at their political narrow-mindedness because it was something I could count against them in a seemingly "objective" way. It isn't like that at all with my grandmother.

My grandmother sees that I'm not eating. "Have another manju," she says. She doesn't remember that I hate bean paste because she has never taken my distaste for it seriously. All children like sweet things, she thinks—even children who are thirty-three. So I take another manju and slowly peel off the leaf. The rice is cold and sticky. The bean paste is too sweet, as always.

Fuku's cup is empty.

"Can I make you more coffee?" I ask.

She shakes her head. "I'm sorry I can't do more for you," she sighs.

"You don't have to do anything for me."

On TV, the bride is about to leave her parents' apartment. Outside a black limousine is waiting to take her to the wedding. Her family, being commoners, are not allowed to attend the religious part of the ceremony. Her father stands at the door in a black suit and bows deeply at her. She is no longer his child but a member of the imperial family.

Fuku points to the bureau in the corner of the room and says, "I have some letters in the drawers there."

"What kind of letters?"

"Letters from everyone. I'm asking people to take back theirs if they want them. Your uncle Shiro did. You should do the same."

The three drawers of the bureau are so full I have to yank them hard. Inside there are hundreds of old envelopes and postcards, some of them tied together with string or rubber bands. The first bunch of envelopes I pull out are from people whose names I vaguely recognize from family stories—relatives long dead before my time, friends of my grandparents from when they lived in Kobe before the war. Small photographs fall on the floor, mostly black-and-white prints.

I bring a handful of these photographs to Fuku, and she tells me who they are of: my mother taking a dance lesson at eight, Keiko in her New Year's kimono at ten, my great-grandfather Takehiko in the uniform he wore when fighting in the Russo-Japanese War.

"I didn't know he went to that war," I tell my grandmother.

"He was a captain. And he was decorated. Look at the medals."

Except for the uniform, the man looks so much like my grandfather that I might have mistaken the two—yet I know my grandfather never went to any war. I know little about my great-grandfather Takehiko. The only story I remember is that, as a young man, he was bitten by a poisonous *mamushi* snake while inspecting the paddies he owned. He calmly asked his sharecropper, who was standing by, for his sickle, and then he cut his own leg open to let out the venom. I stare at the photograph, trying to see some trace of his will to live, his ability to stay calm in a crisis, which were what we were supposed to learn from that story.

"Do you want these photographs?" Fuku asks me.

"Don't you want to keep them?"

"I have no use for them. They're yours."

"Thank you."

Setting the photographs aside, I go back to the bureau to look through the letters. Halfway through the first drawer, I come across the letters I wrote in grade school. The stationery looks vaguely familiar. Each sheet of paper, colored blue or pink, has prints of animals, dolls, stars, or rainbows. My handwriting meanders over the page, dodging these pictures. It sounds like I was always bragging:

about the writing contests I won at school, about the races I won, about how tall I was growing.

"Take what you want," Fuku says. "They'll be ashes when I die."

I set aside my own letters and the weekly postcards my mother wrote. Many of them mention what she is planting in the garden; she often thanks her parents for the seeds, bulbs, or roots they sent her. Some postcards include anecdotes about my brother and me. She almost always mentions our health and our schoolwork, the places we visited together, what she is sewing or embroidering for us. In one postcard, she tells her parents that she is sending some flannel pajamas she made for them because the coming winter is expected to be particularly cold.

In the second drawer I pull out, I come across two envelopes bunched together with a thick rubber band. The handwriting on the first one seems familiar, large and sprawled in blue-gray ink. I take off the rubber band and flip the envelopes—the return address is always written on the back of the envelope in Japan. I am right. The first one is from my father. The blue-gray ink is from his Parker pen, the same one he used to write to my English teacher, Miss Craddock, in tenth grade when I applied to study abroad the following year. He wrote that he could not provide the character reference for me that the scholarship organization had requested because he had very little to say about me that was positive—I was an intelligent but extremely self-centered and arrogant person. I wouldn't have gotten the scholarship if Miss Craddock hadn't torn up my father's letter and asked my friend Machiko to write a reference for me instead. "In the recommendation I'm sending," she told me, "I'll explain why our school asked your friend. I'll explain that you have an exceptional family circumstance." Then she paused and added, "I know your father was wrong. Don't be discouraged by what he said." Stunned by her kindness, I wanted, for a moment, to burst into tears so that she would hug me and I could tell her all about my father, about how lonely I was in my own house. Miss Craddock knew that my mother was dead, but she didn't know half the "exceptional family circumstance" she was referring to. But I just nodded and tried to smile, to say "thank you" without choking up.

I am surprised by how painful this memory is, even now. Looking at his handwriting on the envelope, I wonder what my father ever had to say to my grandparents. The other envelope has my grandfather Tatsuo's name and address on the back. I take out the letters and unfold them. They are both dated shortly after my mother's death. I begin with my father's letter.

June 10, 1969

The rainy season has started. It has rained quite hard in Kobe. How is the weather in the country? I hope you have suffered no severe rain damage.

I am sorry that I have been too busy to respond to your frequent letters. You must have heard from Keiko, who came a few days ago to hear the priest read the sutras for Takako's soul and then telephoned because she did not see the children on her visit. As I told Keiko, my children are quite happy and cheerful.

My daughter has taken to Michiko just as she took to my sister, Akiko. She is quite eager to spend time with her new mother. Jumpei, too, calls her Okasan and follows her around. A friend who visited the other day said, "They don't seem at all like children who have just lost their mother. How fortunate for them." My father has pointed out that until lately, these children have been much too spoiled. They have not had an adequate education in their morals and attitudes, even though Kyoko has always excelled at schoolwork. I did not notice this problem till my father pointed it out to me, but once he did, I had to agree with him. The children have been quite spoiled. At the time, they were in Ashiya at his house, so I asked my sister, Akiko, to be a little more strict with them than their mother had been. I'm afraid Akiko did not make a good attempt. She is too softhearted. Since Michiko's arrival, however, things have improved remarkably. Michiko is enthusiastic about giving the children a good moral education. As a result, Kyoko has become a little less self-centered and conceited. Jumpei is better able to express his naturally sweet temperament without being the weakling he used to be.

I understand how you must feel. Indeed, I feel your pain with you and very much appreciate your concern for my children. Still, I am writing to ask you to let them be for the time being and not seek their company. The best thing for

Michiko, Kyoko, and Jumpei is to be left alone to determine how the three of them will build a future as a family. When the children are older, they may understand the past for what it was; they may be able to give due recognition to the memory of their first mother without losing the gratitude and affection they owe to the second mother who raised them through the difficult years. For the time being, they are too young to attain such a complex balance of emotions. Therefore, though I understand your concerns, I must ask you to forget the children till they are adults.

As you know, Shiro has offered to take them to your house to spend the summer. The children would undoubtedly enjoy the summer in the country. However, in view of all the above reasons, I am not ready to give my permission. I will think it over, consult my father, and think some more. He will contact you after our minds are thoroughly made up.

I have never been good with words. Easy eloquence always escapes me. I can never fully express the thoughts that lie deep within my heart. But I trust that in your wisdom, you will understand my humble attempt to express my duties, obligations, and wishes.

I hope to see you soon myself to discuss how and where Takako's ashes will be dedicated next April. For the time being, however, I want you to know that my children are cheerful and happy. They are well on their way to a new life.

The rainy season is hard on one's health, especially since it will be followed by extreme heat. Please be sure to take care of your health. I wish for your welfare from the bottom of my heart.

Respectfully, Hiroshi Mori

That rainy season, I rode the commuter trains to and from my school every morning and afternoon. The rain, which beaded up and trickled down the large glass windows of the trains, looked like the tears my mother must be crying in heaven to see me so unhappy.

I was never eager to spend time with Michiko, who told me that I talked too much even though I scarcely talked at all at home. One Sunday while we were having dinner, Michiko asked me to get a glass of milk for her. I said, "Why don't you get it yourself? You are sitting closer to the refrigerator." My father got up from the table and beat me until I bent over and threw up. A glass fell off the table and shattered because I had bumped into one of the table legs. My brother started crying. Michiko just sat there and watched the whole thing. This must have happened a week or two before he wrote the letter.

Across the room, my grandmother is watching TV. I want her to understand that what my father said was a complete lie—I never wanted to be happy at the cost of forgetting my mother. But how can I explain this? My grandfather must have believed my father to some extent; maybe that's why he decided that I would be better off living in the city with my father and Michiko. I cannot bear to think that my grandfather might have died still believing I had forgotten about my mother and was happy with Michiko. I will never be able to tell him how things really were.

I put down my father's letter and pick up Tatsuo's. It's addressed only to Fuku.

July 30, 1969

We had a long rainy season followed immediately by oppressive heat. The weather is hard to bear. I hope you are all well at your house.

Four months have passed since the tragedy our two families shared. You must have felt so much sorrow and pain. They say nothing compares with parents' affection for their child. Only those who have suffered the same loss can understand the terrible grief you and your husband must feel.

I am one of the few who can understand. My second son was lost in the atomic explosion over Hiroshima. He was only in middle school. I have thus experienced the same loss and can truly sympathize with your sorrow about Takako's death.

As you must have heard already, the woman who is to become the children's second mother has been here since May. The children returned to their house as soon as she arrived. We were all worried about how they would get along with her. But she is cheerful and straightforward by temperament; she works very hard to build a good home for them and their father. As a result, two months later now, both children are living happily with their new mother.

The most important thing for the children is to forget that tragedy and begin a new life with their new mother. That is essential if the four of them are to find peace and happiness together as a family. Nothing in the world must be allowed to interfere with that happiness. With this in mind, I talked to my son on the day before the woman's arrival. I told him that the four of them must forget the past if they were to have a good future together. For that purpose, though it sounds cruel, the children must not be allowed to see their mother's family and friends until they are in college or even older. At present, if they saw their grandparents, uncles, aunts, they would not be able to forget their first mother. Remembering her would bring them only sadness and resentment toward their new mother. It is of utmost importance, I told my son, to prevent any conflict between the children and their new mother. Getting along with her is the most important thing in their lives now.

Of course, you must think of Takako daily and worry about her children. I feel your pain as if it were my own. Nevertheless, for the reasons I mentioned above, I ask you to give up the children for the next several years. I must, then, decline your invitation for them to spend their summer vacation at your house this year or any other time in the future.

It may seem heartless to make such a request to you and yours, who are related to the children by strong ties of blood. All the same, I ask that you understand and honor our reasoning. You will hardly disagree with me if you think of what is best for them.

Next month when the priest comes to read the sutras for Takako in the morning, I will notify your daughter Keiko to visit the altar. This same priest from my temple has been reading the sutras for my late wife the last eleven years.

Please send my regards to your husband. I hope he, too, will understand my position.

I pray that you take care of your health as the heat continues to be oppressive.

Respectfully, Tatsuo Mori

I picture Tatsuo in his living room, laying his hand on his chest every time he mentioned his heart problems. I am glad that I didn't show much concern for him, that I didn't even say it was good to see him. I can't believe that he would actually use his own son's death to justify his conduct, to appear sympathetic in such a false and insincere way.

"Grandmother," I call to Fuku. But when she turns to me, I don't know how to begin. She is more than twenty years older than when she received these letters. Maybe I shouldn't even bring them up. What if she has forgotten about them? Wouldn't she be better off?

But it's too late. She is staring across the room at the letters I'm holding up. "These letters," I say. "They're from my father and grandfather. Do you remember them?"

She gestures toward the drawer I have pulled out. "There are some more from your father." She turns away to watch TV.

I pull out the rest of the envelopes and shuffle through them. She is right—I find three more letters. I yank them out of the envelopes and skim them. In one, he informs my grandparents of his upcoming marriage to Michiko. "When I think of Takako," he writes, "I wish I could stay single for the rest of my life to honor her memory. But unfortunately, I am burdened with two children. The woman I am to marry has been raising them since last May, and the children both love her. For that reason, I thought it best to make our union official as soon as it was seemly to do so, after the one-year anniversary of Takako's passing." The letter is dated March 21, 1970. The others, from the spring and the fall of the following year, are short and to the point: he reports on the two-year memorial service for my mother, to which he did not invite my grandparents; he announces his promotion at Kawasaki and says that my brother and I continue to be quite happy with Michiko.

I put down the letters, wanting to destroy them. How could Hiroshi use my brother and me as an excuse for his remarriage when he had been seeing Michiko for years? How could he continue to lie about how everything was wonderful at our home? He had told Kenichi about Michiko in those few weeks they spent together after my mother's death. He must have assumed that Kenichi would tell his parents at least some of what he knew. How could he, then, tell them such an obvious lie? I know that in Japan, a person is often excused for lying or concealing the truth if that helps to save face all around, if it spares both the teller and the hearer from scrutinizing the painful truth. Under the circumstances, lying is considered to be harmless or even desirable—a way of showing polite regard for other people's feelings. But what my father wrote saved only his own face. His motive for lying had nothing to do with politeness; he wasn't interested in sparing my grandparents from anything, true or false. He went out of his way to say that my mother had not given us a very good education.

"That's not all I got from your father," Fuku says. "I tore up one letter. I was so angry at him."

"The one you tore up was worse than these?"

"He said I could never see you again, not even after you grew up. He said your mother was crazy, that he wanted you to forget her. I was so angry."

"I'm sorry." I pick up the letters and hold them up in her direction. "What should I do with these? Do you want me to tear them up?"

"No. Keep them if you want to."

I hesitate, half wanting to get rid of them. But the letters are concrete and irrefutable evidence of my father's and grandfather's heartlessness. It's taken me twenty-one years to come across them. I put the rubber band around them and drop them into the pile of things I'm keeping.

"I might burn them later," I tell Fuku. "They're full of lies. I'm ashamed to be my father's daughter. I can't think of anyone more dishonest or inconsiderate."

Fuku is looking toward me, but she says nothing in reply. I cannot read her expression at all. She has never criticized my father's character in my presence or in any of her letters. More than likely, she believes it's my duty to show respect to him no matter how undeserving he is, because I am and will always be his child. I owe my life to him. If I were younger, she might even scold me for my bad manners, for speaking so disrespectfully. I wish she would, so I could protest and explain how I feel. I would tell her that I cannot show respect to people who I know will never return it—it's one thing to humor an older person I love; it's quite another, though, when the other person has never won my affection or respect in the first place. I want to talk about that difference to her. But she is saying nothing, and I don't know how to bring up the subject on my own. So I continue to look through the drawers, now and then stopping to read the letters my younger cousins wrote in high school and college.

"Your father feels very badly now," Fuku says suddenly.

"I beg your pardon?"

"He came to see me and cried."

I stop looking through the letters. "He came to see you?"

"He said he wanted to go up to the family grave and give some flowers to Takako and to your grandfather. He brought the flowers."

"When was this?"

Fuku thinks for a while. "The year before last, in the spring. That was the last spring I could still walk up the hill to the cemetery. I can't manage that now."

"You mean you and he went up there together two springs ago?" That would have been the year before I saw him in New York. He never mentioned it.

"He stood before the grave and cried. Big tears were rolling down his cheeks. He said Takako was such a sweet, gentle person. He feels very badly now. He cried a long, long time. You shouldn't be so hard on him."

I don't know what to say. For a moment, I think that Fuku might be wrong. Maybe she mistook someone else for my father, or perhaps she's remembering him from some other time, though I don't know when my father and Fuku were ever alone together.

"I wanted him to stay for lunch," Fuku continues. "I didn't have much in the house to make him a good meal. So I asked him if he wanted to go to that restaurant down the street. It was new then. I had heard they served good lunches. I thought we could eat together and remember Takako and your grandfather. I hadn't seen your father for almost twenty years."

"Did he have lunch with you, then?"

"No. He had to get back to the station to take a train. He had been on his way to Okayama on a business trip. But when the conductor called out Himeji, he suddenly wanted to come and see Takako's grave here. He said he just jumped off the train, bought the flowers, and called a cab. It was like some spirit was telling him to do it, he said, but he had to leave in a hurry because he was expected at a business meeting."

Now I know that he was really here. The part about leaving in a hurry for a meeting sounds just like him. My grandmother couldn't have imagined or dreamed it.

"It was enough that he stopped by," Fuku is saying. "Your father sure regrets the way he behaved. He feels badly. I understand."

I pick up his old letters from the pile and put them down again. Aside from crying at the grave, my father has done nothing to show his remorse about my mother's death or the way he acted afterward. Even by my grandmother's account, he did not apologize to her. He only said that my mother had been a sweet, gentle person—as if this were news to anyone. He hurried off without having lunch. His crying doesn't mean that much to me. After all, he had cried in front of Kenichi, too. That didn't stop him from having Michiko move in a few weeks later. It didn't stop him from behaving in the most thoughtless and self-righteous way possible toward my mother's family. No matter how much he cries, he can never redeem himself in my mind.

I look up from the pile of letters and meet Fuku's eyes. I would like to tell her my true feelings. It would be a relief to me. But I look away and say nothing. My grandmother is ninety-three. If she wants to believe that my father is sorry now, if that gives her peace, why should I bring up my own anger and stir up the resentment she has overcome? Why should I come back here after all these years to bring her anger and worry and hurt? She wants to remember her former son-in-law as a man crying at his wife's grave, not as the writer of a letter that made her so angry she had to tear it up. By living so far away, by choosing not to come to Japan till now even to see her, I have done nothing to comfort her in her old age. How can I, then, fail to treat her with consideration on this short visit at least—to put her feelings before mine and try to reassure her that she need not worry about me? Why shouldn't I pretend that my father is not such a bad man? Though it's perhaps too late, I want to be a granddaughter who respects her grandmother's wishes, even if it means not saying what I really think. But it's hard. Going through the rest of the letters, I stop now and then to compose myself, to hold back from telling her how much my father has hurt me, how determined I am never to forgive him.

I put the drawers back into the bureau and ask Fuku, "Remember when Ken Nichan and Neine brought over some of my mother's kimonos for you to keep?" I try not to dwell on how this, too, reminds me of the bad way my father acted, showing up without any warning at Kenichi's house one evening to drop off my mother's things.

"Yes, I remember that very well."

"Ken Nichan said I should look for them and take them back with me. I would also like Grandfather's diaries. Remember he said I could have them when I grew up if I kept a journal, too?"

Fuku nods.

"Do you know where these things are?"

"They could be anywhere in the house. But you're welcome to them and anything else you want. They'll be ashes soon when I die."

I begin to open and close the drawers, trunks, and closets all over the house. I don't come across the diaries, though I find four of the kimonos wrapped in thick white paper. Fuku follows me from room to room.

"Look at this," she says, opening the drawers and closets after me. "I want you to look at this and remember."

She shows me drawers full of new dish towels, stockings, underwear still wrapped in plastic.

"If something happens to me," she says, "I want you to tell everyone where I keep things. Did you see? Everything's new. I'm counting on you to remember. When people come to the house for my funeral, Sayo shouldn't dry dishes with dirty towels. You know where the new ones are. You tell her."

"Don't worry. I'll remember." I don't want to insult her by not taking her seriously, so I don't say, "You're not going to die for a long time yet." There is no point in reminding her, either, that I live in a foreign country, that I might not be at her funeral.

"There were so many things I wanted to leave you," she sighs. "But they all turned into rice after the war." I know, from my mother's stories, that Fuku had to sell her best kimonos to raise money to feed her family.

"Here it is." Fuku pulls out a dresser drawer, takes a silver gray kimono, and holds it toward me in both her hands. "Takako felt sorry for me because I had been forced to sell my kimonos. So later, she sewed me new ones with her own hands. This is the last one she gave me. She came all the way from Kobe to see me on Mother's Day to give me this kimono and some peonies from her garden. Here. You take it to remember us by."

In my hands, the kimono is heavy because of its solid weave. It's the color of the sky on days when it rains continuously but not hard.

"When did she give this to you? Which Mother's Day was it?"

"It was the year after you moved from the apartment to that house. Your mother took the early morning train to come to see me and had to leave in just a few hours."

That would have been May 1968, ten months before her death. She had gotten through the first winter in our new house and thought that whatever bothered her was gone. Every morning, she rose at dawn to clear the weeds and overgrown bushes from the yard. She planted lettuce, parsley, tomatoes, eggplant, zinnias, pansies. She didn't foresee that in October, the red leaves falling from the maples would remind her of those red letters summoning people to the front during the war: sure invitations to die.

From another drawer, Fuku pulls out a black *haori* jacket and turns it so I can see the crest embroidered on the back in white silk.

"This is the Nagai crest." She points to the embroidery. "It's an orange blossom. Your great-grandmother Kayo made this haori. She spun the silk herself, wove and sewed the haori, and did the embroidery. I always meant to pass this on to Takako. Now I'm giving it to you."

Fuku puts the haori on top of the gray kimono I'm holding. The silk is closely and evenly woven. I am not the first spinner and weaver in my family, though Kayo's spinning wheel and loom would have been slightly different from the American models I use. I am pleased to know this about her—a great-grandmother I never met, who never imagined that her legacy would continue in a foreign country.

Still, the kimonos provide little consolation. I continue looking for the diaries, for some more of my mother's clothing, but I don't find them. I'm sad for their loss and sadder still because nothing I take back will make up for the time I did not spend with my grandparents or the time my mother did not spend with us because she chose to die.

"I don't know where the diaries are," I say to Fuku.

"All turned into rice," she mutters.

"Not the diaries," I say, almost laughing because she is confusing the times. But I'm disturbed, too, by how her mind seems stuck on her losses—just as mine is. "Maybe Uncle Shiro knows where they are," I say, trying to be cheerful. "He said on the phone that he went through Grandfather's papers. I'll ask him."

I put the kimonos away and go out to the backyard with Fuku. It's midafternoon—overcast and cool for this time of year. Fuku wants me to dig out the potatoes she planted in March. Digging carefully with her trowel, I pull out two of the plants by the stem. The potatoes are the size of children's fists, almost too small to eat. I put them in a large aluminum pan from her kitchen.

"Dig those out, too," Fuku says, waving her hand toward the four remaining potato plants. "I have no reason to save them." She looks even smaller here in the yard, among the rows of plants. While I harvest the potatoes, she squats in the next row and picks the lettuce, breaking off the outer leaves and keeping the heads intact. "Aren't you hungry yet?" she asks me.

"No. It's only three."

"I hope Keiko gets here soon. I want her to make supper. I don't want to ask Sayo, and you're my guest so you shouldn't have to do it."

"Supper is a long time away. Let's not worry about it yet."

The potatoes, the lettuce, and some beans are the only vegetables she is growing. The rest are flowers: garden pinks and lantern flowers, dahlias, zinnias. Purple chrysanthemums are already flowering in the corner where my grandfather Takeo used to plant his tomato vines that grew to be big bushes. After my swim in the river, I would bring a saltshaker and a damp cloth and sit between the rows to eat the tomatoes off the vine. I was allowed to eat as many as I wanted. They were among the few things I ate without being coaxed or threatened.

I stoop down to touch the chrysanthemum buds. They are hard, luminous at the tip. I wish my visits had continued through my teens and twenties; then, coming back here now, I would not feel such a mixture of familiarity and strangeness, this fondness and regret.

My grandmother stops picking the lettuce and looks up.

"Last time I came," I say to her, "Grandfather was still here."

While Fuku goes back to the house to rest, I cut some garden pinks and walk over to see the Yamamotos next door. The couple come to the door and start bowing to me. I bow back. We are standing under the roof I fell from one year. Their daughter, Reiko, who was my age, showed me how to get up on the roof by climbing the maple tree first, but she forgot to warn me about the loose shingle above the front door. I lost my balance while running around on the roof and fell off. I wasn't badly hurt because the part I fell from was lower than the rest of the roof. What I remember most is Mr. and Mrs. Yamamoto scolding Reiko as if the whole thing were her fault, even though my grandparents and my mother told them to take it easy on her.

"Your grandmother said you were coming," Mrs. Yamamoto says. "You've grown up."

"I came to ask you a favor. I want to go up the hill to the family grave. Would you mind going with me? Grandmother doesn't want me to go there alone, and she says she is too old to walk up that hill."

Mr. Yamamoto takes some daisies from the garden because his family's grave is also up on the same hill. It's time to bring more flowers for his parents; they both passed away since I've been out of the country. Reiko is married now and lives in Himeji. He talks about her and her daughter as we climb the hill to the clearing where the two family graves are. Because Mr. Yamamoto's family used to be our family's sharecroppers, our stone is much larger than theirs and closer to the ledge that overlooks the river. Mr. Yamamoto and I get some water at the faucet in the middle of the clearing and start toward the stones.

"Watch out," he shouts. "There's a *habu*."

I stop. He is standing completely still on the grassy path in front of his family's stone and squinting at his feet.

"What is habu?" I ask. "Is that the same thing as mamushi?"

"Yes. Be careful. They always come in pairs." He picks up a stick and beats the grass at his feet.

I peer into the grass around my path. There is no snake of any kind, so I proceed to the stone and put the flowers in the basin.

"It went back into its hole," Mr. Yamamoto says after a while as I wash the stone. "I don't see the other one anywhere. You'd better tell your grandmother."

"She says she doesn't come here anymore. But she'll be glad you were with me. I wouldn't know a mamushi from a garden snake."

Mr. Yamamoto starts cleaning his family's grave. I light the incense sticks Fuku gave me and put them in the bowl under the names. The Nagai stone has more names and dates carved on its side than the Mori stone: my grandfather Takeo, his parents, my mother, and her older sisters who died as young children. Each is identified by the name in this life and the spirit-name given at the time of death, and also by their relationship to the living: Takeo's father, Takeo's mother, Takeo's first, second, and third daughters. Takeo is identified as my uncle Yasuo's father. Blood ties are remembered beyond death here.

The Nagais before my great-grandfather Takehiko are memorialized in a mountain village a few miles north, where the family had lived for centuries, supervising their land from the mountaintop. Takehiko was the first to come down from that village and live among the family's sharecroppers. He chose this site for the family cemetery. In the summers, my uncles, aunts, and cousins used to visit here together.

I still have a picture that was taken on one such occasion. It shows Fuku and Takeo, my mother, Yasuo and Sayo, my uncle Shiro and his wife, Michiyo, Kenichi, Keiko, Jumpei, and me all standing in front of this stone. Jumpei and I must have been four and seven; it was before most of our cousins were born. All the adults in the picture look solemn. Maybe it was irreverent or bad luck to smile at the grave site where you were getting a memorial picture taken with the ancestral spirits. But I'm putting my palms together in a mock gesture of reverence and grinning with all my teeth. Jumpei's face is completely turned away from the camera toward me. His mouth is wide open with laughter.

The smoke is rising from the incense sticks. I close my eyes.

I hope you remember how I made you laugh, I say to Takeo and Takako.

When I get back to the house, Keiko is in the kitchen cooking. She is making a salad, a pot of rice, and some potato stew with little pieces of meat I can easily pick out and not eat. Fuku is in her bedroom resting.

Around five o'clock, Yasuo and Sayo come over with a tray of Chinese food from a restaurant. "Time for dinner," he says, laughing and shaking my hand. Soon we are sitting on the tatami floor of the family room around the big black table. Keiko gives Fuku small portions of everything.

"Whenever I eat Chinese food," Fuku says to me, "I think of your other grandmother, Okiku-san."

"How is that?" I ask.

"A week before your mother's wedding, your grandfather and I came to town. Okiku-san and I had lunch together. She took me to the best Chinese restaurant in Kobe and treated me. She kept saying how happy she was about the marriage. She loved your mother. Okiku-san was a gentle and considerate person, not at all like her husband. She went through a lot of hardships because of him."

"Because he was selfish?"

Fuku gives a discreet small nod. "Anyway, at the Chinese restaurant, she kept ordering more and more food and urging me to eat. We had such a good time together."

If I could go back in time, this is what I want to see: my two grandmothers talking and laughing together over egg rolls or shark-fin soup. They would have worn their going-out kimonos and had their hair done to visit a fancy restaurant. They must have confided in each other about their hardships. I imagine them lifting white cups of chrysanthemum tea to their lips and smiling at each other.

I know little about my paternal grandmother except that her name was Kiku and she was called Okiku-san, like the woman from the Mansion of the Plates. Kiku died before I was a year old. When I go to doctors' offices and they ask what my grandparents died of, I say I'm not sure about my grandmother even though she died young, in her midfifties.

"Okiku-san had liver cancer," Keiko tells me as she puts more rice into my bowl. "She was in Hiroshima when they dropped the bomb. You knew that, didn't you?"

"Yes. Everyone was there except my father."

Yasuo sees me pick out the pieces of meat and set them aside on an empty plate. He shakes his head. "I see you are still a picky eater.

Eating like that, you'll never live a long life like your grandmother."
He peels a summer orange and sets the sweet sections on Fuku's plate.
"These are her favorites ever since I made her eat them when she
stayed at my house with a bad cold. They cured her."

"But remember," Sayo breaks in, "she didn't want to try them at
first when I recommended them. She said they were bitter. How
could she know when she had never tasted them? She said she could
tell by their look. She was wrong, of course. Sometimes she has her
mind set against things, so it doesn't matter what you tell her." Sayo
glances sideways at Fuku.

Fuku continues chewing the orange sections in silence, perhaps
pretending not to hear. Her sisters, Masu and Ko, both lived to be
over ninety-five, though Fuku is the only one left now. She has lived
more than twice as long as my mother. Fuku's family is known for
longevity; her mother lived to almost a hundred.

Yasuo takes another orange into his hands. His thumb circles over
its rough skin to find the soft spot near the stem end.

"Here, Mother," he says. "Eat more."

Until the last two years of her life, my mother thought that she
would live to be a very old woman because of her family history. I
wonder if she ever imagined my brother and me taking care of her in
her old age, spooning Chinese food on her plate, peeling oranges for
her. *Look how attentive Uncle Yasuo is,* I want to say to her; *Jumpei and
I would have done anything for you, too.*

At nine o'clock, I see Yasuo and Sayo to the door.

"Maybe we'll have a big family reunion next year," Yasuo says.
"It'll be the thirteenth anniversary of your grandfather's death. We'll
have the priest over to read the sutras and remember him together.
It'll be a good occasion for your grandmother to see everyone."

"That sounds very good."

"If I can send you a ticket, will you come back for the reunion?"

"You don't have to do that. I'll come anyway."

"Let me get your ticket," Yasuo insists.

I hesitate.

"Don't be polite. I'm your uncle. Your mother took care of me when I was little. Your grandmother would want to see you again next summer. I want to help you come back."

"All right. Thanks a lot."

Yasuo pats my shoulder with his big hand. I remember the crickets, grasshoppers, and butterflies he used to catch, the wild nightingales he tamed so that they sang inside bamboo cages or flew around his house.

"You look like your mother now," Yasuo says. "You have her eyes."

We say good night, and I watch them walk to their car. Then I go back in the house, where Keiko and Fuku are drinking tea.

"Sayo left the Chinese food," Fuku says. "The leftovers won't fit into my refrigerator. They'll spoil."

"Don't worry, Mother," Keiko assures her. "They won't spoil overnight. It's very cool tonight."

"Will you eat the leftovers before you go home, then?"

"If not, I'll take them home for my husband."

Keiko has covered the tray with a cloth. Fuku lifts it and looks at the food. "Sayo should have taken back the whole tray. There's too much food."

I don't want her to stay up fretting about the food. "Grandmother, you should go take a bath and relax," I suggest. "Then we'll all go to bed."

"You two should take a bath, too, but the hot water comes out too sudden. I don't want you to come to my house and get burned."

Fuku puts the cloth back over the food and starts to smooth the cushion she is sitting on.

"We'll be careful about the hot water," I try to assure her.

"I can't eat all this food. Why did Sayo bring so much anyway?"

"But it won't go to waste because Keiko's taking it back."

"The food will spoil while she's carrying it on the train. It won't be any good by the time she gets home."

"Stop worrying," Keiko says. "The train takes much less time now. Besides, it's air-conditioned."

"You two take a bath and go to bed," Fuku says. "Which of you will go first?"

Keiko and I look at each other. She shrugs. We are the guests. Fuku won't take a bath or go to bed until the two of us are in bed. Though I am irritated by her nagging, I remind myself that she wants everything to be perfect on this visit, just as I do.

"You go first, Neine," I say to Keiko.

After we have bathed, we lay our futons in the middle room between the family room and the butsuma. This is where my mother, brother, and I slept during our summer visits. In July and August, we had to sleep inside a green mosquito netting to avoid being bitten. My brother and I crawled around pretending to be lions in a cage. I fall asleep while Fuku is walking around the house after her bath, making sure everything is in order.

At six the next morning, Fuku calls from the next room.

"I bought extra milk when the grocery truck came last. I don't want it to spoil. It's in the refrigerator. You go and drink it."

"She's worried about the food," Keiko whispers from her futon.

"There's some bread in the refrigerator, too," Fuku continues. "We left last night's rice on the table." Now she's moving around. Cloth rustles against cloth. She must be folding her futon and getting dressed.

"I want to sleep some more," I call out to Fuku, too sleepy to hide the crankiness in my voice.

"Go ahead and make yourself a little breakfast," Keiko adds. "We'll get up soon, and you can eat with us again."

"Do you know how to toast the bread on the burner?" Fuku asks, completely ignoring what we said. We can hear her steps. She must be walking toward the kitchen.

Keiko pushes her covers aside, gets up, and puts on a cardigan over her nightgown.

"What are you doing?"

"She's not going to stop till we get up and eat with her." Keiko buttons up her cardigan. "She's worried about the food."

"I'm going back to sleep all the same." I pull the sheets over my head. "I never eat right after I get up."

Keiko is already walking away toward the kitchen.

By now, Fuku has checked the kitchen and come back to the dining room. She is saying something about the tray of Chinese food left on the table. I kick the covers aside and pull a long-sleeved T-shirt over my nightshirt. Keiko is right. My grandmother is not going to be satisfied until we are all eating breakfast. I sit on the futon for awhile, listening to her shuffling around. *Leave me alone,* I want to say. *Why won't you let me sleep?* But that is childish. I have to give in.

As I stand up and begin to fold my futon, though, I can't help wishing that I had been allowed to visit her when I was a teenager. Perhaps then Fuku and I would already have had our fights about eating in the morning, about how her constant reminders bothered me. Our relationship is missing an important middle part: we were together when I was too young for serious rebellion, and suddenly I am here as a grown-up granddaughter, someone who should be attentive to her needs. I could not spend my teenage years challenging her authority and coming slowly to peace; instead I was always trying not to make her worry about me, writing only the good things in letters she was not even allowed to answer. It is too late to make amends for that missing middle. I cannot tell her about the anger I feel toward my father for his part in our loss. I need to do the best I can to make this visit a good one, an experience she can remember with pleasure.

I finish folding the futons and go to dress. Walking toward the big sink by the kitchen, where we always washed our faces, I remember my uncles and grandfather getting me up before dawn to go walking in the mountains, to see the sun rise.

In midafternoon, Keiko and I walk to the bus stop, down the street in front of the elementary school. Fuku follows us in her gray blouse and black skirt, an old pair of brown leather shoes too big for her feet. Keiko is carrying the tray of Chinese food with pink Saran Wrap on top.

The bus isn't here yet. Behind us, a narrow path cuts between the paddies to the river. Ahead, across the street, is the school and then more paddies going up to the foot of the mountains.

"I'm glad you could come," Fuku says to me. "I wanted to see you once before I died."

"Don't say such a thing," Keiko protests.

"I'll be here again," I say. "Uncle Yasuo will send me a ticket to come and visit next summer. He's planning a family reunion to remember Grandfather. I'm sure he told you that."

Fuku tilts her head a little and sighs. "You can remember me then, too. Most likely, I'll be gone by then."

"Grandmother."

"I have lived too long." She looks down at the gray pavement. "Some nights, I think Sayo should put me in her car and take me to some cliff I can jump off from. Or when I'm crossing this road, I think about stopping in front of a car so it'll hit me. But then I think of what an ugly death that would be. The person who hit me would be so inconvenienced. People would gossip, too. They would say, 'That old woman, something must have been wrong with her head.' What a big nuisance that would be to your uncles and aunts. And maybe your cousins wouldn't be able to marry or find work after such a scandal. So I think I have no choice. I just have to live till my time comes."

Keiko and I look at each other. She turns back toward Fuku and tries to laugh.

"Mother, what a morbid way to talk."

"It's the truth," Fuku insists. "I can't wait to die and meet Takako and Takeo. And my sisters."

I look up at the sky. It's a clear day. The sun feels too bright on the road. I am standing between my grandmother in her too-large clothes and my aunt wielding an awkward tray of food covered with Saran Wrap. What can I possibly say to make things right?

"Grandmother," I say, "I wish you wouldn't talk like that. I didn't come all this way to hear you talk about how you want to die."

She looks at me in silence. Immediately, I regret what I've said. It must have sounded petty and resentful, as if I cared more about my feelings than about hers. But before I can say anything else, the orange-and-cream–colored bus comes down the road. I put down my backpack and touch Fuku's thin shoulder.

"I'm so glad we could see each other," I offer, wishing there were a way I could put all my love and regret and apologies into my voice. "I missed you so much. Please don't think about dying. I want to see you again." What I really want to say is, *I am sorry about all the years I couldn't be a good granddaughter to you because my father kept me from you, because I had to go and live in a foreign country. Forgive me.* But I cannot tell her that, now or ever.

The bus is waiting, its doors wide open.

"Thank you for coming," Fuku says, her cheeks wet with tears. She hesitates a second and adds, "Come and see me again. I'll be waiting."

"Yes," I nod. "Next year."

I squeeze her shoulder, pick up my backpack, and head up the steps while Keiko says her good-bye. The bus is empty. I give the driver my change and walk all the way to the back. As soon as I sit down, I turn back. Fuku is waving. Keiko comes to sit across the aisle and carefully lays out the tray of food next to her. The bus lurches forward. I continue waving.

Every summer, my brother and I cried as soon as we sat down on the bus. We sat in the very back and waved as though we never expected to see our grandparents again. Grandmother always sent us home with some kind of food—tomatoes and eggplant from the garden or rice cakes she had made. Watching us cry, she would say something about how she was getting old, and that it would be so lonely without us. She was always more pessimistic than my grandfather, who waved to us with a big smile on his face. My mother and I used to laugh about it later. "Your grandmother," she used to tell me, "she's the biggest pessimist I know."

I keep waving until the bus has moved so far that we can no longer see each other. Then I turn to face forward.

Keiko reaches across the aisle and lays her hand on my wrist.

"Grandmother just talks like that, right?" I ask her. "She was always kind of pessimistic, wasn't she?"

"Yes. Your grandmother's even worse than before because she is older. Sometimes she speaks that way because she's lonely. But she was glad to see you. It made her very happy. And she has Yasuo and Sayo to take care of her."

I watch the river to my left. Every summer during my childhood, the river looked the same but was in fact slightly different. The place where we were supposed to swim—because the current was slow and the depth just right—changed from summer to summer due to rainfall and erosion. It was the kind of thing you knew only if you lived here. I will never live in this village or even in the same country. In a week, I will be separated from this river, this village, by an ocean, another time zone, another language. My eyes hurt, and my throat feels tight. How do I know what has changed and what remains the same when I live so far away? How can I feel comforted by the past when loss is the most constant thing in it? Holding my aunt's hand, I continue to look out the window at the green paddies that once belonged to my mother's family. I am leaving behind a village where all my life, under different circumstances, could have taken place.

A Thousand
Cranes

After our dinner together, my uncle Shiro brings out a bottle of wine while his wife, Michiyo, clears the table. Their fifth-floor condominium overlooks one of the many rivers of Hiroshima. On the busy street below, white headlights move like beads rolling down along the black water. When Michiyo returns from the kitchen, Shiro uncorks the wine and pours us each a glass.

We have been talking about my grandfather's letters and papers, which Shiro is keeping in his office. He has the diaries and will send them to me.

"When I couldn't find the diaries," I tell Shiro and Michiyo, "Grandmother said, 'Maybe they turned into rice.' She was thinking about the kimonos she sold after the war. She forgot that Grandfather passed away years later."

Shiro and Michiyo both laugh.

"That was the only thing she was confused about. Otherwise, she remembered everything."

"Her memory is remarkable." Shiro frowns and smiles at the same time. "She gets confused sometimes because her mind is stuck on a detail she can't forget, like selling those kimonos after the war. She's not losing her memory in any way."

"You're right. She kept reminding Keiko and me to do things. She was afraid *we* might be forgetful."

Shiro shakes his head. "She is as *shitsukoi* as ever."

Shitsukoi means, literally, "thick-willed" and therefore "maddeningly persistent."

"She was shitsukoi all right," I admit. "She woke us up to have breakfast because she was worried about all the food she had bought. It was early, so we wanted to sleep some more, but Grandmother kept talking until we gave in."

Shiro and Michiyo look at each other.

"She's done that to us, too," Michiyo says.

"Your poor grandmother," Shiro sighs. "She wants things to go exactly her way. She can be a terrible nag sometimes."

"But she doesn't nag in a mean way," Michiyo puts in. "She worries because she wants to make sure her guests have enough to eat and they're comfortable and everything is all right. She worries because she's kindhearted."

"Of course," I agree. "She just doesn't understand that people might be more comfortable if she could leave them alone now and then. I know she means well."

"It's the Nagai curse," Shiro laughs and sips his wine. "All of us are like that in some way. We don't know how to leave well enough alone. We can't help being shitsukoi."

I look at him wanting to say, *Not me.* I have no problem leaving people alone.

"Your brother, Jumpei, is not like that," Shiro says. "And my son, Takeshi. But they're exceptions."

"How about me? I'm not a nag. I don't worry when people come to my house."

"I don't mean that," Shiro says. "I mean the way we can't do things halfway. Whatever we do, we go all out. We don't know when to let up."

I want to protest again, but Shiro keeps on talking.

"Look at your uncle Yasuo. When he goes fishing, he doesn't just catch a few fish and come home. He spends the whole afternoon and brings back more fish than his family can eat. It's the same thing with his business. He works from dawn to midnight and goes in on Sundays to do his accounts."

"He used to trap birds, too," I add. "My mother told me."

"Birds, crickets, beetles. When we were growing up, Yasuo had jars and cages all over our house. He used to hide behind bushes in the winter with a net to catch nightingales. Even if it was snowing and cold, he could sit there all day. He didn't know when to give up."

"He almost flunked out of high school because he was too busy catching birds and crickets."

"That's right. Now, with Keiko, it's her religion. Why can't she be moderately religious like other people? Instead she gives all her money to this hirameki shrine and stands in front of train stations handing out tracts. It's all or nothing with her, too."

While Shiro refills his glass, I take a sip from mine. The wine is fruity and sweeter than the German wines I am used to. It reminds me of the cooking liquers, fruit rinds, and spices my mother kept in her cupboards. They were arranged in orderly rows of glass jars, each labeled in her meticulous handwriting.

"I suppose my mother was like that, too."

"You bet."

My mother used to get up at five to weed her vegetable garden. She built trellises and arches for her morning glories and roses, the bamboo sticks cut, bent, and tied neatly with white twine. In her desk drawer, her embroidery floss was sorted and arranged by color, boxes of pencils were sharpened to perfection, and she had several notebooks in which she kept records of her gardening, her embroidery projects, her plans for outdoor excursions.

"You're right," I say to Shiro. "My mother did everything all out, too. She was more cheerful and energetic than anybody's mother I knew. But when she became unhappy, she didn't feel just a little depressed. She thought her life was completely worthless. So it *was* all or nothing with her, too."

Shiro nods. "People in your mother's generation were prone to depression when they got to be thirty-five or forty. Your mother had one of the worst cases."

"You mean people in her generation suffered because of the war?" I ask. Every time age or generation is mentioned in Japan, the Second World War is the dividing line: people belong to different generations according to how old they were back then.

"Your mother was in middle school when the war broke out," Shiro says. "She spent her most impressionable years being told to sacrifice everything for her country. She had to eat watered-down rice and go hungry, walk through neighborhoods full of dead bodies after air raids. She was prepared to die for her country, and then it came to nothing. The war turned out to be nothing worth dying for." Shiro pauses to sip his wine and continues. "When the war ended and we lost our land, she had to work hard to support us. Then she met your father, nursed him through TB, and married him. She worked hard to make a good home, but her marriage wasn't happy. By the time she was nearing forty, she felt as if she had spent her whole life sacrificing for one meaningless cause after another. A lot of people her age went through that. I was lucky to be a few years younger. I don't remember the war quite as vividly."

"I suppose."

"Remember Takeshi Ogata, your mother's and my cousin?"

I nod.

"He was your mother's age and very similar in temperament; both of them were very intelligent. They tended to think a lot and take things to heart. Once they started thinking depressing thoughts, they couldn't stop. That's what I mean by the Nagai curse. Other people went through the same things and were able to shrug them off. Your mother and Takeshi couldn't."

I don't say anything for a while.

Michiyo gets up from the table. "Let's have some tea," she suggests in her bright, cheerful voice. "*Bancha* or oolong tea?" she asks me.

"Either sounds very good."

She goes to the kitchen, part of which is visible from the dining room over the countertop. I watch her fill a kettle and put it on the stove, open a tin, and measure the tea leaves into a glossy brown pot. When she comes back to the dining room, she sits with her face partially turned toward the kitchen to watch the kettle. "I think some hot tea would be wonderful," she announces, smiling at me.

"I didn't mean to have a depressing discussion," Shiro says. He drains his glass. "The Nagai persistence can be a good thing. It doesn't have to be a curse."

I wait for him to go on.

"I've always been able to get more research done than my colleagues at the university because I know how to work hard even under stress. I can really concentrate. In that way, I'm lucky to have our family's persistent nature. You must know how that is."

For a moment, it seems strange that Shiro and I can now talk about work. When we last saw each other, I was in high school. Now I have a doctorate and an academic position just as he does, though our fields are different.

"I'm pretty disciplined about my work," I say, "but I'm not a perfectionist the way my mother was. Maybe I don't have the Nagai temperament. I'm not all that persistent."

Shiro shakes his head and almost guffaws. "You are more persistent than all your cousins combined. You inherited more of the Nagai temperament than anyone else."

"I don't know about that."

"Remember when you used to make origami cranes?"

I nod.

"Once you learned how to make them, you wanted to make them smaller and smaller. You had to use your mother's sewing needles and tweezers to fold them because they were too small for your fingers. You had a cookie tin full of origami cranes smaller than your thumbnail."

"But that's just one thing."

"You also filled at least one notebook a week with your stories and pictures during summer vacation. You collected seashells with holes in just the right places so you could string them into necklaces. When we walked on the beach, you were always picking up shells and looking at them. You were just like Yasuo. Both of you could do the same thing for hours."

"All right," I concede. "But I'm not like that about everything. I do most things less than halfway. If I have a class that's not going well, I don't lie awake worrying about it. When I knit sweaters, if I find a minor mistake several rows later, I don't rip out the stitches to correct it. I'm not a perfectionist."

"Good," Shiro says, grinning. "That means you've learned your lesson."

"What lesson?"

"The lesson about living with the Nagai curse. Choose one or two things you can't leave alone and make sure they are good things. Then back off from everything else so you don't have to be shitsukoi all around. That's what I try to do with my research. I obsess on that, but I try to let up about everything else."

"Does that work?"

"Sure. It works for me. I wish Keiko had done the same. Keiko would have made a great scholar because she's smart and hard-working. She would have done a lot of good for other people and been happier herself if she'd found something other than this crazy religion to obsess about. It's too bad she couldn't go to college and find something to study."

For a long time, I have had similar thoughts about my mother: she might have been happier if she had found a vocation, an art, a cause to pursue professionally. Then she wouldn't have been so quick to think that her life was worthless.

Michiyo goes to the kitchen, where the water is boiling. She lets the tea steep and then brings it to the dining room.

"Try and see if you like it," she says, pushing a brown ceramic cup toward me.

I lift it and drink. It's bancha, the roasted Japanese tea that, unlike green tea, is sweet.

"It's delicious."

Smiling, she pours a cup each for herself and Shiro, goes back to the kitchen, and returns with a plate of manju. Each manju is shaped like a maple leaf.

"These are specialties of Hiroshima. You'll like them because they don't have bean paste inside. The outside part is like pancakes. Inside they have chocolate or jam. Try one." She holds the plate toward me.

I take one of the manju and bite into semisweet chocolate. "This is great."

Michiyo and Shiro are looking at each other and nodding. *See, she likes the manju,* they must be thinking to each other. I can imagine what it's like for my cousin Takeshi to come home on his vacation from his job in Okayama, two hours away by train. Though he hasn't lived at home for a few years now, Shiro and Michiyo would remember exactly what food he liked and disliked; they would tell him things he had forgotten about his childhood. If my mother had lived on, my homecoming would have been the same way. I smile at Michiyo as she pours more tea into my cup and puts another manju in front of me.

An hour later, lying in bed in Takeshi's old room, I remember saying good-bye to Keiko at the train station in Himeji.

"I won't have a chance to see you again," she said as we stood near the ticket gate. "You'll be in Kobe only a short while after this."

"I'll be back again. Maybe next year."

"I'm glad we got to see each other. Your mother would be happy."

"Yes."

"I'm praying for her every day." Keiko smiled and tilted her head, as if to say, *Is that all right?*

"I'm glad to hear that. Thank you," I said. "See you next year."

I began to walk toward the tracks. Before turning the corner, I looked back one last time and saw Keiko waving. Her other arm was wrapped tight around the tray of Chinese food, more an inconvenience than a welcome gift since she wasn't going straight back to Kobe. She had to stop at the Himeji branch of her shrine. Still, Keiko had accepted the food so my grandmother would stop worrying and feel at peace. In the same way, I thought, it was all right for me to thank her for praying for my mother. Prayer is Keiko's way of honoring and mourning my mother. It doesn't matter that I don't believe in her religion. Just as Keiko had wanted to give Fuku some peace of mind, I wanted Keiko to feel that she was doing me some good.

Keiko believes that the souls of dead people are caught in limbo between this life and the next world, waiting for the prayers of surviving relatives to help them move on. She wants to get a genealogy chart done so she can pray all our ancestors into the next world. Shiro is right about one thing, Keiko is going all out: she wants to bring our entire family, living and dead, into peace, into enlightenment. But Shiro may be wrong to say that her pursuit is crazy, that she would have been better off as a scholar. All weekend, Keiko was considerate toward my grandmother, toward me. She smiled and laughed a lot. She must be happy. Who can say that she would have been happier some other way or done more good for other people?

To Keiko, hirameki must be a flash of light just as its name suggests, something that brightens up her life. As she sits at the altar every morning to pray, she might notice a stream of light coming through the window. Dust in its path would glitter and be transformed into specks of light, into souls. The world is full of lost souls waiting for her to claim them as kin, to help them move on. She is so eager to do good. I fall asleep imagining her at a train station. "Look behind you and around you," she is calling to tired people coming home from work or school. "Don't you see that flash of light? It's all around you. Don't you see it?"

The following afternoon, Michiyo and I make our way through the Peace Memorial Park, the site of another kind of hirameki forty-five years earlier. It's been gray and windy all morning and afternoon. The rain starts when we are halfway through the park. Shiro is at the university attending a meeting. He wouldn't have come here even if he had been free.

"You two should go alone," he said at breakfast. "I don't feel up to it. It's too depressing, especially in this weather."

He has a point. This is a place for grieving. The statues and memorial stones along the path are covered with flowers, one thousand cranes of peace, letters and banners addressed to the souls of people who perished here. Wet paper and petals glisten against gray stone. At the end of the path, we come to the largest commemorative stone, which is surrounded by flower arrangements sent by the current mayor of Hiroshima, the U.S. ambassador, someone from the prefectural office. Michiyo and I stop to read the words carved on the stone: "Please rest in peace. The mistake will not be repeated."

In silence, we cross the plaza and enter the museum building. Inside, the exhibit is spread out into a series of small rooms. The first room has fact sheets and charts about the power of the atomic bomb; the second is lined with glass cases. Metal and glass fragments pulled from the skin of the dying, burned shirts peeled off their backs, curled fingernails and singed hair they had shed are all preserved under lock and key.

Walking a few steps ahead of me, Michiyo doesn't pause long to read the tags under each item. She and Shiro have lived in Hiroshima for the last five years. She must have seen these displays over and over with guests, but they are not things she would remember from her childhood. She was born in Kobe during the war and was only two or three at its end. Unlike my mother, she doesn't remember the long lines at the ration stands, sitting in the dark all night while the air raids went on, the constant talk of dying for her country.

"Your uncle is right," she says when I catch up. "This is very depressing, isn't it? But I always come with guests. I think it's my duty to see these things, somehow."

Underneath one of the burned blouses in a display case the identifying tag explains that the young girl who had worn it died from her burns and radiation poisoning. There is a small photograph of her back. Next to the blouse is a church organ, its wood charred, its cords snapped. Walking away from it into the third room—more burned clothing, photographs, stopped watches, fragments of walls—I think of Keiko again.

When Keiko came to live in Kobe, several years after the war, she worked at an office downtown and took piano lessons on weekends. Because she had no money for her own piano, she painted the keys on a piece of cardboard, exactly the right size and proportion. She practiced on this silent paper piano every night after work. Eventually, she married her piano teacher, who said she was the best student he'd ever had. But a few years after their marriage, her husband quit giving lessons and went to work at his father's fruit shop. He and Keiko were too busy to play the piano. When the shop went bankrupt a few years after my mother's death, Keiko's husband got a clerical job and both of them joined the hirameki shrine, pledging their small income.

Standing among the preserved rubble of Hiroshima, I know that Keiko's disappointments, my mother's death, and my personal sorrow are nothing by comparison. Still, I cannot stop thinking of Keiko pounding on her paper instrument night after night. I imagine her, years later, longing for that silent music as green bananas ripened in the cellar of her husband's failing store. Even now, Keiko hasn't given up on discipline and persistence. She prays morning and night for the dead of our family; she carries bundles of tracts in her purse to distribute on the street. Shiro is right about our family curse. None of us can give up on our hopeless causes. Why do we want to pray for the dead and remember their pain when our persistence does little except to keep us in pain?

Michiyo turns back toward me and puts her hand on my shoulder. I look away, afraid of bursting into tears. On the wall, there are notices the American planes dropped in Hiroshima a few days before the bombing. They warn of further air raids; they urge the people of Hiroshima to surrender.

"We don't have to see any of this," Michiyo says.

"It's all right. I want to see it."

In the next room, a group of schoolchildren are clustered around two large dioramas placed side by side. One shows the city as it was before the bomb; the other shows it right after—nothing but a jumble of gray ashes and charred sticks. The teacher, a middle-aged man, is standing behind the dioramas and talking. The children are growing restless; their heads in identical yellow caps begin to move up and down, sideways. They look very young, no more than second or third grade. As Michiyo and I enter the room, two boys, standing near the diorama of the city before the bomb, begin to point at various buildings.

"Look, here's the castle."

"The Sumitomo Bank Building downtown. I've been there."

They are too young to understand that the buildings shown here were destroyed and then reconstructed.

The first boy waves his hand over the general area between two of the rivers. "This is our neighborhood," he says. "Look."

"Let's go," the teacher calls. "There is more to see."

The children file out in orderly double rows. Michiyo and I follow them into yet another room, this one much darker than the others. Lit by one fluorescent light from overhead, two mannequins stand in a gray landscape behind glass. They are a mother and her young daughter, their kimonos burned and coming off in black strips, their hair and faces singed and bloodied. Their feet are covered by rubble: shattered roof slates, charred cloth, burned wood. The painted background is an eerie orange. The schoolchildren walk on in hushed obedience. The teacher does not stop to comment.

I want to hurry past the rows of yellow caps and catch up with the teacher to tell him something is going wrong with their well-intended visit. If these children are getting anything out of the displays, it's that war is bad because bad things happen to us and to our families. But that isn't why war is bad.

When my mother told me about the Second World War, she didn't just talk about the deaths of her friends, her own hunger, the destruction of her city by firebombs. The worst thing about the war, she told me, was the way she had been taught to support it. "I believed we were fighting to bring civilization to the rest of Asia," she said. "I thought we were going to China and Korea and Burma and all those places to chase away the Americans, the British, and the French who oppressed the people there. We were bringing them a better government." She had no idea, during the war, about the Japanese soldiers' cruelty toward the native populations of Asia, toward prisoners of war. She never heard, until much later, about the massacres of civilians all over Asia. She was angry that the textbooks in my brother's and my history classes still did not mention such things. Rather, they emphasized how Japan was "forced into conflict" by unfair trade practices, how the Russians broke a treaty to attack us in the last year of the war to win the northern islands, how

Japan, nobly, vowed never to fight again. "This is all wrong," my mother said.

She was an exception. My teachers at school seemed unimpressed by the objections I raised because of what she had told me. It was clear that other kids didn't hear the same stories from their mothers. Later, my stepmother, Michiko, would say that I could not invite people of Korean ancestry to our house because they were inferior and unhygienic. Asked about the war years she had spent in Shanghai, Michiko talked only about the French movies she used to sneak into. She complained that her family had been forced to return to Japan after the war, without time to sell their property at a fair price. As soon as Japan had lost the war, she said, Chinese people broke into her house and stole things. To her, the war was like some natural disaster that inconvenienced her family; it had no other implications.

In a way, the displays in the museum are no different, however noble their original intention. The atomic bomb is still portrayed as a cosmic disaster that befell innocent people, burning them and destroying their homes. Even the inscription outside, on the memorial stone, is too vague: "Please rest in peace. The mistake will not be repeated." What mistake? Does the word refer only to the bomb, or the Second World War, or all war? And why does the inscription use the passive voice, "will not be repeated," as though we had no control over the outcome? Exactly who or what is accountable for the "mistake" that ended up in the tragedy of Hiroshima?

I know that the people of Hiroshima were "innocent" in the way all civilians are innocent, but dying in a war, even for them, is not the same as being killed in a natural catastrophe like a typhoon or an earthquake. The worst thing about war, as my mother told me, is that we are encouraged to contribute in words and action to the machinery of destruction. The people who died here had been trained, just as my mother had, to support the war, to participate in the "civilian war effort" of building weapons and ammunition. They had played a part, however small, in the destruction that ended in their own deaths. If we don't scrutinize that aspect of their tragedy, if we gloss over the complexity of their circumstances, then we have learned nothing.

Michiyo and I, behind the schoolchildren, enter the last room of the exhibit. It is more of the same: burned clothing, photographs, watercolor pictures of the disaster by the people who survived it. We have come through several rooms and not found one explanation of why this war took place, in what ways each side was responsible and guilty. If they had been paying attention, the children ahead of us would have learned only one thing: war is bad and scary. They would have learned this in the same simpleminded and emotional way that the children before the war had been taught that war is good or necessary.

Leaving the last room, I cannot get over my disappointment. It isn't right to scare people into peace. The exhibit is incomplete without a detailed discussion of how the Japanese and American governments both contributed to the escalation of war, to what led up to the dropping of the bomb. I know that most people would applaud the total lack of anti-American sentiment in the displays, the restraint from finger-pointing. Being a gracious loser is an essential part of Japanese culture. It is shameful, we are taught, to engage too much in the after-the-fact analysis of our defeat, to be eager to assign blame to ourselves or to our opponent. Maybe this exhibit shows a typically Japanese attempt to save face all around, a desire to be polite: by treating the bomb as a cosmic disaster, we eliminate human responsibility—it's as if the bomb caused itself to be dropped. But that is not the truth, and the atomic destruction of a city is scarcely a fit occasion for politeness. The whole point of politeness is to shield people from unnecessary embarrassment or pain on various social occasions. That principle should not apply here. Commemorating the bomb is not a social occasion, and if the only honest way to advocate peace involves assigning blame all around and causing embarrassment, guilt, and pain, then such feelings are far from unnecessary. To stop short of a full investigation, in the end, is only an abuse of politeness, not true courtesy or consideration. It is false to represent the bomb as a disaster we can all mourn together.

As Michiyo and I descend the stairway toward the exit, I have a sudden mental picture of my father crying in front of my mother's grave. Anyone can give way to dramatic seizures of remorse, to tears and sadness. Even my father could do that much. Then, five minutes later, he could decline my grandmother's invitation to lunch and go on his way, as thoughtless as ever. If my mother's spirit had continued on in any way, she would not have wanted his flowers, tears, or remorse; she would have wanted him to tend to her mother's need to talk, to be sad together. My father, crying in front of Fuku, had only wonderful things to say about my mother: she was a gentle, sweet person. But maybe it would have been better if he had blamed her some and also blamed himself for their mutual unhappiness. After all, they were both responsible for the failure of their marriage; even my aunt Keiko has said that. If my father could have reflected on exactly how she had been responsible, how he had been responsible, then he could have come to some understanding. Then he could have truly honored her—by some act of honesty and consideration.

Michiyo pushes the door that leads outside. "We've seen enough, don't you think?" she says. "Fresh air would be good for us now." She opens up her blue umbrella and holds it over us.

Through the park, the yellow umbrellas of the children are moving under the wet trees ahead. Michiyo and I stop in front of the memorial for the middle school boys who died in the ammunition factories downtown where they had been mobilized to work.

"My father's brother, Tsuyoshi, was one of them," I tell her. The names of their schools are carved on the stone. "I don't know which one of these schools he attended." The boys' names, the explanation reads, are written on a scroll stored in a vault inside the museum. "Whatever happened to him, I hope it was very quick." I can't stop thinking of the burned blouses, singed hair.

"Your father's family lived in Hiroshima, right?"

"All except my father. When they moved to Hiroshima, he stayed behind in Kyoto to finish high school. His family lived in the suburbs, so no one except Tsuyoshi was hurt on the day of the bomb. But they went looking for him later and got exposed to radiation. Keiko said my grandmother died from liver cancer. Aunt Akiko has always had problems with her liver, too, and she just had surgery this summer. Maybe radiation poisoning has something to do with their problems."

"How about your father? Did he come back to Hiroshima to look for his family?"

"I don't think so."

"He must have. People didn't have telephones in their houses back then. Letters were slow, especially after the bomb. Most people who had family came back here when they heard the news. They didn't know about radiation poisoning. They were anxious to find out what had happened to their family. I'm sure your father came back, too."

"I doubt it."

We begin to walk away, past the domed building at the old epicenter. There are scaffolds around the skeleton of the building that was standing after the flash.

"They're trying to repair that," Michiyo says.

"Repair it, how?"

"So the building doesn't completely fall apart. They want it to look exactly the same as it did the moment after the bomb."

We exit the park and follow the riverside street toward the tram stop. After a few blocks, we are at a busy street corner that looks like any downtown shopping area. Cars are everywhere; people walk in and out of department stores and office buildings.

"I'm sure your father came back here," Michiyo says again. "Otherwise, he wouldn't have known for weeks if his family were alive or dead."

A tram clatters its way down the street toward us, all its cars painted bright yellow. The writing on the front and sides is in French. The tram is followed by another, this one green, with German words.

"Those trams come from all over the world," Michiyo explains. "The tram company here buys cars from discontinued services. They don't repaint the cars because they look more interesting that way." She shrugs. "A sort of tourist attraction, I guess."

Watching the tram cars of the world converge, so close to the old epicenter, I imagine this same street forty-five years ago—crowded with people looking for their families. I don't think my father was here then, though I am not sure. I know so little about him. He has never talked about his younger brother's death. I don't know what my father did during the war, how he felt about it then or later, if he went hungry like my mother and resigned himself to death and then was angry about the lies he was told. He never mentioned the years following the war when he was hospitalized with TB. I know almost nothing about my father's past. He might as well be a complete stranger.

All I can say for certain about my father is that he surely wouldn't have returned to Hiroshima to look for his family if he had known about the danger to himself from radiation. That is the one thing I can count on him to do: to act with an unswerving dedication to his self-interest, which doesn't even include his family. My father's concept of self stops only and wholly with himself. Other selfish people—even his father, Tatsuo—include their own family in the consideration of their self-interest. They talk about "my house and my family" as extensions of themselves, as part of their emotional territory. My father never loved me even in that selfish way. That is why he doesn't seem like family to me. So long as I can live thousands of miles away, I can almost believe that I have written him off, forgotten him. Then I can go on with my life and think of him as someone who has no influence over me regardless of how much he has hurt me in the past. I wish, more than anything, that I hadn't seen him at all during this visit.

Michiyo looks sideways into my face, no doubt trying to make sure that I am all right. She tilts the umbrella farther in my direction to shield my hair, which is blowing in the wind.

I am suddenly reminded of the purple hair of the doll she gave me on the morning she married my uncle, when I was three. I had been crying all morning, my mother told me later, because Shiro's friends had stopped by to move some of his furniture from the house he and my family shared. Shiro was to live with Michiyo's family for a month and then move to Tokyo for his graduate studies. That morning, before their wedding, Shiro and Michiyo stopped to see me because my mother had called them at Michiyo's parents' house and said that I was crying. I remember the hallway of the house where I was standing, and Michiyo handing me the doll with a soft cloth body and long purple hair.

Now Michiyo walks next to me in silence; she doesn't want to ask me needless questions or intrude on my thoughts. Though she and I are not connected by blood, I have known her almost all my life. She is my family in the way my father never will be. I can count on her to remember what I like and dislike, to notice when I am too upset or preoccupied to talk. When the time comes for me to speak, she will listen to me as carefully as she now matches her steps to mine. But if I say nothing, it will also be all right.

As we walk on, away from the memorial of pain, raindrops keep hitting the stretch of fabric over our heads. A thousand words are falling, every second, from the sky.

Smoke

The phone rings on Wednesday evening while I am straightening out my room at Sylvia's. I pick up the receiver by the porch.

"Kyo-chan," my cousin Kazumi says. "Your father just called. He wants to take us out to dinner."

"When?"

"Tomorrow night. That's the only time he's free, remember?"

My father must be alone. Michiko is supposed to return from Hokkaido early Friday morning to accompany him to the hospital. The surgery is scheduled for Saturday, the day Kazumi and I plan to visit her mother, Akiko, at her hospital. I'm not going to visit him at his. I'll be flying out of Osaka the following morning.

"What do you think?" Kazumi asks. "Can you go?"

"Would you come with me?"

"Of course."

"I'll go then."

When we hang up, I open my desk drawer, pull out my plane ticket, and look over the itinerary. Seattle. Minneapolis. I imagine myself sitting in an airport coffee shop with a newspaper, a cup of coffee, and a bagel. I wish I could skip forward to that moment, into the relief I will feel then, but I am stuck in this cluttered room. The desktop and the floor are covered with clothes, books, piles of letters. I bring the ticket, back in its blue envelope, to the phone stand and slide it underneath the receiver. The corner of the envelope sticks out, a sliver of blue I can see from any place in the room.

The next afternoon, a little after four, Kazumi and I wait for my father in the kitchen of her home. She gets up to make a pot of Earl Grey tea. Outside on the patio, her dog is pacing back and forth. The nails of his paws click, and the chain makes not quite a squeak, more like a whistling sound, against the concrete. Kazumi puts a thin lemon slice in each cup before pouring the tea. Then she sits down at the table across from me. This is where we used to do homework the spring after my mother's death. I sprinkle a teaspoon of sugar on the lemon slice, which has floated to the top.

"My grandmother told me something I can't figure out," I say.

"What's that?" Kazumi asks, stirring her tea.

"She said my father came to visit her two years ago. He showed up out of the blue and wanted to bring flowers to the family grave. Isn't that strange?"

Kazumi puts down her cup and narrows her eyes. "He never told you about the visit?"

"No. Why? Did he tell you?"

She shrugs. "He didn't tell me, but I knew about it. The visit was Grandfather's idea."

My hands around the warm teacup, I wait for her to go on.

"Two winters ago, Grandfather got very sick. He stayed in bed for weeks, coughing and burning up with fever. My mother and I had to change his pajamas every few hours because he said he was suffocating in the smell of his own sweat. Every week, he sent us to Shinto shrines to buy amulets. He really thought he was going to die."

Kazumi pauses to sip her tea. I don't comment because I can't feel sorry for him.

"Anyway, when he recovered, he called your father to the house and gave him a big lecture. He ordered your father to visit your mother's family grave, offer flowers, and apologize."

"Apologize for what?"

"Grandfather thought his sickness had come because your father had angered the ancestral spirits of your mother's family. Your father had to make amends so no more bad things would happen. Grandfather said your father had been particularly wrong to forbid you and Jumpei from seeing your mother's family."

I drink my tea in silence, thinking of the letters I found at my grandmother's house.

"I don't understand," I tell Kazumi. "Grandfather and my father were in agreement about not letting us see our mother's family."

"Grandfather is old. He conveniently forgets what he wants to forget." She gets up and takes a pear out of the fridge. Peeling the skin in one piece, she cores and slices the pear and puts the slices on a plate.

"I remember what Grandfather said to your father," she says, sitting back down. "He said, 'Go apologize to the spirits of your wife and your father-in-law. Bring them flowers. Make sure you are humble to them. Humility is an essential part of human character.'"

"You heard all that?"

She grins. "I'm the one who brings them tea."

She pushes the plate toward me. The slice I take tastes cold and hard. Pears in Japan have the texture and tartness of apples.

"My father lied to my grandmother, then," I tell Kazumi. "He said he had been sitting on a train when, all of a sudden, he was overwhelmed by an urge to visit the grave. Afterward, he rushed off without having lunch with her. And just think—the visit wasn't even his idea to begin with."

Kazumi shakes her head.

"I'm embarrassed to be his daughter. Grandfather, too. I wish I wasn't related to them."

We each take another pear slice and eat in silence. I think of my grandmother's wrinkled face and thin hair. In her garden, she wanted me to dig all her potatoes because they were the only things she could offer me to eat. I remember the way they hit the bottom of the pan, hard and small. How could my father refuse to have lunch with her? How could he look her in the face and tell her a lie—such an elaborate and sentimental lie—about why he was there? I imagine my grandfather sweating and groaning in his sleep when he was sick. Even in that state, he was a tyrant, ordering Kazumi and Akiko on errands, contributing nothing but a pile of dirty laundry. He wanted to appease the spirits of my mother's family only to protect his own health.

Kazumi pours more tea in my cup and pushes the sugar bowl toward me. "I called my father in April," she says, "when I thought my mother might die. He had nothing to say to me. He didn't even ask me if I was okay. I hung up crying. He never called me back. I would have felt like an orphan if my mother had died. I know how you feel."

I put another spoonful of sugar in my cup, trying to think of what to say to break the sad mood we have fallen into. But suddenly, the dog stops his pacing and barks loudly. Someone is knocking on the door.

"Hey, Ran-chan," this person says to the dog from the other side of the wall. "How are you today? You recognize my voice, don't you? What a smart dog."

Kazumi gets up from the table. The dog changes from barking to whimpering.

"That's not my father, is it?" I ask her.

"Of course it is. I'd better get the door."

"It doesn't sound like him," I insist. "Besides, he hates animals. He never even once petted my dog."

"Your father is old now," Kazumi says, slipping on her shoes. "He likes our dog."

I stay at the kitchen table while she goes outside. As soon as she opens the door, the dog dashes toward my father, barking. The chain rattles; the paws click as he jumps up and down. "What a good dog," my father is saying. "Are you happy to see me? Oh, I'm so happy to see you, too. Roll over for me, can you?" The chain rattles some more. My father must be bent over petting the dog. I can hear the thump-thump of the dog's tail against the concrete. When my dog Riki was lost, about a year after my brother and I had moved back to his house, Hiroshi said nothing to console us. Who would have expected that years later he would be gushing over this dog? I wait, sipping my tea. I will not get up to meet him outside.

Finally, Hiroshi comes into the kitchen, dressed in the navy blue suit he must have worn to work. He takes off the jacket and hangs it on the back of the chair. He is wearing a white short-sleeved shirt underneath. After he sits down, he unknots and slips off his tie, rolls it up, and tucks it into the pocket of his jacket.

"I have to go upstairs for a minute," Kazumi says, "to get Grandfather's room ready in case he comes home while we're out."

From his breast pocket, Hiroshi takes out his lighter and a pack of cigarettes. He taps his cigarette against the table a few times before lighting it. He smokes in his usual way, taking many nervous puffs, scarcely letting the cigarette rest on the edge of the ashtray to burn by itself.

The tea left in my cup is cold. The uneaten pear slices on the plate are beginning to look bruised.

I don't know what to say to him. He looks so thin, scrawny, even. His arm keeps jerking back and forth like a wound-up device between the ashtray and his mouth. I reach out to lift the teapot, but it's empty.

My father continues to smoke, not even looking at me.

"Kazumi and I were having tea," I say. "There isn't any left, but I could make more if you'd like."

"No," he shakes his head. "We're leaving as soon as Kazumi comes downstairs. Let's try the Chinese restaurant near the bridge—not the one by the station." He takes a deep drag of the cigarette and looks into my face for a brief second, then looks away. "Michiko called yesterday from Hokkaido," he exhales. "She sounded like she would rather stay at the hospital with me than go out to dinner with you. Of course, I told her she didn't have to stay with me, so she'll still take you to that other restaurant by the station."

"She doesn't have to take me to dinner," I say. I can hear the icy politeness in my own voice.

Hiroshi doesn't even notice. "Michiko worries too much about me." He sighs in an exaggerated manner. "There's no need for her to be with me tomorrow night. They won't be doing anything yet. But she wants to be there just in case. I decided to take you out tonight so she would feel less of an obligation toward you if she couldn't make it."

I shrug.

"She will call Kazumi tomorrow morning either way."

"She really doesn't have to do anything for me. I don't expect it. Besides, I'm hoping to see some of my school friends tomorrow. Maybe I can spend more time with them if we don't go to dinner."

"You have to see things from her point of view." Hiroshi frowns as he leans forward, sticking out his scrawny neck. "You never understood about obligations. You think they are the same as expectations. You should have learned the difference a long time ago."

I pick up my cup and drink down the cold tea. *Did you go to my mother's grave out of your sense of obligation?* I want to ask. *Then why did you cry? Were you faking that, too, or were you giving way to some temporary feeling of guilt?*

"Doing the right thing is very important to Michiko," Hiroshi continues. "She was going to cancel her trip to Hokkaido because of my surgery, even though she'd been planning this vacation with her friends for a long time. I convinced her to go. I said, 'Go now, because once I have the surgery, you'll be busy taking care of me. I want you to have a vacation first. Besides, you have obligations toward your friends, too. You can't inconvenience them.' So she went, but she was very reluctant. You have to admire her for taking her obligations seriously. You have no right to dismiss her concern out of hand just because you don't understand." Hiroshi squashes out his cigarette and immediately lights another.

I can hear Kazumi's footsteps upstairs. She must be straightening out Tatsuo's room and the sitting room, laying out a change of clothes. She said Tatsuo changed three, four times a day so he "wouldn't smell like an old man." He didn't care how much laundry she had to do every day.

My father, in the last years of his marriage to my mother, used to come home once or twice a week to put a fresh supply of clothes into his suitcase and leave again. Though I seldom saw him, I knew when he had been home the night before because his shirts were hanging in the backyard. The way my mother stretched the sleeves out and pinned the shirts side by side, they looked like a gathering of invisible people holding hands.

My cup clatters when I put it down. Hiroshi looks sharply at me, as if offended by my clumsiness.

"I heard you went to see Grandmother a couple of years ago," I say, trying to sound casual. "You wanted to visit the grave. Is that true?"

He doesn't answer. Instead, he takes a long drag from his cigarette, squints at me, and blows out the smoke.

"Did you really go there?" I ask again.

"I went there," he says, flicking his ashes.

"Well," I say when he doesn't go on. "How was your visit?"

He sighs, blowing out more smoke. "I took a cab from Himeji because I'd forgotten how far the place was. What a mistake." He pauses. "The cab ride took forever and cost me a fortune. When I got near the house, I couldn't remember exactly where it was, so I stopped at a gas station to ask. I had a lucky break there. The attendant happened to be her grandson."

"My cousin Akira?"

"I don't know. I didn't ask his name."

"Did you tell him who you are?"

"No. But he obviously knew where she lived, so he gave me directions." He puts out the cigarette, grinding it hard.

"Was Grandmother surprised to see you?" I prompt him. "You hadn't called ahead of time, had you?"

"No. I guess she was surprised. But she recognized me right away." Hiroshi squints as he lights another cigarette.

"You went to the grave together, right?" I ask.

"We went most of the way in the cab. I told the driver to wait at the bottom of the hill. The car wouldn't make it up that dirt path." He turns away and looks out the window, not offering another word.

I don't know how I can get him to go on to the next part. Will he admit to crying at the grave? I want to memorize everything he says so later, when I'm alone, I can compare his version with Fuku's. It's like saving the letters he wrote to my grandparents. What I am after is evidence. I want to see if he will lie to me. Trying not to sound too eager, I ask another question. "You had time to talk to my grandmother?"

"We talked some." He frowns and closes his mouth on the cigarette. "Kazumi is taking a long time," he says, pointing at his wristwatch.

Almost the next moment, I hear her steps down the stairway. "Sorry I took so long," she says as she enters the kitchen. She must have heard him.

"No problem. We have plenty of time," Hiroshi says, jumping up from the chair. He grabs his jacket and heads toward the door before she can say anything more.

No one talks during the five-minute walk to the restaurant in the afternoon heat. Watching my father shuffle on, a few steps ahead of Kazumi and me, I think, just for a moment, that I imagined our conversation in the kitchen. I can't believe that he really went on about the expensive cab ride and mentioned meeting my cousin as a lucky coincidence. Did he dwell on these things to avoid talking about the actual visit because he suspected me of trying to draw him out, to catch him in a lie? Or is the expensive cab ride really what he remembers most about the occasion? I wish Kazumi had been there to hear his words with me.

We arrive at the restaurant, which is a white building with red and jade-green pillars. Inside, no one else is at the fifteen or so tables covered with white cloths. It's not even five-thirty. A waiter in a black uniform seats us by one of the red pillars: Kazumi and I on one side and Hiroshi on the other. The air-conditioning is working full blast. Hiroshi puts on the jacket he has been carrying.

While the waiter is getting silverware, water, and menus, Hiroshi says, "Let's make sure we leave by six-thirty. I worked late the last couple of nights. I want to go to bed early." He waves his hand toward the waiter even though he is already coming back our way. Hiroshi reaches out and grabs all three menus and then says without opening them, "We'll start with some egg rolls and shark-fin soup." The waiter has to stop in the middle of laying out our silverware to write down the order. He walks back to the kitchen at a brisk pace.

A few minutes later, lighting a cigarette, Hiroshi opens his menu but doesn't hand us ours.

"What do you think, Kazumi?" he asks my cousin, turning his menu and pointing so she can see. "I'm thinking we should order family style. We'll get the sesame beef, pockmarked tofu, and spicy chicken. Then we can always order more things as we go along."

Kazumi looks from him to me, as if trying to connect the two of us through her glance. Hiroshi does not so much as move his head in my direction.

"Whatever you think is best," she says.

My father is smoking his second cigarette when the waiter brings the soup and the egg rolls. I don't touch the soup. Even before I became a vegetarian I never ate fish because it made me sick. Cutting the egg roll in half, I scoop out the stuffing, dunk just the skin into my mustard sauce, and eat it. Hiroshi eats his soup with relish, sucking the liquid from the tip of his big spoon. He has not put out his cigarette. It continues to burn in the ashtray next to him.

The last time I had Chinese food with him was in New York, a year ago. The time before that was in Kyoto when I was ten. My family had a reunion dinner with three other families, all of whose fathers had gone to the same university with Hiroshi. The food was served banquet style, with large platters placed on a revolving-top table. One of these platters had a boiled carp with its head and fins, a yellow eyeball swimming in the eye socket. Coated with a brown sauce the color of pond scum, the carp looked worse every time it made the round—the skin broken into tatters, the flesh flaking off where people had poked with chopsticks. After about ten minutes, I threw my napkin over the carp, got up, and waited outside for everyone else to finish eating. When we got home, my father told my mother that she should make me eat fish at home once a week. "Her allergy is all in her head," he said. "I don't care if she breaks out. She'll have to get used to it." My parents argued for a long time, but my mother let the subject drop in the end. She must have realized that it was pointless to keep on. My father wasn't home often enough to see whether or not she fed me fish. That reunion dinner in Kyoto was one of the three or four times he ever went out to eat with us.

"What's wrong with your egg roll?" Hiroshi asks me now. The cigarette is still burning, as if he planned to take a puff from it between mouthfuls of soup.

"Nothing. I don't eat meat. The filling has pork in it."

He grimaces as he lifts his spoon to his mouth.

"I told you in New York that I didn't eat meat. That was a year ago. You made a big deal about it, so how could you forget?" Hearing a sharp edge in my voice, I stop, look away.

Hiroshi puts down his spoon with a clatter and waves at the waiter. Once the waiter is at our table, his pad and pen ready, Hiroshi opens the menu and picks up his cigarette. He smokes while he looks over the menu, taking his time. The waiter stands at attention. Finally, Hiroshi says, "Bring us this broccoli and carrot dish. And the fried noodles with vegetables." Taking the cigarette out of his mouth, he cocks his head toward me. "The one with the long hair is my daughter," he says. "She's been living in America. She doesn't eat meat."

Hiroshi closes the menu and glares at me. The waiter is smiling politely and uncertainly. Nobody says anything for a while. I turn my head toward the window, which is covered with pale green venetian blinds. I want to raise them and put my face against the cool glass. I imagine what would happen if I just stood up and left. But I turn back in time to see Kazumi smiling at the waiter.

"That's all for now," she says, nodding. "Thank you very much."

I pick at the rest of the egg roll without eating any more.

Soon the waiter is back with four large platters of food and a bowl of rice. We start to help ourselves.

"I keep thinking of those East Indians," Hiroshi says as he dishes the sesame beef onto his plate.

"I beg your pardon?"

"They're vegetarians, like you. Look at them past forty. Their faces are wrinkled and dried up. It's because they don't eat enough protein and fat. You don't want to look like that, do you?" He sticks his chopsticks into the pockmarked tofu on his plate. The surface glistens with grease from the ground pork as he stirs the sauce toward the sesame beef, the two dishes overlapping on top of the rice.

"Maybe they get more sun," I say without thinking. "But who says they have more wrinkles than other people? Each person is different. It's racist to say that all East Indians have wrinkles."

"Take my word for it. They have more wrinkles than anyone else. I see enough of them in Kobe." He waves his chopsticks at Kazumi. "Don't be shy. Eat more." He opens the menu again. "How about lotus-leaf-wrapped rice? That's good. I've had it before."

"I'm getting full," Kazumi says.

I reach over and take one of the menus he hasn't handed us. "The rice is prepared with ground pork and sauteed in oil with special spices," I read. "I can't eat that."

Hiroshi sighs. "We'll order two and ask them to prepare one without pork." He raises his hand. The waiter walks toward us at a fast clip and writes down the order. After he leaves, we eat in silence.

"Do you walk Ran-chan twice a day?" Hiroshi asks Kazumi when the waiter returns with the rice.

"Yes," she says, unwrapping the rice and spreading it on the plate for us. She folds up the lotus leaves and puts them in the center, to divide my meatless rice from theirs. She has always acted like my older sister, though I'm six months older and was a year ahead in school. Our mothers were the same way. Mine was seven months older than hers. Mine was quick and funny; hers was steady, reliable. Kazumi and I are playing the same parts, each of us like her mother.

"Ran-chan is anxious for his walk," Hiroshi says as he spoons some rice onto his plate. "Let's get you home before dark."

"It's nowhere near dark yet," Kazumi protests. "Besides, we only go a short way the second time. It doesn't matter whether it's dark or light."

Still, he calls for the bill as soon as we are done with the last course—fried sweet potatoes in a tangle of sticky sugar threads. He examines the bill quickly and shuffles over to the counter to pay while Kazumi and I are still drinking our tea.

"Tell me one thing," I say to Kazumi as we get up and begin to walk toward the door, where Hiroshi is waiting, another cigarette between his fingers. Kazumi is a few steps ahead of me. I raise my hand and touch her back. "Does he seem weird to you?" I ask. "It's not just my imagination, is it? He really is weird."

We both stop a moment among the empty tables and chairs. She cranes her neck and turns back to me, her lips pursed into a half-smile. "He certainly is strange. My mother says he has turned into a strange character. Wait till you see her."

I squeeze her shoulder lightly and then let go as we begin walking. I want to tell her how relieved I am that she sees him the way I do—I'm not imagining his behavior or being unreasonably critical. But we are almost at the door, so I shrug and smile.

"All the same, Aunt Takako would have been happy you had dinner with him," she whispers.

"Maybe," I say.

Outside, Hiroshi drops his cigarette and grinds it out with his shoe. He takes off his jacket, beads of sweat trickling down his forehead. We walk back to Tatsuo's house and stop in front of the door. The house is dark. Tatsuo is not home. Kazumi puts her key in the lock. "Would you like to come in?" she asks.

"No, we'd better go," Hiroshi says.

Kazumi opens the door all the same. The dog dashes out, dragging his chain, and jumps up on Hiroshi.

"Ran-chan." He stoops over and lays his hand on the dog's head. "It's good to see you again. We came home early so you can take your walk." The dog's ears go back and he sticks out his tongue. "Michiko will call you about dinner tomorrow," Hiroshi says to Kazumi.

"Thank you for taking us out tonight," she says. "Good night, and good luck on your operation."

"Time for me to go home," Hiroshi says to the dog. He nudges him away. "Be a good dog."

"How are you getting home?" he asks me when Kazumi closes the door.

"I thought I'd take the train."

"Well, I was going to take a taxi home," Hiroshi says after a few steps. "I can give the driver enough money to drop me off first and then drive on to your friend's house from there. It won't add much to the fare."

"You don't have to do that."

"It won't be any trouble."

"Okay," I say. "Thank you."

"The taxi stand is a few blocks away."

"I know where it is."

We begin to walk in silence. Hiroshi is a few steps ahead of me when we come to an intersection. He continues straight ahead through a red light while I stop to look. A car comes from the left. Then another from the right. Then the light changes. Just as I step into the intersection, a car comes from the side and turns in front of me. By the time it's gone, Hiroshi is far ahead, on the other side. He doesn't even look back. I begin to run after him. I'm just catching up when we get to the taxi stand. There is no one in line, with three cars waiting.

"Good," he says. "We don't have to wait." He marches up to the first car and taps on the window for the driver to open the automatic door.

"Take me to Asahigaoka-dai first and then drive her to Mikage," he says, climbing in. "I'll pay the whole fare."

The cab pulls away from the stand. We ride several blocks in silence. Hiroshi is staring straight ahead, at the back of the vinyl seat.

"Are you nervous about your surgery?" I ask him because I can't think of anything else to say.

Trying to light a cigarette, he looks down his nose at the tip of the lighter. "No," he shakes his head.

"Grandfather said you were going in for nine weeks. I didn't realize it was so serious."

"It's not serious." He takes the first drag and exhales, spreading smoke in the interior of the cab.

"You're not in pain now?" I don't even know why I am asking, except to be polite. Whether he feels pain or not is of no concern to me.

"Of course not," he answers. "The hospital wants to keep me for nine weeks because they can get my insurance to pay. That's all. The doctors want to make money. Besides, this isn't America. They don't just cut you open, sew you up, and expect you to leave in a week." He grimaces as if to criticize me for what he considers to be the inferior medical practices of the country where I have chosen to live.

What is the use of talking to him? I turn away and watch the houses along the hill while he gives the driver his exact address. Soon we are in front of his condominium.

Hiroshi says, *ja*, "well." *Genki-de*, "Stay well." He shoves some bills toward the driver and gets out. He doesn't look back or wave. I don't roll down the window to thank him for dinner.

That was my father, I want to say as we start back down the hill. *You'd never know it by the way we acted.*

Now we are halfway down the hill. The grade school I attended is behind us, its cream-colored buildings blurring against the mountainside at dusk. On the first day of first grade, my mother had walked up this hill with me and stood waving at the gate. She waited while I joined the other children in the school yard, and we followed the teacher into the building. She was still waving when I looked back just before entering the building. Inside, the corridors were made of dark wood. We were supposed to walk and never run. On rainy days, the whole building smelled of old wood, oil, and varnish. In my memory, those corridors are a tunnel of time—long, narrow, and dark. On one side, I was in first grade going to school with my mother; on the other, I was leaving, alone.

My graduation ceremony from sixth grade was a week after my mother's death. Though it was held on a Sunday so both parents could attend, my father went to play rugby, leaving my aunts Akiko, Keiko, and my uncle Kenichi to accompany me. Because I was one of the three students chosen to recite our poems after the principal's speech, I sat up on the stage with the teachers. My mother had sewn me a black velvet dress for the occasion; she and I had chosen the black patent leather shoes I was wearing. When I walked up to the microphone, I was nervous because I had missed the rehearsals. It was quiet in the auditorium except for my breath scratching against the microphone. I said the first word, trying to concentrate. When I was finished, there was a moment of silence and then applause, louder than I had anticipated.

After the ceremony, almost everyone I talked to said, "Your mother would have been so proud of you." It was as though my mother, dead, still cared more about me than my father could if he were to live to be a hundred years old.

When I turn away from my old school, the sky is dark blue. The lights are beginning to come on near the bay. The cab proceeds south toward the highway, past the east-west street that would be a shortcut. I don't say anything. Going from one hilltop neighborhood to the next, cabdrivers always take the longest way possible if you don't complain. But it isn't my money. I could care less.

At Sylvia's house, the porch light is on, but no one's home. The note on the fridge says, "We went out for dinner downtown. We'll be back around ten. Hope your dinner with your father was OK. Love, Sylvia and Cadine."

Upstairs, my room is in the same state of disorder as before. Switching on the light, I startle the cat, Ophelia, who has been napping on my pile of clothes. She runs down the stairs and clonks out the cat door. It's too early to go to bed. I turn off the light and walk over to the window by the porch.

Down the hill, my hometown sinks into the dark and then floats back out of it, transformed into the language of light. The outlines of buildings disappear and are replaced by the white squares of office windows and the neon signs on rooftops. The two highways that cut across the city become two strings of white lights with orange beads moving under them. To the left, the bay curves toward Osaka, where clusters of red and yellow lights illuminate the factories. Halfway between these factories and the port of Kobe, the new landfill in Ashiya is mostly lit in white and orange lights. North of there but south of the highways is the old seaside neighborhood where my mother had been happy. It, too, is a blur of orange and white.

Leaning against the window ledge, I continue to look at the city. When I first came back, I didn't know where the landfill was, but now I couldn't miss it—I can read the view as though it were a map of light. Though I ordinarily have a poor sense of direction, I don't even need a compass here. This is the one place in the world that is completely familiar to me. I know the names of the streets and neighborhoods, the famous landmark buildings now lit in neon. I knew their names even before I learned to read. No city I lived in or visited since then could give me the same unchanging sense of familiarity.

I open the screen door and step out on the porch. Up here on the hill, a cool breeze stirs the air at night. All the "good" neighborhoods in Kobe are on hilltops, away from summer heat, overlooking the "million-dollar night view." The house in which my mother ended her life and the house to which my father moved us after his second wedding were both on hilltops—a sign of the status he had achieved by then. Both are within five miles of here. Though I went to see the house of my mother's death, I have no desire to see the other.

My bedroom in that house was on the second floor; because the second floor was smaller than the first, part of the roof jutted out under my windows. Once a week, late at night, I climbed out onto that part of the roof and walked around to where the house connected to the garage. Then, crawling down to the top of the garage, I would sit on the edge with my feet dangling. I imagined what it would be like to jump to the street from there. First, I would lower myself carefully, my hands grabbing the slates; then I would have to let go.

"If you cause Michiko to leave me because you can't get along with her, I'll stab you with the meat knife and kill myself before the police get me."

That's what my father said about once a month when my stepmother threatened to leave him because of me. Without much warning, she would start yelling and screaming in the middle of dinner about something I had said or done. It was all Hiroshi's fault, she said, for having allowed my mother to raise me wrong. Then, with her suitcase packed, she sat in the living room while my father beat me so I would cry and apologize. If the beating didn't work, he talked about my mother—she hadn't loved me, he said; if she had, she would still be alive. Sometimes I apologized right away. Then he said I was just saying I was sorry, that I didn't really mean it. He threw me against the wall, he picked up a heavy dictionary and hurled it against the side of my head, or he slapped my face so hard his fingers made red blotches on my cheeks.

When he finally allowed me to go up to my room, I closed the door, locked it with its metal latch, and put both of my chairs between the doorway and my bed. I didn't lie down until I had scattered books and tennis balls on the floor and put masking tape over the light switch so he would not be able to turn on the light. I slept with my clothes and shoes on. It would take him a few minutes, I thought, to break the latch and force the door open. He would then stumble around and lose more time. By the time he was at my bedside, I would be halfway across the house on the roof. If I broke my legs jumping from the roof of the garage, I would still call for help so that the neighbors would come running out of their houses. My father, I was sure, would not kill me with people looking on. He never even hit me in front of anyone except Michiko.

Sitting down on the concrete floor of Sylvia's porch, I think of my father this afternoon. To say that he was insensitive and rude today doesn't even begin to describe how he was. He rushed through the Chinese dinner, smoked a pack of cigarettes, and made everyone nervous with his impatience. The waiter must have thought of him as a rude customer, one of the worst he had ever served. Still, something is wrong with my recollection; something important seems to be lacking from my mental picture of him from this afternoon. It doesn't match what I remember from thirteen years ago.

Maybe that's what gave me a strange feeling as we were walking to the restaurant or even while the three of us were eating. The whole time we were together, I was trying to observe and memorize every detail of his poor conduct. Even though there was plenty of that for me to notice, I felt, now and then, that I wasn't seeing the whole picture. I couldn't get over how thin and old he looked. Hiroshi poses no threat to my life now. He will never hit me again. I will never again have to sleep with my clothes and shoes on, tennis balls scattered on the floor to trip him. That's what I can't get over.

Of course, it isn't as though I were simply imagining how bad Hiroshi's actions were this evening—even my cousin said that he was a strange character. Maybe it's fair to say he is just as despicable as before, only in a different way: he makes up for the lack of violence in pettiness and insensitivity. If I were trying to be completely fair, though, I would have to say I was petty, too. In all my interactions with Hiroshi, I did nothing to promote goodwill, I did nothing to think better of him in his old age. Even in such small matters as food, I wasn't prepared to give him the same break I gave everyone else. When Keiko made the meat and potato stew at Fuku's house, I picked out the meat and ate the rest of the stew. The Chinese food Sayo and Yasuo brought had some meat in it. I carefully dished out only the vegetables and ate them. When Fuku wanted me to drink milk the next morning, I drank a big glass of it in front of her, even though I always hated milk, and the way Fuku remembered everything, she might have remembered that. Irritated as I was by her nagging, I still wanted to please her. I would never see her nagging as a moral failure or criticize her for forgetting that I hated milk. Her obsession about food was just a bad way of showing love.

But if Hiroshi forgot that I didn't eat meat, I passed the harshest judgment: he was insensitive; he had no respect for my beliefs. If he took me out to dinner, I was offended because he was just doing his duty. But if he hadn't, I would have been equally offended, taking the omission as an insult. Every time I saw Hiroshi, I was determined to find fault with him. I even felt a sort of vindication, really, when he acted the way he did.

Instead of feeling sorry, though, I keep picturing him as he sat at the table in his father's house, smoking one cigarette after another while he talked about his visit to my mother's grave. He would have told me nothing if I hadn't asked. The smoke hung between us like the choking silence in which we interpreted each other's words and actions in the worst light possible. Each white puff from his cigarettes was a trace of some word that should have been said between us long ago. By now, all the right words are gone, vaporized into smoke. Perhaps I have contributed just as much as he has to that pollution between us.

In the dark room behind me, I can make out the wooden telephone stand by the door. Though it's too late for love or peace between my father and me, there could perhaps be some minimal but genuine courtesy, something more than the icy politeness I have resorted to. Maybe even my father recognizes that possibility. Maybe that was why he took me out to dinner and paid for my cab. Maybe he wasn't doing it only because of his sense of obligation. I didn't give him the benefit of that doubt. As the cab moved away from the curb, I didn't thank him for dinner or wish him luck on his surgery, as Kazumi had done. Perhaps in this round of events between us, I have been downright rude; I have not even lived up to simple politeness. If I wanted to call him now to change that, it would take just five or six steps to enter the house and dial the number, to say something, to be fair.

He is alone in his condominium now, perhaps sitting at the kitchen table with a cup of tea, looking at this same view. With a major operation coming up in two days, even he might take stock of his life. Maybe he is remembering the last time he was hospitalized—how my mother sat at his bedside every day to care for him. Everybody who has known both my mother and stepmother comments on how cheerful, humorous, and sweet-tempered my mother was, how abrasive and rude my stepmother is by contrast. It's possible that my father has noticed that, too, and felt some regrets, though he has confided in no one about such feelings. If he ever felt lonely, remorseful, or worried, it would be tonight when he thinks about the surgery. My stepmother isn't home to ridicule him and remind him that he and I never got along. If I called him, it is possible that we would part on some note of courtesy and good intentions.

I stand up and look back into the dark room, waiting for some urge, some inspiration that would make me open the door and step in. If my mother were watching over me now, as Fuku believes, would she want me to forgive him? Would she be happy, as Kazumi said, that I had dinner with him tonight? Would she agree with Keiko that the grudge I hold against him would do her no good and that it will bring me endless unhappiness? No. My mother would not have chosen to die alone if she had known how Hiroshi would beat me and threaten my life. If my mother had foreseen me crawling across the roof in the dark to practice my escape, she would have gone on living to protect me. Or else she would have despaired for both of us and tried to include me in her death. But even that would have been the result of love gone wrong.

I have long forgiven my mother for having considered, at least for a short while, taking my life as well as hers. The anger I felt at her for that, and for leaving me, was an obstacle I could overcome because I knew she had loved me. It's a different story with Hiroshi. With him, the obstacles stand alone, without any love. I cannot say that I will forgive him for what he did in the past; nor can I say that I will overlook his faults and offenses because there are other things I like about him. In the end, the things he did to hurt me are the only things I know about him. They hang between us like the smoke from his cigarettes—constant, ever growing. If I removed the smoke, there would be nothing behind it except his mouth blowing out more smoke.

I turn away from the dark room. The view floats toward me like a net of light. My back against the door, I sit down again. In three days, when I am back in Wisconsin, I will miss these mountains, the bay, my old school, the clustered lights. I might regret the way I left— with just as much resentment as before. Still, nothing can cancel out my anger. My father is sixty-four. Most likely, his health will never be the same after the surgery. He will never again play rugby or stay up drinking all night with his friends. But I cannot feel genuine pity or concern for him. I cannot feel the loss of a relationship, warmth, or love that we never had in the first place. I cannot make myself believe that I will regret my failure to make peace with him. What I regret instead is the loss of this city—how I had to leave it thirteen years ago because of him. That's what I keep thinking about instead of peace, forgiveness, or even courtesy and fairness toward my father.

The breeze continues to stir the darkness around me. I remember Hiroshi saying, at the restaurant, that he was anxious to go to bed early. Perhaps he is already sleeping. It's foolish of me to try to imagine him sitting in the kitchen, regretting the past. More likely, he is snoring in the room where he slept through my visit last week and got up only to criticize me for not knowing the way back to Sylvia's house. No matter when I talk to him, and how, he will always disappoint me, always fill me with new resentment. If I were ever to make peace, it would be with that fact, in my own mind, not with him. I continue to scan the map of light below me. I don't go back into the house. It is too late to call him, to say anything at all.

The Child of Wisdom

At eleven o'clock the next morning, Friday, I am sitting on the steps in front of Sylvia's house waiting for my friend Miya. Heat vapors are rising from the ground under the orange trees. The rainy season is slowly coming to an end. In the neighbors' yard, the pomegranate trees have bloomed. The red flowers are ruffled and almost artificial looking, like the paper roses we made to decorate the stage for school plays. Miya is late, as usual. She is probably just leaving her apartment right now.

During my last semester at Kobe Jogakuin, Miya gave me a ride to school every morning. Always ten or fifteen minutes late, she would speed up the hill, park in the lot reserved for visitors, and never get a ticket. We would run to our British drama class and get in, barely on time. Paul Bennett, who taught the class, locked the classroom door promptly at nine and did not let latecomers in.

During our middle and high school years at Kobe Jogakuin, Miya and I had been close friends with other girls who played on sports teams. There were about twenty of us who practiced after school, walked together to the train station, and sometimes stopped on the way for coffee. Though none of us played team sports in college, we still met for lunch or studied together in the library. When I left for the States, at the beginning of our junior year in college, all of those friends wrote to me every month. Within a year and a half, they were sending me news of their wedding plans.

In February of my senior year, Machiko, a friend I had been particularly close to, wrote, "I finally feel settled and at peace. I can't believe that just a few years ago, I used to lie awake all night worrying about my future. How silly I was back then. Now that I am engaged, I don't have those terrible ups and downs of emotions and I'm grateful for this change." Reading her letter on a snow-covered path between the mail room and my dormitory at Rockford, I knew I could never write back to her. She had written as though the whole struggling part of her life were now ended, when mine was only beginning. I had decided, by then, to go to graduate school to study writing. I expected the next few years to be full of hard work. I had just had my first short story accepted for publication, and I could not forgive Machiko for thinking of her marriage as the crowning achievement of her life.

In the next few years, I lost touch with all the friends from our group except for Miya, who kept writing to me, whether I responded or not. She must have written three or four letters for every one I sent to her.

The door opens behind me, and Cadine steps out.

"Someone's on the phone for you," she says. "She only speaks Japanese. She kept saying your name."

I follow her back into the house, thinking that Miya must have gotten lost or even decided to cancel our plans. Cadine hands me the phone in the hallway.

A high and clipped voice says *a chotto,* "well, anyway."

It's my stepmother. She gets right to the point. "I can't go to dinner with you and Kazumi. I already called her. She gave me your number at your gaijin friend's house."

"Fine," I say. I cover the receiver and turn to Cadine, who is still standing next to me. "Could you do me a favor? Can you watch out for my friend Miya so she knows she's come to the right house? She should be here any minute."

"Okay." Cadine puts on her shoes and runs out the door.

On the phone, my stepmother is saying, "I came back from Hokkaido just a while ago. We're leaving for the hospital as soon as your father's ready. He's packing a few things now." She clears her throat. "I'm going to stay with him instead of going out to dinner. He says it's not necessary because all they'll do is prepare him for surgery. But I'm his wife. What would the doctors think if I weren't there?"

"I understand."

"I got you something from Hokkaido." She sighs as though I had made an imposition, even though I never asked her for a gift. "I hear you and Kazumi are going to Akiko's hospital tomorrow."

"Yes."

"Well, I'm glad Akiko changed her mind about seeing you after all. It would have been a shame for you to come all this way and not see her. She must have postponed the visit as long as possible to avoid the intrusion, but at least she's decided to see you. That's something. Just be careful not to overstay your welcome. Be sure to leave early."

I have an urge to simply put down the receiver, but I don't.

"Anyway, I'll drop off your gift with Kazumi on the way to the hospital. She can give it to you tomorrow. Their house is a little out of our way, of course, but it's all right. We'll just have to leave twenty minutes earlier. Anyway, your father and I don't expect you to be at the hospital for him. If you'd rather visit Akiko, we understand. Why should we ask you to sit and wait while he's in surgery? Hospital chairs are always uncomfortable."

"You didn't have to get me anything from Hokkaido," I tell her.

"You probably won't even like it. It's a set of jewelry. Earrings and a necklace made of milkstone. That's the special product of Hokkaido; you know, they make it by boiling milk and cooling it so the milk fat turns into a gem. I thought the jewelry was quite stylish."

"So milkstone is boiled milk fat?"

"You can give them away if you don't like them. I never know what to get you. Our tastes are so different. We have nothing in common. But you can always stay at our house if you need a place."

"I'd better go," I interrupt. "I'm going out with a friend in a minute. She might be outside right now." I pause and add, saying each word slowly and clearly, "Please tell Father that I wish him the best on his surgery." I let a moment pass, to make sure she heard, but hang up before she can respond.

Outside, Miya and Cadine are standing on the steps. Cadine sees me first and says, "There you are." She runs back into the house before I can introduce them.

"I must have scared her. I was trying to think of something to say, but nothing came to my mind." Miya laughs a little, a dimple on each of her cheeks. She is wearing pale green eyeshadow, light pink lipstick outlining her small mouth. Her hair is shoulder length, curled slightly to frame her face. "I haven't spoken any English since college," she says.

"I'm sorry. I was talking to my stepmother on the phone."

We begin to walk toward her blue Mazda parked across the street. Miya's long green linen dress swishes around her legs. She is wearing green high heels to match.

We get into the car and sit down.

"You haven't changed at all," we say simultaneously as we close the doors and then burst out laughing. With her fingers, she smoothes the wide ruffles around the square neckline of her dress, the same kind of dress she used to wear in college.

I have not been expecting her to look like this. When she got married, during my first semester in graduate school, she sent me pictures of herself in the traditional bridal kimono, her head bent under a huge wig of upswept hair and white cloth. Her face, painted white with rice powder, looked like a doll's face with the eyes and the mouth penciled in. She had looked more like herself, I thought, when she had played boys' roles in our high school plays. Even her going-away outfit, a mauve two-piece suit and a pillbox hat, seemed staged. She was like someone from a different period of history, Jackie Kennedy in the early sixties. The few pictures she sent me shortly after, of herself and her husband playing golf, didn't take away this impression. They were too perfectly dressed for their parts: white shirts and pants, cotton sweaters with varsity stripes. Now, ten years later, she looks more like before. This is such a relief that I almost want to thank her.

"Your hair's longer," Miya says as she starts the car. "It suits you."

When I first went to Kobe Jogakuin in seventh grade, I still wore my hair the way my mother had liked: straight down to my waist. After my stepmother came and I cut my hair, my friends were always trying to talk me into growing it back. But every time my hair got past the tips of my earlobes, my stepmother began to complain about finding shed hair around the house. No matter how often I swept or vacuumed the floor, she found the one or two strands I had missed and said, "I don't know anyone whose hair sheds so much." She grimaced to show her distaste—as far as she was concerned, the excessive hair shedding was another of my shortcomings. After two or three weeks of her constant complaining, I would go to the corner barbershop and say, "Cut my hair as short as you can." The old man there would chop it off so what was left stood straight up from my head like bristles on a kitchen scrub brush.

"My hair looked terrible when it was short," I tell Miya now as we drive down the hill.

"But you still looked all right because you had such natural good looks. I used to envy that. If I had gotten my hair cut so short, I would have looked ridiculous. You still looked pretty in a dramatic way."

"I never thought about it like that."

"But everybody thought so. Remember the red wide-brimmed hat you used to wear? Yoshiko and I were walking home one day in eighth grade, and we could see you ahead of us. Yoshiko stopped in the middle of our conversation and said, 'You know, if any one of us wore that hat, people would just laugh at us. How can Kyoko look so good in that?' "

I laugh, surprised that Miya would remember my hat.

At the bottom of the hill, Miya turns west to get on the highway toward downtown. "I drive here often," she says. "I give my husband a ride to work when he oversleeps."

Cars and trucks are zipping by. Trying to merge, we seem to be driving right into their path. One of the cars slows down to let us in. Miya smiles, waves to the driver, a man in a blue business suit.

"I don't think I can drive here," I say. "I'm used to driving on the other side of the road."

I didn't learn to drive until I was in America, though most of our friends took driving lessons at eighteen as part of what is called Bride Training—acquiring skills to marry well and be a good housewife. The other lessons, all of them expensive, were in flower arrangement, tea ceremony, European and Japanese sewing, various types of gourmet cooking. Though I had no desire for that kind of training, I was envious of my friends, whose parents were so eager to spend money on them while, at least once every month, my father threatened to stop paying my tuition. He said that going to college was making me even more selfish than before. "It's too bad you're not the kind of person who wants to learn tea ceremony," my stepmother said from time to time, though she never offered me the opportunity.

"Too bad you're so different." I wanted to have parents who would offer me Bride Training so I could decline it and be irritated by their misguided expression of love.

In ten minutes, Miya and I are downtown. We drive into the parking garage below the Daimaru department store, where my mother and I used to shop. The exit of the parking garage leads us into the basement level of the store, the gourmet food section: bottles of wine, blocks of cheese, chocolate, and pastry are displayed behind glass. The smell of coffee reminds me of how my mother and I used to visit coffee shops in the middle of our shopping. Our favorite place was on the roof of another department store overlooking the bay, where we had tea and cake and counted the ships in port.

"So where do you want to go?" Miya asks after we come up a set of stairs to the street level.

"I don't know. How about you?"

"No, you choose. I can come back here any time."

"Okay. How about Gaylord?" I mention one of the Indian restaurants. "Is that still there?"

"Yes. I went there in the spring with my husband and his friends from the Jaycees."

"Jaycees? The Junior Chamber of Commerce?"

She nods.

"I didn't know they had Jaycees in Japan."

"Sure they do. My husband was elected vice president of the local chapter. He has a meeting tonight."

We cross the street to Kokusai Kankan, the International Hall, and go down the stairs to the basement. Gaylord is to our right with its bright red door, a tapestry of Indian elephants hanging above the entrance. In the dark interior, everything looks exactly as I remember, candles flickering on the black tables against wine-red walls. A woman in a sari seats us in plush red chairs. Only a few of the tables are occupied. The waiter, an East Indian man, takes our order in Japanese and bows to us.

While we wait for our food, Miya updates me on what our friends have been doing. She has kept in touch with all of our close friends and a lot of people who had simply been classmates. Listening to her, I begin to miss everyone—even those classmates I hadn't particularly liked. Our graduating class from high school had only one hundred and fifty girls, all of whom had attended Kobe Jogakuin since seventh grade. There wasn't anyone I didn't know well.

Unlike the girls who attended public schools, we never used *keigo*—the polite and honorific language. We talked as though we were sisters or cousins, calling one another by our first names or nicknames, while the public school girls used the polite combination of the family name and the suffix *san,* the equivalent of "Miss." Their polite talk—which we overheard on the train or at athletic meets—reduced us to fits of giggling. My mother, who had attended a girls' school before the war, had addressed her friends informally also. Even at forty she and her best friend called each other Oshi-chan and Taka-chan, as though they were still kids.

"Yoshimi and I get together once every month," Miya says, mentioning a girl who used to take my photographs because she liked my eyes. "We usually invite several other people so it's like a class reunion. A lot of people got married and moved to Tokyo. The rest of us are really happy to see one another."

The waiter brings out large platters of food and goes away.

"I went to Shima-chan's wedding in April," Miya says. "I told you that she'd been divorced, right?"

"No."

"Well, she was. Her second husband seems like a nice man. He just graduated from college, but he's not like other really young guys." Cutting her chicken with her knife, Miya meets my eyes and then looks down. I know what she wants me to understand without saying it: Shima-chan's husband is much younger than she, but it's okay.

Miya smiles and then brings the fork up to her mouth with her left hand. She is eating in the way we were taught—using the fork in the left hand, the knife in the right, and never putting down either except to pick up the water glass or bread. I'm cutting up my spinach pakora with a fork in my right hand, eating like an American, but she doesn't seem to mind.

"Both Shima-chan and Yamako were married a very short time and had no children," Miya says, "so their divorces were simple. I hear Yamako is engaged now to someone from the hospital where she works. She's a surgeon, and now she and her fiancé want to go into private practice together."

Miya picks up her glass and sips the water.

Maybe things are changing after all. In high school, none of us had parents who had been divorced. We didn't know any woman who had been married more than once, even if she had been widowed at an early age. When we went to college and studied with a professor who had been divorced and lived with her parents, we were in awe of her. "She was married only for a few months," we used to whisper to each other, as though there were something almost romantic about her life. "She left her husband because she was unhappy." Though this woman was only in her early forties and very attractive, we would have been amazed if she had gotten remarried, especially to a younger man.

"Everyone's proud of you," Miya says. "You're a professor. You teach American kids how to write English."

"I don't think it's so special."

"I'm not surprised. You were always smart." She breaks a tiny piece off her nan, steam rising from her fingers.

"So tell me about your tutoring jobs," I ask.

"Oh, it's nothing." She shrugs. "You are a real teacher. I just help a few high school students who are having trouble at school."

"That's hard work. How many students do you have?"

"Five right now."

"One at a time?"

She nods. "I have someone every night except Fridays and Sundays. Tonight is one of my free nights."

"Do they come to your apartment, or do you go to their houses?"

"They come to my place after school and stay till eight or nine. My husband is pretty good about it. He doesn't mind if I can't cook dinner till they're gone. If it's really late, he goes out alone to eat so I don't have to cook. He's very easygoing." Miya tears another piece off her nan. "Maybe it's because we don't have children." She lowers her voice. "Because we can't." She smiles, the slight upturn of pursed lips that says, *It's okay, don't worry.* She takes a sip of water and adds, "When Machiko comes back from Tokyo to visit her parents, she brings her two boys. She's planning to have another baby so she can try for a daughter. When I see her, I feel envious. Otherwise, I'm used to it."

In college, when she worked part-time at a boutique, Miya put a small amount of money every month in a separate savings account. She said it was for her children's college fund. *How does she know that she'll get married and have kids?* I wondered then. *What if she doesn't meet anyone she likes?* I was saving money myself, to go to graduate school. My plans included only myself while hers included other people—other people she hadn't met yet. Now it seems so sad that she ended up not having children after all. I lift my glass and take a sip of water, wondering what to say without offering unwanted sympathy or consolation.

"We all have some expectations that don't come about," Miya says. She straightens out the coaster with her fingers so that her glass is sitting right in the center.

"Yes," I add. "That's how life is." As I say this, I understand that such platitudes are meant to comfort without going into the painful specifics. If I lived here and saw my friends often, I would learn to say these things at the right time, without being prompted. Knowing how to offer comforting words without unnecessary intrusion would be part of learning to speak Japanese like an adult.

By the time we finish eating, all the other tables are empty. The waiter takes away our plates and brings two cups of coffee. I take a sip of mine and then add two sugar cubes. Even at an Indian restaurant, the coffee is Japanese—much too bitter to drink by itself.

"So are you busy this afternoon?" Miya asks. It's almost three.

"No. I was supposed to have dinner with my stepmother, but I don't have to. I have no particular plans."

"I talked to Hitomi last week," Miya says. "She wants to see you. Would you like to go to her house? She lives in Nishinomiya, close to my apartment."

"That sounds good."

"And tomorrow, can you meet Yoshiko, Hiroko, and me for a drink? It's your last night."

"I'm free in the evening."

"Good. I was hoping it would work out. I already canceled my tutoring appointment so I can come. Is there anyone else you want to see?"

"How about Toshiko?" I mention one of the two girls I used to walk home with from the train station. Last I heard, she had gotten a master's degree in philosophy. "Is she still in town?"

"She lives with her parents and teaches English at a women's college in Himeji."

"English? I thought her degree was in philosophy."

Miya shrugs. "There were no jobs for philosophers when she was looking. Because most of her reading was in English, she got a job teaching basic reading courses."

"Can we invite her?"

"Sure, and anyone else you'd like. I have a directory at home from the alumni office. Maybe you can look through that and see if there's anyone else."

We finish our coffee, pay the bill, and walk across the street to the department store. Miya stops in the aisles of the gourmet food section and says, "Let's get a cake to bring to Hitomi."

At the bakery counter, she points to a round strawberry cake behind glass. The clerk takes it out, puts it in a white box, and wraps it in glossy pink paper, finishing with a white ribbon tied into a huge butterfly bow. Miya hands her the money and then gives me the box.

"You carry it. But it's my treat."

She calls Hitomi from a pay phone before we go into the parking garage to find her car.

Hitomi comes to the door apologizing.

"I had to clean the bathtub while the boys were at school. I didn't have time to change." She is wearing old jeans and a faded blue T-shirt, her hair pulled back into a ponytail.

"Don't worry. I'm not exactly dressed up." I point to my denim shorts and purple T-shirt.

Outside, two men are standing on the neighbor's roof, pounding nails and ripping out the roof-slates.

"Come on in," Hitomi says. "The house is a mess. I have two boys in grade school. Did Miya tell you?"

I nod.

In the small kitchen, where we sit down around a dark brown table, I put the cake box in front of Hitomi.

"This is Miya's treat."

"A strawberry shortcake," Miya says, "from Daimaru."

"How kind of you. I'll make some tea." Hitomi jumps up from her chair to fill the kettle. After she turns on the stove, she opens the cupboard and rummages in there for a long time. Finally, she says, "I only have green tea, bancha, and Twinings English Breakfast tea. That's not a very good selection. Wait, maybe there's some more in the drawers."

"Hitomi, why don't you settle down?" Miya says. "Here, sit down. English Breakfast tea sounds fine. You don't have to find anything else."

"I don't know. Maybe I should make coffee instead. My tea's no good."

Miya sighs and turns to me. "Hitomi always gets this way when we come to visit. Relax, Hitomi. Sit down."

In her chair, Hitomi pulls at her ponytail to straighten it. Even with the windows closed, we can hear the pounding and ripping from next door.

"It's been such a long time," Hitomi says to me, blinking. "I really wanted to see you."

"I'm glad to see you, too." I say. She looks thinner than before, but otherwise, not that different: "Everyone looks the same."

The three of us look at one another and laugh.

After a while, Hitomi pushes her chair back and goes to the glass cabinet to take out a teapot, three cups and three saucers, a sugar bowl, all of them thin white porcelain with tiny pink rosebuds. "I'm sorry about the noise." She sits back down. "My neighbors are building an addition over the garage. It'll be darker in here when they're done." She sighs, gets up to check the water again, and sits down. "I get nervous when my friends visit me. I'm so happy to see them. I don't know what to do with myself."

"Come on," Miya scolds. "You make it sound as if we never visit you."

"I know, I know." Hitomi waves her hand in front of her face. "But I sit at home by myself all day otherwise. It's a treat to have company." She reaches out for the cake box. "Shall I open this now?"

"Go ahead." Miya nods.

Hitomi unties the ribbon, rolls it up, and sets it down on the table. The ribbon unrolls a little, the outer circles of white loosening up, while Hitomi unwraps the paper without tearing it, smoothes and folds it up. Tightening up the rolled ribbon, she puts it on top of the paper, right in the center. Only then does she open the box and say, "The cake looks wonderful. Thank you. Would you like some?" This is the Hitomi I remember: meticulous and correct. She used to get mad at me for being sloppy and careless.

By now, the water is boiling. Hitomi gets up, measures the tea into the pot, and tilts the kettle over it. She sets the timer for three minutes. Immediately, I remember Mrs. Sakai, the home ec teacher, telling us we should brew tea for no more and no fewer than three minutes. Otherwise the tea would be bland or bitter.

Hitomi and I had big arguments in ninth grade because I hated Mrs. Sakai and considered her unfair while Hitomi thought she was wonderful. Hitomi and her cooking group were Mrs. Sakai's favorites. They always got things done the fastest, with the least mess. Nothing my group did ever turned out. In our woks, vegetables would burn or be undercooked. Our bread rose too much and over-flowed in the oven or else turned into fist-sized rocks. We burned the shells for our cream puffs so there were holes in the bottom. When it came time to stuff them, we turned them upside down and put the cream in. No-need-to-cut cream puffs, we called them. Mrs. Sakai flunked us for not having baked a new batch, to get them right. She said we hadn't taken the assignment seriously enough. Turning the shells upside down had been my idea. Hitomi couldn't believe that I would try to get away with such sloppiness.

When the timer goes off, Hitomi pours the tea into our cups, cuts and serves the cake.

"Is the tea all right?" she asks, sitting down.

"It's great," I say.

As we drink and eat, Hitomi tells me about her husband and her two boys.

"But you've gotten married, too," she says to me at the end.

"Yes."

"Remember you used to say you would never get married or have kids?"

"Well, I was right about one."

She laughs. "You and I fought a lot in junior high school."

Back then, we drove each other crazy with our differences, even in the way we studied. I refused to do assignments that I thought were stupid and as a result, almost failed a few classes. Even when I did all my work, my performance was always spotty, and this infuriated Hi-tomi, who did well in everything. "You are so inconsistent," she yelled at me. "How can you almost fail your math test and get the highest marks in English and history both? You only study what you want." In return, I accused her of being a perfectionist, a hypocrite, even.

"Sometimes I couldn't believe we were such good friends," Hitomi says. "I was mad at you so often. But when I heard other girls criticizing you, I got mad at them. I defended you, even though these girls were saying the same things I said to you."

"I know. It was the same way with me."

Miya, who seldom fought with anyone, sips her tea and shakes her head.

Hitomi looks at the clock as she gets up to clear the plates. "My children are coming home soon. I want you to meet them. They're very fond of Miya, too."

"We'll wait for them and then leave," Miya says, "because you'll be busy once they get here."

"It's strange to have sons," Hitomi says, "after growing up with only girls. I didn't have brothers, and all my friends were girls. I didn't even go out with any other boy. My husband was my first boyfriend."

Hitomi was the first in our group to be engaged, in our sophomore year in college. By then, she and I never had arguments: we'd gotten more polite but more distant. One afternoon shortly after her engagement, we happened to take the same train home. She asked me what I had been up to. I said I was applying for a scholarship to finish my B.A. in the States, and that I hoped to be gone by the beginning of the following year. She told me about her fiancé, her Bride Training classes. Then she said, "Remember when we used to fight a lot? I think I was jealous of you. You were always so smart. I didn't want to admit you were smarter than I." We continued to talk about school and our other friends, smiling, speaking in quiet, polite voices. Her stop was before mine. After she got off and I continued to stand by the door, my eyes and throat hurt. I realized that I had been holding back tears. I wished she and I could have our big fights again. I wanted her to go on thinking she was smarter and better than I.

Now she turns to me and confides, "I had some trouble right after my second son was born. Seven years ago. Miya knows." She nods toward Miya.

"I didn't tell her anything," Miya says. "I wasn't sure if you'd want me to."

"Are you all right?" I ask.

She tilts her head sideways and smiles. "I'm okay now, but I wasn't then. I had a nervous breakdown. I couldn't leave the house, not even to walk to the corner grocery store. I sat on the couch all day crying. Every morning, I begged my husband not to go to work. As he stood in the doorway ready to go, I would grab his arm and try to pull him back into the house. I was afraid something bad was going to happen to him if he went out. One time, I ran after him in the driveway in my pajamas and then passed out. After that, my mother had to come and stay with me for three months. I had to see a doctor."

We are very quiet for a while.

"That was a long time ago," Hitomi says finally. "After I was well again, I thought about you. I knew you had been through a lot, in the time before we were friends."

"Hitomi, I'm sorry I didn't know," I say. That doesn't seem enough. I want to hug her or take her hand, which is curled around her teacup. Her wedding band is a little loose. She must have lost weight since her marriage. I pick up and put down my cup, trying to think of the right thing to say. I know Hitomi meant my mother's death when she referred to the time before we were friends. Though none of my friends at Kobe Jogakuin had known my mother, they had known that her death was an important fact about me. Now Hitomi is saying that, after her own trouble, she understood the pain I was carrying around back then. I want to thank her for thinking about me in that way, but I don't know how to say that without intruding. Still, I want her to see I got her point.

"My trouble, too, was a long time ago," I attempt, smiling just a little. "It's something I'll always remember. We've both been through a lot."

Hitomi nods. We look at each other and nod again.

Soon after, her boys come home. Running around the house and rolling on the floor, they tell us that they are airplanes dive-bombing enemy ships. Hitomi asks them to settle down and show Miya and me their schoolbooks and toys. They stop running around just long enough to empty the contents of their knapsacks on the tatami floor, talking all the time. Miya and I get ready to leave so Hitomi can start supper. She walks us to the car, followed by the kids.

"I'm sorry I can't go out with all of you tomorrow," she says over the noise of the construction. "But I'm glad to have seen you."

"I'll be back," I assure her. "Stay well."

As we drive away, I imagine her sitting in that kitchen day after day. It's half the size of my kitchen. She doesn't have much room to move around between the glass cabinet, the fridge, and the stove. I hope that the neighbor's addition will turn out to be smaller, that more sunlight than expected will continue to come through her windows.

Miya parks her car in a small lot in front of a gray stone building. I follow her up the stairs to the third floor. "It's very small. Don't expect much," she says as she turns the key and opens the door.

The room we walk into has a beige carpet, a brown couch, and a TV set near the door. On the opposite side, beyond a dining table and chairs, a doorway opens into a small kitchen. A narrow hallway connects the kitchen to the bathroom and the bedroom. The low ceiling is painted white.

"My parents-in-law own a big house in Osaka," Miya says as we sit down on the couch. "They want us to move in with them. I know that makes sense, but I don't want to give up this place, cramped as it is."

"Of course. It's your own place. Why should you give it up?"

Miya shrugs.

"You should never move if you don't want to." I realize that I am repeating Keiko's advice.

"You don't think I'm being selfish in wanting my own apartment?"

"No. I think it's only natural."

"Thanks." Miya smiles and gets up. "I should get the directory before I forget." She goes down the hallway to the bedroom and returns with a thick book with a blue cover.

We sit side by side on the couch, the directory open between us, looking first at the table of contents, which is arranged by years of graduation. Anyone who graduated from either the high school or the college of Kobe Jogakuin between 1935 and 1990 is listed. Miya finds the pages listing our graduating class from high school: 1975. Her name appears near the top as Miya Akatsuka. We are listed alphabetically according to our birth names; the current names, if different, are given in parentheses. Though I never sent anything to the alumni office, my name and business address are printed. I glance up and down the columns, remembering faces of classmates. In my mind, everyone is between eighteen and twenty.

"Remember Buko?" Miya points to one of the names. Next to it, the address says, "Hilton International: Kobe Office."

"Buko is the regional director for Hilton," Miya says. "She's a very important businesswoman."

"How did she get a job like that?"

"The year after you left, she transferred to a hotel management school in Switzerland. She came back fluent in English, French, and German. She has a good chance to be the next executive director for Hilton-Japan."

I try to imagine Buko as an important executive in a business suit, but I keep remembering her bangs cut straight across her forehead.

"Do you see her often?" I ask Miya.

"I ran into her a few months ago downtown. She was coming out of a health club where she swims during her lunch hour. I was just standing across the street. We went and had some coffee, before she had to go back to her office. She seemed very happy."

"Does she live in Kobe?"

"No, she stays with her parents in Ashiya when she's in town, which isn't often since she is always traveling on business. She's the only one left at home. Her brother and sister got married."

I look through the rest of the names, stopping once in a while to inquire about different classmates.

When I get to the end, I think of a friend who was a year older. "How about Chieko Seki?" I ask Miya. "I lost touch with her during my senior year at Rockford. Did she go on to graduate school?"

"Chieko? I didn't know her except through you."

"You don't hear anything about her?"

"No." Miya shakes her head. "I don't know."

"I should look her up." I turn the pages forward to the graduating class of '74. Chieko graduated with them and then went to Kyoto National University to study psychology. In between, she took a year off to study for the entrance exams. That was my senior year in high school. I had gotten back from Arizona, where I had spent a whole year not having to worry about going home to Hiroshi and Michiko every night. It seemed almost unbearable to be back home again, hearing Michiko nagging him about me downstairs, late at night, until he came up to my room to hit me. At school, too, things were different. My friends had gone through some transformations while I was away.

During our sophomore year in high school, we had all worn jeans and T-shirts to school, and no one had dated boys. When I returned from Arizona, my friends were wearing dresses or silky blouses and long skirts to school; they got their hair permed and on weekends went to mixers with boys from the nearby boys' schools. On the few occasions when I went with them, boys looked at us across the dark room while the music played on. Eventually, they would start to walk up and down in front of us, stopping to take a closer look. I could tell by the way they walked that some of them were a little drunk. When a boy asked me to dance, I could smell a sickly sweet combination of alcohol and hair oil or aftershave. The boys I danced with seldom talked to me—except to ask me if I wanted to dance more or if I was tired. When some of them called me a week later, I couldn't match the names with their faces. I always turned down the dates.

All my friends, except Chieko Seki, thought I was silly and perhaps even conceited. Because Chieko had spent her junior year in Boston, she had come back, the year before, to the same thing. She understood when I said I missed the boys I had dated in Arizona—with whom I had watched movies, gone hiking, or helped on community projects like recycling cans. She knew the kind of boys I was talking about: they were serious and talkative boys from our classes and church groups. We had discussed and even argued about books or politics or our own rebelliousness toward our families and teachers. No Japanese boy ever asked us what we thought of these subjects. Chieko and I met once a week in Ashiya to talk, to complain, and it was a relief for me to know I was not alone in being puzzled and irritated by the whole situation.

I should have thought about her earlier, I think as I page through the directory. Maybe I can still call her and ask her to meet us for a drink tomorrow. When I find the right page and am looking down the column, Miya suddenly reaches out and takes the directory away from me.

"Let me see this a minute." Her eyes scan the names. She turns forward a few pages, finds whatever she was looking for, and closes the book. She doesn't say anything.

"What's going on?" I ask.

"Actually," she says, "I did hear something about her."

"About Chieko?"

"Yes. I heard that she passed away."

"She what?"

Miya shakes her head. "I'm sorry," she says.

I reach toward her. "I want to see that for myself," I tell her.

She hesitates.

"Please."

When she hands over the directory, I find the page I was on before and go down the columns. Her name is not listed where it should be in the alphabetical order. I turn the pages and find what Miya has seen: a single entry at the end of the class. There Chieko's name is printed without an address, a black dot to its left. The word above it, *eiminsha,* is a euphemism for the dead. Literally, it means, "a person who sleeps eternally."

I close the book and put it back on the coffee table. "When did this happen?" I ask.

"I think it was the year after we graduated from college."

"Was Chieko sick?"

"I'm not sure." Miya frowns. "I didn't hear the details. I don't know anything for sure."

The year we were meeting for coffee, Chieko had long hair parted in the middle, a big smile that softened the square outline of her jaws. I used to love the way she laughed, tipping her head backward a little. Her name meant "a child of wisdom."

"She must have been only twenty-two," I tell Miya. "That's so young. She was just a year older than us, and now we're in our thirties."

"I'm sorry," Miya says. "You liked her a lot."

Miya gets up, goes to the kitchen, and brings us each a glass of iced tea. As we drink the tea in silence, I know that Miya took the directory from me to prevent me from coming upon Chieko's death on my own, in print. She wanted to break the news herself, but because she wasn't friends with Chieko, she doesn't want to talk about her death. She doesn't want to pass on information that might only be hearsay or unfounded rumor.

"So who would know more?" I ask after a while.

"Maybe Kanko." She names a girl Toshiko and I used to walk home with. "Kanko was studying psychology at the national university at the same time, you remember. She's in Kyoto. Here, let me copy her number." She opens the directory again, copies the number, and hands it to me. I fold it and stick it into my pocket.

"Are you okay?" Miya asks me. "I wish I didn't have to tell you."

"I'm okay, but it's a big surprise."

"I remember she was very smart and considerate," Miya says. "I wish I'd have known her better."

Drinking my iced tea in silence, I keep looking at the blue directory on the coffee table and thinking of the way it lists the dead with black dots next to their names, no addresses given. It's as if they were floating in the air forever like lost balloons or kites, unable to come back down to the earth.

At eight o'clock, when Miya drops me off at Sylvia's house, Vince is waiting for me in the kitchen with Sylvia and Cadine. He has to leave town tomorrow on business and won't be back until after I'm gone. I don't want to say good-bye right away, so the four of us sit in the kitchen talking. Cadine and I check on the caterpillars, which have completed their chrysallis. Brown and mottled, they look like dry leaves. It's hard to imagine that anything could come out of those shells.

After Vince leaves, I go to the upstairs phone to call Kanko. She answers on the first ring.

"Hi, Kanko. This is Kyoko. I'm in Kobe. Miya gave me your number."

She is speechless, no doubt with surprise.

"I'm sorry to call so suddenly," I apologize.

"No. It's good to hear from you. Are you staying long?"

"I'm leaving the day after tomorrow. I should have called sooner. I'm meeting Miya, Yoshiko, Hiroko, and Toshiko tomorrow night for drinks. You're invited, too."

"I don't think I can make it. My husband and I live on the other side of Kyoto. I seldom get into Kobe. But we can at least talk on the phone. I've been wondering about you. Tell me what you've been up to."

For a while, we exchange news about ourselves. Since she got her master's degree, Kanko has been teaching at a women's college in Kyoto. Last year, she got married to another psychologist, who is working on his Ph.D.

"We'll look for jobs when he finishes next year," she says. "It's hard for both of us to get jobs. But I want to work at least part-time, after all the time I put into getting my degree."

"That can be hard, too. Some of my friends in the States have part-time jobs where their husbands have full-time jobs. They often feel that they are treated more as someone's wife than as a colleague."

"I have already thought about that. I want to go back for my Ph.D. after my husband finishes his."

"Good for you."

"At least," she says, "I'm lucky to be teaching in my area. I talk to Toshiko on the phone every couple of weeks. She doesn't even get to teach her specialty."

We talk some more about our work. Then I finally say, "There's something I want to ask you."

"What is that?"

"It's about Chieko Seki. You and she were in the same master's program."

"Yes. She did some research for a professor I had classes with."

"Did you see her much—you know, the year she died?"

"I saw her some, but not all the time. We had mutual friends, though we weren't in any of the same classes."

"You know she and I were friends my senior year in high school, the year she took off to study. She was very kind to me. She took time off from her studying to meet me for coffee."

"She was a very generous person," Kanko says.

"I need to know what happened to her, if you know."

She doesn't say anything.

So I ask her what I already know from her silence, from Miya's silence.

"Did Chieko kill herself?"

Kanko still hesitates.

"Was it suicide?" I ask again.

"Yes," she answers, her voice lowered.

"Do you know why?"

"I think it had something to do with love." She pauses. "I don't know the particulars because she didn't tell me anything herself. But the friends we both had said she was in love with someone and it didn't work out. That's all I know."

It could have been another graduate student, I think, or even her professor, the one she was doing research for. I imagine Chieko in a white lab coat, in a large desolate-looking room. I will never know what her life was like that last year.

"I ran into her on the train," Kanko says, "about two weeks before her death. She looked run-down, like she hadn't been sleeping well. We talked about how tough graduate school was. My stop was before hers. As I was getting off, she patted me on the shoulder and said, 'We'll both be all right. We'll hang in there.' I said I would call her and we would have coffee. After I heard the news of her death, I kept remembering that train ride. I didn't realize how unhappy she must have been. I thought she was just tired."

"That's how it is," I tell her. "We never know until it's too late. I know what that's like."

We talk about other things for a while and then hang up, promising to see each other on my next visit.

As I stand by the window after the phone call, the neighborhood Kanko, Toshiko, and I used to live in is to my left, lit up—like the other hillside neighborhoods—in white residential lights. In ninth grade, Kanko and Toshiko played on the basketball team while I went out for volleyball. Every afternoon around five-thirty, we took the same train to our station and walked home, first stopping at a bakery for a large bag of cinnamon rolls. During the twenty-minute walk up the hill, we ate the rolls, their sticky spirals unraveling in our fingers. Sometimes Kanko and Toshiko were mad at each other because of something that had happened at practice. They gave each other the silent treatment, each of them keeping a separate conversation with me as I walked in the middle with the bag of rolls and handed them out one by one. Toshiko left first because her house was the closest to the station. After Kanko and I walked another block and she went into her house, I had to turn the corner and walk the last few blocks alone. When my house came into view, I felt a sinking sensation in the pit of my stomach. School was a day-long break from the house I had to return to every night. Now it seems strange for all three of us to have become teachers when I remember them—and myself, too—as young girls too hungry to walk home without those sticky rolls. If she hadn't killed herself, Chieko, too, might have been a teacher or a researcher, trying to find a position she could be happy in. She and I might have talked over the phone or met for coffee and complained about our jobs.

As I step away from the window, I catch a weak reflection of the room, my own face, blurred over the light of the city below. Turning away and getting ready for bed, I imagine Chieko riding a train. She is on one of those expresses that used to pass by the platform where we waited for an all-stop. The express trains always slowed down a little on their approach so that, for a second, we could catch the faces of the passengers in their lit interior. Her long hair falling over the shoulders of her gray tweed coat, Chieko stands against the glass doors, waving. She is smiling and telling me, telling Kanko and Toshiko, telling everyone to hang in there, carry on.

Milkstone

When Kazumi and I enter her hospital room on Saturday afternoon, my aunt Akiko is sitting up in her pink pajamas, her hair brushed back into a neat bun.

"I'm glad you came to see me," she says to me. "Let's go to the lobby." She points to the other patient, who is sleeping.

Kazumi and I help her out of the bed, and together we walk to the lobby and sit down on the yellow couch, Akiko in the middle.

"You look well," I say.

She reaches for my hand, lets go, and reaches for it again. "I wanted to get well fast so I could see you."

"My father never told me about your illness."

She lets go of my hand and shakes her head. My father is undergoing surgery at another hospital right now, doctors in blue or white surgical garments bending over him.

"He made it sound like his own surgery was nothing serious," I add. "He said the doctors wanted to keep him for nine weeks so they could make money."

"Your father has turned out to be a strange character," Akiko says. "I can't believe he is actually my brother."

Kazumi pats her shoulder.

"I don't wish him ill," Akiko explains. "But I don't feel related to him in the least."

"Did Kazumi tell you about our dinner with him on Thursday?"

"She did."

"He was in a hurry the whole time," I tell her anyway. "As soon as we sat down, he wanted to leave early to get some sleep. I wasn't surprised, of course. Last week, when I visited him and Michiko at their place, he got up from the table in the middle of our conversation and went to take a nap."

"I don't know how I ended up with a brother like that," Akiko sighs.

"Maybe I shouldn't complain because I wasn't very nice to him, either," I admit. "Both he and Michiko could tell that I wasn't eager to see them. I did nothing to hide my reluctance."

"What do they expect?" Akiko's voice rises a pitch in indignation. "After the way they treated you, why should you be eager to see them? If they want to improve things, it's up to them to start."

"You really think so?"

"Of course. He is your father."

"That doesn't mean much in our family," Kazumi says.

Akiko wrinkles her nose. "I don't know how I ended up with these men. Father, brother, husband, all three of them such insensitive people. I'm glad I didn't have a son."

"There's something I want to ask you about my father."

Akiko turns to me and waits.

"I don't want to upset you," I hesitate. "Maybe I'll ask another time."

"I'm all right now. Ask me anything."

"Okay. It's about when you were in Hiroshima—you, Grandfather, Grandmother, and your brother Tsuyoshi." I pause.

She nods for me to go on.

"My father was in Kyoto then, right? Did he come back to Hiroshima to find out what happened to you all? My aunt Michiyo said that most people who had families went back to find out. Otherwise, they wouldn't have known for weeks. How about my father? Did he come back?"

Akiko leans forward and takes a deep breath. She glances at Kazumi and then at me. "No. He didn't."

"Why not?" I ask, not at all surprised, really.

Akiko frowns slightly. "He never gave any reasons. He was living in a rooming house. The landlady, who was a friend of our family's, later said that she had offered him money to make the trip. But he didn't come."

"So, how did he find out what had happened, then?"

"He got my father's letter after a man showed up at our house carrying Tsuyoshi's school cap with his name and address sewn on the inside. This man had seen Tsuyoshi fall down and die by one of the rivers downtown. He could do nothing but bring the cap and tell us."

"When did Tsuyoshi die?" I ask. "The day of the bomb?"

"No, the next morning."

So Tsuyoshi hadn't died instantaneously, as I wished when I saw the displays at the memorial museum.

"This man came about a week after the bomb. He took one look at my mother and knew that he had come to the right house. Tsuyoshi looked a lot like my mother." Akiko sighs. "Anyway, my father wrote to your father and said Tsuyoshi was dead and we were coming back to Kyoto as soon as we could."

"My father didn't travel to Hiroshima to be with you first?"

"No, he sent us a letter saying he would wait for us, since we were coming back anyway."

"So that's how it was." He had just sat in his cramped room waiting for news. What would he have done if a letter never came? How long would it have taken him to assume that his family was dead? Would he have gone back then, or would he have considered it unnecessary? If it had been my mother whose family was in Hiroshima, she would have taken the first available train as far as it went and walked the rest of the way into the heart of disaster.

"I just remembered something your father said." Akiko's eyes tear up.

"Don't tell us if it makes you sad." I put my hand on her shoulder. Her pajama top has a fuzzy nap.

"He told us that after hearing about the bomb, he wondered what would happen to the life insurance if we had all died but the records had been burned as well. He didn't know how he would be able to collect the money. Why would he say such a thing to us?"

Kazumi pulls a white handkerchief out of her purse and hands it to Akiko. It has lace edges like the ones my mother used to carry. Long ago, Kazumi and I had handkerchiefs with cartoons printed on them, while our mothers had white ones with lace or small embroidery.

"Did he say that right after the war?" I ask.

"A few years afterward. We were celebrating New Year's Day. He had had one cup of sake, and he was laughing when he said it." Akiko presses the handkerchief to the corners of her eyes. "I don't know why your mother married such a strange character."

"Maybe he was different back then, at least to her. Aunt Keiko said he used to be very attentive. He actually seemed like a kind person, even."

"No," Akiko insists. "He was always selfish and cold." She presses the handkerchief to her eyes one last time and then puts it in the breast pocket of her pajama top. "I don't know why your mother didn't see that right away. She was so smart about everything else. She could have married anyone else."

Kazumi pats the back of her hand.

"Still," Akiko continues, "I'm glad she married my brother and had you and Jumpei. She was such a good friend to me."

"You were a good friend to her, too."

A few months before her death, my mother wrote in her journal about how Akiko had come to visit her in the rain to cheer her up because she had sounded depressed over the phone. They sat in the living room in their thick sweaters and ate the hothouse strawberries Akiko had brought, listening to Takako's old Doris Day and Peggy Lee albums. The strawberries were large and sweet. They reminded my mother of fairy-tale cures: dew from a moonflower, oranges in the dead of winter, an apple from a snow-covered mountain—always something nearly impossible to get. She told Akiko that sometimes she wished she could die in her sleep. "Please don't say such a thing," Akiko asked her. "You can't die and leave me alone. Promise you'll grow old with me." Outside, the rain was turning into sleet. The trees looked gray and dead forever. *Akiko-san, daisuki,* Takako wrote in her journal: "I love Akiko." She promised that she would try to cheer up.

"I was afraid you and Jumpei might forget her," Akiko says. "Your father and grandfather wouldn't let me speak about her in front of you."

"I never forgot anything, but Jumpei says he was too young. He scarcely remembers her."

Akiko pulls out the handkerchief again. "Jumpei didn't understand what death was. About a month after the funeral, he told me something. He said, 'I'm going to save a lot of money. Maybe I can buy her back when I grow up.' "

Nobody says anything for a while.

"Jumpei's famous savings," Kazumi says, trying for a light tone. "Remember Aunt Takako was worried about his turning into a miser? He was always counting the coins in his piggy bank. He got less allowance than we did, but he always had more money saved. You and I always spent everything we had."

Akiko puts away her handkerchief.

"I want to come back next summer to spend a few weeks with my mother's family," I tell her.

"Stay a few weeks with us," Akiko says.

"You don't have to worry about seeing Grandfather," Kazumi adds. "He'll be busy working."

Akiko grimaces. "He's eighty-six, and he won't quit working. He's afraid of going senile. He thinks work keeps him young."

"He's fussy and vain as ever. If I don't press his shirts the right way," Kazumi says, "or if I don't clean his room the way he likes, he calls me a freeloader."

"That's terrible."

"It's all right." Kazumi smiles. "My mother and I know he couldn't last a day without us. He doesn't even know how to make a cup of tea. So we just laugh to ourselves when he calls us names."

"I saw Grandfather only once," I tell Akiko. "I didn't even say good-bye to him."

"Don't worry about him or your father," Akiko says. "You don't have to see them or Michiko."

"Even Grandfather doesn't get along with Michiko," Kazumi says. "She takes offense at the smallest things."

"She's always been like that," I say. "She used to get mad at me for the most trivial things and then threaten to leave my father. I doubt that she really meant to leave him. Maybe she was just trying to make him angry at me."

Akiko holds my hand. "If I had known how mean she was to you, I would have done something. I would have talked to your grandfather every day till he broke down and let me take you back. I'm really sorry I didn't do that."

I squeeze her hand and then let go. "It isn't your fault. You didn't know what was going on. None of us did. I even believed Michiko when she said I was bothering you by visiting you every Sunday. I should have talked to you instead of listening to her."

"Kazumi told me," Akiko says. "That still made me angry, after all this time. Michiko lied to me, too. When you stopped coming, she said you were busy with friends, and that you were a teenager now and didn't want to spend time with relatives."

"My friends were with their families on Sundays. I went to the library alone."

"It turned out all right," Akiko says, trying to smile. "I'm glad you were able to get away from Hiroshi and Michiko. They've done you nothing but harm. You owe them nothing."

We begin to talk about my life in Wisconsin. I don't tell them how out of place I often feel in Green Bay. I don't mention the long winter months and the bleak restlessness they bring. What good will it do to worry Akiko and Kazumi about my life in a place they can only imagine vaguely? For a long time, I have thought my closeness to people was defined by my ability to talk about what bothered me, what made me unhappy. But that isn't the only thing. The closeness I feel with my aunt and my cousin, my mother's family, and my old friends is based more on unspoken trust or respect. No matter where and how I decide to live, all these people I love will assume that I am doing my best, that my life is good, that they can be proud of me in some way. Unlike my father and stepmother, they will not criticize me for where I choose to live and with whom, what job I hold, how much money I make. They will never ask pointed questions about my relationships, my qualifications, my income, or anything. Their politeness, their desire not to intrude or criticize, is a relief. If I were unhappy where I was, and moved, my friends here would shrug their shoulders and say, "Well, a lot happens to a person in her life," or "It's all part of experience." Many of them have already been unhappy or dissatisfied. When we were young, I felt that tragedy had set me apart from them. That was true back then, but it's no longer the case. Though I haven't been part of my friends' lives in the last thirteen years, time and events have reduced the barriers. Akiko, too, is talking to me differently now, without the restrictions imposed by her father and brother, because I am no longer twenty. We can speak more easily now, even though we haven't been speaking to each other for so long. This is a comfort: time solves some of our problems even when we haven't been consciously trying to cope with them.

The nurse comes in and hands Akiko a small tray with several pills and a glass of water. Akiko takes the pills one at a time, carefully swallowing the water after each. It's four o'clock.

"I'm going to leave and let you rest," I suggest. "Maybe Kazumi can have supper with me before I go back to pack my bags. I'm going out with some of my high school friends, but that's not till later."

"Let me walk you to the elevator," Akiko offers.

"No, we'll walk you to your room."

"I can walk there by myself. I've been walking every day. It's good exercise."

Kazumi and I stand up first and reach down. Akiko puts one hand in each of ours and leans forward. We walk slowly down the hall, holding hands. At the elevator, she lets go.

"I'm so glad I saw you," she says. "I missed you."

"I missed you, too. Get well soon. I'll see you next summer."

Kazumi and I get into the elevator and push the button for the first floor. The gray doors shut while Akiko is waving.

A couple of hours later, after our supper at a coffee shop, Kazumi and I have to say good-bye at the train station in Ashiya. She has to walk home to get the house ready for our grandfather.

Standing at the gate, I can't believe we are actually saying good-bye, that in about thirty hours, I will be back in Wisconsin. Kazumi and I will not go on seeing each other every weekend, the way our mothers did. "I would have felt like an orphan," Kazumi had said, "if something had happened to my mother." *Come and live with me,* I want to say. *Let me take you out of here.* But she won't, and I know it.

"Kai-chan," I say, using her childhood name. "Kai-chan, daisuki." *I love you.*

She starts crying. I lean forward and hold her.

"I'll be back soon," I say.

"Be happy," she says.

"Seeing you was the best part of my trip," I tell her.

I don't want to let go. Still, I turn away and put the ticket in the slot. It makes a clicking sound, and the metal arm goes up on the other end. I begin to walk away. Kazumi is still waving at me when I look back from the corner. I climb the steps to the platform, where the train is waiting. Soon it lurches forward and retraces the route between Ashiya and Kobe that we used to ride as children, going downtown in the identical dresses one of our mothers had sewn for us.

Back at Sylvia's house, I begin to look through my belongings: books and gifts I bought or was given, letters and kimonos from my grandmother's house, brochures and postcards from the places I've visited. I need to make piles of things to take with me on the plane, things to pack into boxes for Vince to send to me, things to throw out. I stick my hand inside my backpack and touch something hard. It's the package Michiko had dropped off with Kazumi. I had forgotten about it.

The glossy white wrapping paper I tear off has "Hokkaido" printed all over in blue. The necklace and the earrings are inside a clear plastic package. Shaped like lilies of the valley, they shine a glossy orange, the color of boiled shrimp in cooking magazines. The pamphlet inserted at the bottom explains how milk fat is boiled and cooled to form a paste, which is then carved and polished. The result is a dull shine like plastic. The earrings are clip-ons. Last year in New York, my stepmother noticed that I had gotten my ears pierced. "Very American," she commented, even though some women in Japan also have pierced ears.

"Our tastes are so different," she said on the phone yesterday. That was exactly what she said when I began to buy my own clothes in eighth grade, after she had thrown out the dresses my mother had made because they were too small for me. I never wore dresses again except when Akiko sewed them from the same material she used to make Kazumi's. I went shopping downtown and bought blue jeans and T-shirts in bright red, sky blue, indigo, various shades of purple.

"You would never look very good in those pretty tailored dresses your friends wear," Michiko used to say, looking at my T-shirts and shaking her head. "You and I certainly have different tastes. But you are lucky to be healthy looking and not too pretty. You can wear simple things and look comfortable rather than shabby. I'm sure you wish you were pretty like your friends. But looks aren't everything. You're smart and studious. They say heaven doesn't give us too many gifts."

I take out the necklace and the earrings and hold them up to the light. They would never match anything I wear. Even Michiko must see that my favorite colors are still the blues and the reds, never oranges or yellows. I picture milk fat boiling in a black vat and someone pouring the cooked-shrimp pigment over it. The liquid would bead up to the top and smell faintly sweet. Milk fat is milk fat no matter what you do with it. It never turns into a true gem. Nevertheless, I put the earrings, the necklace, and the pamphlet back into the plastic box and stuff it into my carry-on bag with the other gift items the customs inspectors might ask to see. I want to have all of them in one place so the inspectors won't unpack my suitcases and go through what is personal: the letters, the notes I've taken, my mother's kimonos and photographs.

At seven o'clock, Miya comes to pick me up in her car, and we drive to Ashiya to meet the others at a bar run by another classmate of ours, Kayoko.

When we get there, Yoshiko, Toshiko, and Hiroko are sitting at one of the round white tables. They wave at us as soon as we enter. Miya and I go over to their table.

"Let me buy you a drink," Toshiko says when we sit down. She is wearing a white linen jacket and pants, her hair cut very short. Leaning forward just a little, she lights her cigarette with a silver lighter.

Across the table, Yoshiko and Hiroko are smiling at me in their print dresses, their fingers delicately wrapped around the stems of wine glasses.

"You haven't changed," Yoshiko says to me.

"I was just going to say that about you all," I say.

Kayoko, our classmate, brings the drinks to the table and sits down. She is wearing a black low-cut dress and a silver necklace with a pendant shaped like a musical note.

"This is very nice," I say, waving my hand to indicate the maroon-and-green interior. Etude is the name of the bar, written in a fancy script on the awnings outside the window. I remember that Kayoko used to play the piano.

"I started this business right after my divorce," she says, laughing. "My parents put up the money for it because they felt sorry for me."

I smile and nod, not knowing what to say. Kayoko says that she is now living with the man she hired to cook at the bar. They have no plans to get married.

"One marriage is enough." She shrugs her shoulders as she gets up to go back behind the bar.

I am too astonished to speak. In high school, Kayoko was a very serious and studious person. She sat in front of me in Western civ, taking meticulous notes. She even copied the maps Mr. Kaneko drew on the blackboard, though similar maps could be found in the last pages of our textbooks. "Oh," she would sigh very quietly if Mr. Kaneko erased the map before she was done copying it, but she would never ask him to wait for her.

"Kayoko went through a very difficult time with her divorce," Hiroko whispers to me.

"We always come here when we get together," Yoshiko adds, "to give her some business."

Sipping her scotch and water, Toshiko tells me that she's been reading Kazuo Ishiguro this summer. "I just finished his second book, *An Artist of the Floating World*."

"I read only his first book," I tell her. "I've been meaning to read the others."

"The second is much better," she tells me. "The third one is excellent, too, but maybe you'll think it's too philosophical. You never liked books with big ideas." She laughs because we both remember that in tenth grade I hated Hermann Hesse. "Too philosophical," I kept saying. "Too many ideas."

"I can't believe that you've become a college professor," Toshiko says, "when the thing I remember most about you is how you almost passed out during the math exam during our entrance exams to Kobe Jogakuin. Remember that?"

"Of course I remember that."

"She and I were in the same exam room," Toshiko says to everyone else. "Kyoko raised her hand in the middle of the math test and said, 'Excuse me. I need to go to the nurse's room and lie down.' "

"I was in that exam room, too," Yoshiko says. "She sounded so casual, like she was going to take a nap or something."

Everyone laughs.

"I wasn't taking a nap," I protest. "I felt sick because I didn't know any of the answers."

"I felt really sorry for you," Toshiko recalls. "I thought for sure you wouldn't get in. Then I saw you on the first day of school in that red dress, with red ribbons in your hair. I couldn't believe it. I thought you had to have done really well on the other exams."

"Maybe I was lucky."

I remember going back after the math exam to the big cafeteria where all our mothers were waiting for us to have lunch. When I said to my mother, "I took my exam in the nurse's office," several other women turned around to look at me with pity. They must have thought, too, that I had surely failed. A week later, when we found out the results, my mother and I could not believe that I had gotten in. That was in February 1969. I didn't know then that I would come back to school in April without my mother for the first-day ceremony.

Now, though, I'm glad to have Toshiko and Yoshiko remember me from the day of the exams, from the time my mother was still alive. Though they don't remember my mother, we were all in that same cafeteria having lunch once, all of us anxious and a little tired.

Toshiko starts talking about how the two of us used to get into trouble. In ninth grade, our homeroom teacher, Mr. Hayashi, showed us a one-hour film about V.D., during which he stood in the back of the classroom instead of going to the teachers' lounge and sending a woman teacher to supervise us. The next morning, Toshiko, I, and another girl named Yuko went to school an hour early and scrawled on the blackboard: *Hayashi's a pervert, Hayashi has V.D. of the mind, Hayashi is preoccupied with sex.* Because Yuko confessed, our parents were called to school. My stepmother told Mr. Hayashi, in front of Toshiko, Yuko, and their parents, that I had possibly done these things because I had a crush on him. "You know how young girls are," Michiko said, smiling and simpering. I walked out. Toshiko and I can't remember now what the punishments were except for the letters of apology we were supposed to write. I never turned mine in.

"I was so mad at Yuko for confessing," Toshiko says. "She had to be such a Christian about it. She wanted to be honest. She even felt guilty."

"Not me," I insist. "I still think Mr. Hayashi should have gotten a woman teacher to show the film. We were only fifteen. We never talked about sex, even with our parents."

"But you two were always getting into trouble," Yoshiko says. "If someone had asked me back then which of us were going to be teachers, I wouldn't have chosen the two of you. Life is strange."

Yoshiko says she might come to the States to visit her sister in Virginia. "Her husband is stationed there till next year. I'm hoping that my mother can look after the kids for a couple of weeks in the spring so I can make the trip. My husband can be on his own for a while, but the kids are too young."

Hiroko says that her husband is applying to M.B.A. programs at American universities. If he gets admitted to one, his company will pay the tuition and give him enough money so he and Hiroko can live in the States for two years.

"What about your job?" Because they have no children, she has been working at an airline company. "Can you take a leave of absence?"

"No, I'll just quit."

"You'll go back to school, then?" Hiroko is bilingual. Like me, she spent one year in high school in the States.

"I keep telling her to enroll in an English as a Second Language program," Toshiko puts in, lighting another cigarette. "It's a good degree to have if she wants to teach when she comes back to Japan."

Hiroko shrugs. "I might be busy taking care of my husband. He scarcely speaks any English. Besides, I've forgotten how to be a student."

"That's nonsense," Toshiko says, blunt as ever.

Yoshiko and Miya are smiling, sipping their drinks. Hiroko laughs. But the irritation in Toshiko's voice is real. I turn sideways and see her frowning, taking a deep drag of her cigarette. I know, in that instant, that a line has been drawn that separates the two of us from the others. Yoshiko, Miya, and Hiroko have chosen to arrange their lives so that their plans will always revolve around their husbands' needs and abilities: whether the husbands can be left alone for two weeks or not, how the husbands will adjust to life in a foreign country. Toshiko and I have chosen another way: our work shapes our lives, our sense of who we are. I think of myself primarily as a writer, not as a wife. I would never have married someone who did not understand that about me. I take it for granted that both my husband and I know how to cook and clean, how to be alone when we are not together. Toshiko has not married, perhaps, because she has not found a Japanese man with similar understanding or self-sufficiency. No wonder she is irritated by the way Yoshiko, Hiroko, and Miya choose to let their marriages influence their plans. Still, that difference does not have to be a barrier between us. After all, we have spent the whole evening together and this is the only time Yoshiko, Hiroko, and Miya have mentioned their husbands. The five of us have known one another since we were too young, even, to have boyfriends. Who we did or didn't marry, in the end, is not important to our friendship.

"Well," I say to Yoshiko and Hiroko. "I hope you will visit me in the States."

"Of course." They smile.

"You, too," I turn to Toshiko, nudging her elbow. "We can go out for drinks and argue about books."

She shakes her head and gives me a crooked smile.

"It's almost ten," Yoshiko says, finishing her drink. "My mother's watching the kids. I'd better go home."

We all get up. Kayoko walks us outside.

"I'll be back soon," I tell everyone as I get into Miya's car.

Miya drives me back to Sylvia's. I don't have to say good-bye to her because she'll be driving me to the airport tomorrow.

Through the night, I wake up every few hours. Except for the cats running around in the hallway, it's very quiet. At four o'clock, I put on my glasses and walk to the window. The lights are still on in the city. The sky is a dark gray, the color of old stones placed in moss gardens. Over the water in the distance, there is a lighter band of gray, almost white, spreading slowly upward. I go back to bed one last time and wake up at eight.

An hour later, Sylvia and Cadine are walking me to Miya's car.

"Thanks a lot for everything," I say.

"Come back," Cadine says. "I liked having you here. I felt safer with you here when Mom was working."

"Stay with us again."

As the car turns the corner, Sylvia and Cadine are still waving. Like all the people I saw in Japan, they keep waving until they can't see me anymore.

During the half-hour drive to the airport, Miya and I continue talking about old friends.

"I didn't tell you before," Miya says, "but Yoshiko has been through a lot in the last couple of years."

"How do you mean?"

"Last year, her husband was asked to resign from his job because he was embezzling some money from the company where he worked. It was a big scandal. In the end, the company agreed to drop the charges if he would just resign." Miya continues as the traffic thins out a little past Ashiya. "So for a while, Yoshiko and her husband were very poor, and they have two children."

"How terrible."

Miya turns to me briefly and nods. "I think they are doing better now. Yoshiko's father decided to help out. He took her husband in as a partner in his business, since no one else would hire him after what happened."

"Is Yoshiko feeling all right?"

Miya doesn't answer.

"She didn't know that her husband was doing anything wrong, did she?"

"I don't think so."

"It isn't hard for her to be married to him now?"

Miya turns her head and looks at me.

"Well," I say, feeling flustered. "I would have a hard time if I suddenly found out that my husband had been a thief and I didn't even know about it. Wouldn't you? You'd start wondering if he'd been dishonest in other ways, too."

"I don't know how I would feel," she says, turning back to watch the traffic.

"But how about Yoshiko? How does she feel?"

"I don't know," Miya says. "We never talked about her husband's troubles."

"Not at all?"

"Of course not. The details were in the newspapers, so she must know that we all know. But I never let on that I knew. How could I? Poor Yoshiko. She would be so embarrassed."

"You didn't say anything because she didn't bring it up."

"That's right."

We drive on in silence. Perhaps eight weeks ago, I would have been stunned or even appalled by what I might have considered a superficial politeness on Miya's part. Back then, I thought that friendship always involved full disclosure, no secrets. But why should Yoshiko be expected to confide in her friends about what is most painful or embarrassing in her life? Knowing that your friends would never force or even expect you to talk about painful subjects is as satisfying as knowing that you *can* talk about them if you want to. It's just that my Japanese friends emphasize the former (at the risk of avoiding too much) while my American friends emphasize the latter (at the risk of prying too much). I am not sure, any longer, which emphasis I prefer. Before I came here, I had assumed that all Japanese politeness was false—an attempt to create a smooth, fake surface, the way I acted toward Hiroshi and Michiko. I didn't understand that there was this other, genuine politeness—an attempt to keep the conversation smooth and calm to honor the other person's dignity. Because I didn't know that, I had preferred assertiveness and confrontation, what I call "honesty." But I realize now that if I have been irritated at times by my Japanese friends' indirectness, I have also felt oppressed by American friends who wanted to know and discuss too much, who would ask point-blank, "So do you really feel accepted and at home in Green Bay?" "How do you feel when your colleagues make sexist comments?" Why should friendship always be about discussing personal pain rather than about taking our minds off it? I look out the window and then turn back toward Miya. I'm sorry that I have said the wrong things, but I know that she will let it pass if I change the subject now.

"The traffic's not so bad, is it?" I say.

"No." She turns back to me smiling. "I like driving on the highway. Machiko thinks I drive too aggressively. She says people in Tokyo don't even drive like I do. Did I tell you about her last visit?"

"No," I answer. "Tell me now."

We park her car at nine-forty, but by the time I've stood in the various lines to check in my bags, it's almost ten-thirty. The lobbies are crowded with people going on group tours. Miya and I stop for one last iced coffee, but as soon as we take our first sip, my plane to Tokyo is announced. We finish the coffee and hurry to the boarding area. Already there are two separate gates: one for domestic travelers and the other for those continuing on to international destinations. No visitors are allowed beyond the gate. A man stands ready to check my passport.

"Oh, I forgot about the picture." Miya pulls her camera out of her purse and holds it out to the man waiting to examine my passport. "Would you mind taking our picture?" she asks him.

The man reaches out for the camera as if by reflex.

"Thanks," Miya says, letting go of the strap. She's already stepping back. I follow and stand next to her. "Ready any time." She nods at the man.

We smile, the man snaps the picture, and Miya takes back the camera.

"Thank you for everything," I say to her. "I wish we'd had more time together. I'm sorry I didn't give you time to write back to me before I left Wisconsin."

"Don't apologize." Her eyes are wet.

"I'll see you soon. You can come and visit me, too."

She tries to smile. "You'd better go," she says. "You'll be late."

"I know."

I hand my passport to the man, who looks at it quickly and gives it back. I have nothing to do but proceed down the narrow hallway. I wave back to Miya one last time and then turn the corner toward the customs gate.

The customs officer waves me through without opening my bag. When I board the plane, everyone else is already seated. In a few minutes, it taxis onto the runway and then takes off. As it gains altitude, I look back to the west toward Ashiya and Kobe. Framed in the small round window, the landscape turns into a rock split open, a sunburst of glass and metal glittering below the dark moss-colored mountains.

A few minutes before one in the afternoon, we land at the Narita International Airport. My connecting flight back to Seattle and then to Minneapolis leaves at five. In the waiting area, there are no empty chairs. People are clustered around the food booths and around the telephones against the wall.

I know I should have called Michiko last night to ask about my father's surgery. But when I got in, it was late, and I felt good about seeing my old friends. I didn't want my phone call to her to be the last thing I did on the last night of my stay. If I call right now, I will still have hours left here so it won't be the very last thing I did in Japan. *Better late than never,* I say to myself in the halfhearted way I try to get motivated about tasks and obligations. I don't want to go away from here being at fault, not having fulfilled my part in demonstrating superficial politeness, which is all I can hope for—more than I can hope for—with them.

I stand in line at one of the phone booths. After twenty minutes or so, it's my turn. I dial their number in Ashiya.

"I just got back from the hospital," Michiko says, immediately recognizing my voice. "I'm going back there again in a few hours, but I needed a break."

"How is Father?"

"Yesterday he was in surgery for nine hours while you were visiting Akiko. The chairs were very uncomfortable. Most of the time, he didn't even know I was there. I thought you might call last night or this morning."

"This is the first chance I had. Is he okay?"

"The operation went without a problem. Now he'll be recovering for the next couple of months. He says I don't have to visit him at the hospital every day, but he just says that. He fully expects me there."

She keeps talking. Behind me, two men are waiting to use the phone.

"I wanted to give you some money," Michiko goes on. "I know your father gave you some when you came to the house the other day, but it wasn't much. I saw what he gave you. Right now, we have to be careful. We're not sure how much the insurance is going to cover. Maybe I'll send you a check when things settle down."

"I don't need any money," I say.

"It's hard to do right by you," Michiko says. "You came to our house only once, as if we weren't even related. I told your father he shouldn't expect much from you. You and he were never close because he was seldom home when your mother was alive. Jumpei's different. He's close to me but not to your father. You never appreciated anything I did for you even when we lived together. We were always strangers. Well, that's fine. I never expected more. But at least I wanted to give you some money."

"Thank you for the thought. But it's not necessary. Look, I have to go now. People are waiting to use the phone. Tell my father that I wish him a speedy recovery."

I hang up, collect my change, and start walking, relieved to be done with this final obligation. There are still over three hours before my flight, but not a single seat is open on the benches along the walls. Even the floor around them is covered with luggage. But it doesn't matter. I don't feel much like sitting around anyway. Checking the map of the airport, I head for the duty-free shops. What I would really like to do is to change the Japanese money I have left into dollars, but according to the map, the place for that is on the other side of the airport, past the customs offices. The duty-free shops, though, are scattered all over the airport, several in every wing. Carrying my overnight bag because there are no lockers in sight, I continue on in what I think is the right direction toward the nearest set of stores.

In front of the stores, a crowd of people is milling around, coming in and out, staring into the large display cases that contain cassette players and cameras. Two guards in black uniforms are stationed at the doors, periodically checking people's bags. A week before he came to New York last year, my father called me from a store like this at the Osaka Airport. He wanted to know what he should bring me as a gift.

"Do you want a camera or a walkman?" he asked.

It was eight in the morning in Wisconsin. I had just gotten back from running.

"I don't need either. You don't have to bring me a gift," I said.

"You must want something. Which could you really use? A camera or a walkman? Do you have either one of these things?"

"No, but I don't have a preference because I don't need either."

He bought both and presented them to me in their hotel room after he asked me how much money I made annually and told me he was disappointed because I knew nothing about Japanese literature. I thanked him and put the gifts in my bag, but I never used either of them once I got home.

I pull out my wallet and count the money inside: almost ten thousand yen. Even after eight weeks here, I'm not sure exactly how much that is in dollars because I can't do simple math in my head. Still, I step into the nearest store, ready to spend it all.

Slowly, I walk down the first aisle where a young man is looking at cotton kimonos stacked up on the bottom shelf, each kimono folded and wrapped in a plastic package. I kneel down next to him to look. The patterns are too flashy: huge blue and purple flowers, indigo and red cranes the size of my palm, black fish jumping all over the white background. Nobody I know would wear such patterns. I stand up and continue on down the aisle, bumping into other customers or their bags every few steps. After the kimonos, the shelves continue on, full of books, records, folk toys. Three older women are going through the records. I stop and watch what one of them puts back on the shelf—popular Japanese ballads and love songs sung by young men and women photographed in flimsy shirts with collars open.

The next aisle has dolls and children's costumes and games, and the one after, foods and ceramics. Every aisle is crowded with people who look vaguely anxious. These people have that worried look we all get in shopping malls near Christmas: there's something we have to buy, but we don't know what, so we grab whatever's nearby and hope for the best. But even as we head for the cash register, we can't get over the feeling that we are forgetting something essential.

All around, people are lining up to make their last-minute purchase in this way. Because most of them are Westerners and don't know how to count the Japanese change, they hand the attendant all their money and trust her to do the counting. I've looked at all the aisles by now, of things thrown into bins, wrapped in plastic, or protected behind glass doors. There is nothing I want or need. I hesitate, watching the line of people. It's two o'clock now, three more hours before I am lifted into the sky between here and where I am going. Because I am traveling against time, I will arrive in Green Bay only a few hours from now. This same minute I am standing here will happen again on the plane, somewhere over the Pacific.

I straighten the shoulder strap of my overnight bag and walk out of the store. There is no need to spend all my money here. Why should I buy something I will never use or need?

Back in the crowded gate area, I sit down on the floor next to the windows, leaning against the cool glass. It's sunny outside. Green rice paddies stretch in every direction around the airport. A plane begins to lift off to my left, gaining altitude. My eyes hurt from trying to follow its course in the hazy white distance where the rice paddies border the sky or perhaps the glittering water I cannot see.

Blinking from that brightness and then looking back at the crowded gate area, I suddenly know that I will never come back to this country to spend more than a few weeks at a time. My impending departure seems as final as the one before, thirteen years ago. In the last few days, I have told my friends, my aunt Akiko, and Kazumi that I plan to come back next year to see my mother's family, that I might even try to spend the whole summer then. I was even beginning to think that someday in the future, if I could get a leave of absence from my school, I would like to spend a semester or a year in Kobe.

Now, from this airport in the middle of flooded paddies, Kobe seems such a long way off, already a foreign country. No matter how much I love its mountains and the sea, the downtown, the familiar neighborhoods and the streets, it is a place I left thirteen years ago to save my life. I will never spend a whole summer, a semester, or a year there. I can't believe that I could even consider it. How can I possibly spend more than a few weeks in the same city as my father? Even if I never saw him, even if he were dead, his presence would continue on in the place where he has spent all his adult life. Kobe will always be a lost land to me, a place to think of with nostalgia, from far away. That is the price of my anger. Aunt Keiko was partially right: anger can bring a curse or unhappiness. I am losing the city I love, the place of my childhood, because I won't forgive my father. But I must accept that loss because there is no other way. After this visit, I know that I can never forgive Hiroshi no matter how much time passes.

Outside, another plane lifts off and disappears in the distance. More must have landed on the other side of the building. New passengers are arriving, squinting at the electronic displays of flight schedules. On the wall behind some of the benches, there is a map of the five continents advertising an airline. Somehow, the map looks slightly skewed or wrong, until I realize that it doesn't have the United States at its center, like the maps I have been looking at in the last thirteen years. This is the map of my childhood, with Tokyo at its center. From that center, lines, indicating regularly scheduled flights, run all over the world, thin as webwork, blue and red like bloodlines diagrammed in schoolbooks.

"The world is a large place," my Japanese friends might say, offering me a platitude meant to comfort by its ambiguity, shifting the focus from a particular hurt to a general wisdom.

I take a deep breath, trying to take consolation, however small, in the inevitability of my situation. My leaving is the logical conclusion of everything that has happened to my mother and her family: the loss of our land, the choices she made because of that loss, her letting go of me in the end to die alone. Sitting here and waiting for my plane, I am continuing our legacy of loss, which might, in the end, turn out to be a legacy of freedom as well. I am the daughter my mother had meant to set free into the larger world through her losses. That is the most essential thing about my past here. Having lost the city of my birth and childhood, I can go anywhere in the world and not feel the same loss again. My mother wanted me to move on, not to be afraid of uncertainty, not to be bound to old obligations.

I open my carry-on bag and pull out the package of milk fat jewelry from my stepmother. Walking up to the trashcan against the wall, I pitch the package into it and return to my seat. I have reached the end of my trip. My face pressed against the window, I wait for the plane that will propel me out of this center of the world into the blue light past its pull.

Katherine McCabe

About the Author

KYOKO MORI'S award-winning first novel, *Shizuko's Daughter*, was hailed by the *New York Times* as "a jewel of a book, one of those rarities that shine out only a few times in a generation." Mori has also published short stories and poems in the *Kenyon Review*, *Beloit Poetry Journal*, and other leading literary magazines. She teaches creative writing at St. Norbert's College in DePere, Wisconsin, where she lives with her husband.